CON RESPETO

Bridging the Distances
Between Culturally Diverse
Families and Schools

AN ETHNOGRAPHIC PORTRAIT

Guadalupe Valdés

TEACHERS
COLLEGE
PRESS

Teachers College, Columbia University
New York and London

Published by Teachers College Press, 1234 Amsterdam Avenue, New York, NY 10027

Library of Congress Cataloging-in-Publication Data

Valdés, Guadalupe.
     Con respeto : bridging the distances between culturally diverse families and schools : an ethnographic portrait / Guadalupe Valdés.
          p.   cm.
     Includes bibliographical references (p.   ) and index.
     ISBN 0-8077-3527-2 (alk. paper). — ISBN 0-8077-3526-4 (pbk.)
     1. Mexican American children—Education—Social aspects—Texas—Case studies.   2. Mexican American families—Social conditions—Texas—Case studies.   3. Home and school—Texas—Case studies.   4. Educational anthropology—Texas—Case studies.   I. Title.
     LC2687.T4V35   1996
     371.96′75′09764—dc20   95-50331

ISBN 0-8077-3526-4 (paper)
ISBN 0-8077-3527-2 (cloth)

Printed on acid-free paper
Manufactured in the United States of America

03   02   01   8   7   6   5

CON RESPETO

Bridging the Distances Between
Culturally Diverse Families and Schools

AN ETHNOGRAPHIC PORTRAIT

Dedicated to the memory of
Guillermina Valdés-Villalva, scholar/activist,
who cared deeply about justice
and about the women
who live and work on the Mexican border.

CONTENTS

FOREWORD

Con Respeto explores the quandary of well-meaning educators and policy-makers who care, who want solutions, and who are willing to experiment with immigrant lives and family values in order to give the "gift" of American dreams to Mexican-origin children. But with her heart and mind of two worlds, Guadalupe Valdés, noted linguist and educator, locates her analysis inside the ordinary, hard-working, inner world of families in Las Fuentes. When the mothers speak, their voices leave no doubt of the immediacy and clarity of their dreams. They want respect from their children and compassion and care toward the extended family; they want their children to grow up to be hard workers like themselves, who will live nearby and who can be counted on when their parents grow old.

For every rhetorical flourish in the media these days on the theme of rugged individualism, there are ten celebrations of the long list of old-fashioned virtues: respect for elders, sacrifice for others, long-term commitment, self-restraint, discipline for children, and so on. It is widely assumed that some families have attained all this and that others are lacking. To the extent that family values can be portrayed in this sense, it is obvious that the ten families who have traveled the long and short distance between Mexico and the United States, as portrayed in Guadalupe Valdés' new book, *Con Respeto,* are among the blessed: they have strong family ties, they are headed by robust role models, and they are populated by men and women on whom others can rely.

Parents in Las Fuentes have patterned a "good life," as Valdés tells us, drawn from long-tested, traditional, familistic values—and Valdés appraises their "quality of life" in deeply textured, culturally relevant terms. Family life is a resource, sometimes the only readily available resource that people can turn to in difficult times; however, strong family values do not necessarily turn Mexican-origin children in the border community of Las Fuentes into successful students. When children do not do well in school, "disorganized families" are blamed. But this book makes clear that, when the children of Las Fuentes do not succeed in school, it is not because their families are weak. Still, family values and school values remain at odds.

This rich and absorbing study of Mexican parents in border communities leads to more complex, rather than single-minded, solutions to school success. Valdés sees to the center of things and deftly questions the merit of typical educational interventions aimed at promoting school success. Specifically, she explores the social impact and long-term consequences of family interventions that target the childrearing styles of mothers, and of programs that focus on language deficits. Valdés argues that these interventions, grounded in mainstream values, do more harm than good. They do not show respect for deeply ingrained familistic values—the cultural capital that immigrant parents bring with them on their backs and in their hearts from their homeland; and they devalue the social and linguistic competence of immigrant parents and their children.

What can parent education accomplish given the social and economic conditions immigrant families face? Is the child who "labors tediously" at school work a more valuable child than a hard-working, job-holding youth who does not respond in school but may be "la mas lista" (the brightest) in the family? Does school success lead to self-seeking individualism rather than the moral basis of everyday reciprocity taught by mothers in Las Fuentes? Is the moral basis of parenting in these families antagonistic to school success? Should parents be taught to step into the role of "teacher" as well as parent to promote school success? Does school success inevitably promote the best interest of children and families in Las Fuentes?

And what of ambition? Valdés learns from parents that children, when they grow up, should give back to their families and not stray far from the nest. And how can parents protect a child who they feel has acquired "misplaced" ambition, given the meager chances for social mobility? Mothers and fathers and grandparents share pride in modest personal goals and robust family goals. That is what defines success in Las Fuentes.

In the late 1960s Gunner Myrdal wrote in *Objectivity in Social Research,* "There is an inescapable a priori element in all scientific work. Questions must be asked before answers can be given. The questions are all expressions of our interest in the world; they are at bottom valuations" (1969, p. 9). *Con Respeto* takes account of the subjectivity in the lives of ten families. This study is an appraisal, a valuation that challenges each American deep to the core of our belief in socializing—and in social experimentation. All too many of us think that problems, however defined, have solutions. As educators and planners we jump to experiment with interventions. Valdés does not provide solutions. She does, however, lead the search with her strong but cautious narrative voice for a sufficiently complex and multi-leveled understanding of the challenges facing families who move across borders as immigrants.

Carol Stack
University of California, Berkeley

Reference

Myrdal, G. (1969). *Objectivity in social research.* New York: Pantheon.

ACKNOWLEDGMENTS

There are many people to whom I am indebted for helping me with the writing of this book. Through the six years during which it was written, my life changed in important and dramatic ways. Many individuals sustained me through those changes and gave me the space and the room to talk about "my families."

I am indebted first of all to Rosalinda Barrera, with whom I carried out the research that led to this book. The experience of working with another Chicana was a very special privilege for me. I know that had she been involved in the writing of these materials, I would have profited much from her advice and wise counsel.

I am also indebted to Lily Wong Fillmore—colleague and friend—for her faith and belief that this book would indeed be written. By mentioning this work in progress in her many talks over a period of years, she persuaded me in subtle but important ways that I should not abandon this endeavor. I am grateful for the enthusiasm she offered when I shared bits and pieces of the work in progress. I am particularly grateful for her invaluable suggestion that I videotape the families before the study ended.

I owe a special thanks to the field workers who worked on this project at different times during the three-year period: Ninfa Cárdenas, Irene Rodríguez, Alicia Villa, Stanley López, and Laura Spenser; and to Jesús Adame and Sergio Díaz, who transcribed many hours of tape recordings. I am especially indebted to Maria Paz Echeverriarza for her important insights about the families that we both visited together.

I have dedicated this book to my sister, Guillermina Valdés-Villalva, who did not live to see it published. It was, however, her inspiration that allowed me to see what I might never have seen. It was her work with the Mexican people of the border that opened doors for me into worlds that neither of us had lived in. Through her eyes, I saw the impact of both oppression and poverty and came to understand why she struggled untiringly to change the world around her. I think she would have liked this book and would have understood why I tried to write in friendship. I know that if she had had the opportunity to argue with me, this would have been a far stronger and better book indeed.

Arguing and persuading were left instead to my husband, Bernard Gifford. It was he who read multiple versions of many chapters and suggested changes and corrections—some of which I refused to make. In every case, however, his suggestions and arguments gave me clarity and allowed me to find a direction I could follow. I am grateful for his patience and his friendship.

PREFACE

The ethnography to be reported on in this book is part of a larger study that was carried out by Rosalinda Barrera and myself between 1983 and 1986. The project, entitled "The Role of Oral Language in the Development of Literacy: A Descriptive Study of Ten Bilingual Children," was funded by the National Institute of Education (NIE-G-83-0043) for a three-year period and had as its purpose investigating the acquisition and development of academic-related abilities (specifically English language and literacy skills) within the family, the community, and the school itself. The project was designed as a largely ethnographic longitudinal and descriptive study that was to follow 10 children in ten families (beginning at ages 4 and 5) over a 3-year period.

Very specifically, we sought to examine how the family environment prepared children to survive and succeed within the family itself and within the surrounding community. In particular, we hoped to discover how bilingual language and literacy skills developed in newly arrived immigrant children outside the school setting. We hypothesized that as a result of the demands that bilingual communities make upon their residents, children would acquire a number of real-life abilities in English within the home and neighborhood contexts. We hoped to come to understand how this development might affect school performance.

As was expected by the initial design of the study, additional questions were raised and original assumptions were reevaluated and reformulated as the investigation progressed. As data were gathered, interviews analyzed, speech samples collected, and elicitation tasks carried out with the children, it soon became obvious that in order to understand why these children succeeded or failed in school, a number of dimensions, which seemed at first glance to be secondary to our original focus, also needed to be explored. It became clear that while the development of English language skills might directly relate to school performance, it often had little to do with teachers' *perceptions* about children's abilities in general.

This book, while a product of the larger study, reflects my concern about the fact that teachers' perceptions about children in the study were often influenced by the views that they had about Mexican-origin families. In writing this separate account and interpretation of the family data that we collected, it is my purpose to provide information about the circumstances in which newly arrived Mexican immigrants live their lives.

In this book, then, I address different questions than those that were raised in our original conceptualization of the three-year study. I have utilized data that were collected during the project's duration, but I have carried out a separate analysis and interpretation of these data.

I take sole responsibility for the summaries and descriptions that I will present here. However, I refer to activities carried out by both Rosalinda (Rosie) Barrera and myself in the plural (we) and use the singular pronoun (I) to refer to my own conclusions and observations.

Even though I have profited greatly from my collaboration with Rosie, and even though my interpretation of the behavior of the children at school owes much to our discussions, the description, generalizations, and explanations found in this volume are exclusively my own. All the errors found here, of course, are exclusively mine as well.

CON RESPETO

Bridging the Distances Between
Culturally Diverse Families and Schools

AN ETHNOGRAPHIC PORTRAIT

INTRODUCTION:
BETWEEN TWO WORLDS

SAÚL AND HIS FAMILY

Saúl Soto was a husky, brown-skinned child whose pudgy little belly usually peeked out from underneath his too-small T-shirt. He smiled often and laughed easily. During his kindergarten year and even during his first-grade year, winning was important to Saúl. Of all the cousins who played together, it was he who ran the fastest and pushed the hardest. *"Yo gané, yo gané"* (I won, I won), he would say enthusiastically after winning a race or beating the other children at a game they had been playing.

Saúl's mother, Velma, wished that he would win just a bit more quietly. She grew tired of Saúl's fights with other children, especially with his brother, Juan Pedro. *"No seas peleonero"* (don't be so quarrelsome), she would say. *"Es importante llevarse bien con todos"* (it's important to get along with everyone). For Velma, it was important that all her children get along. Any energy devoted to refereeing intensive family disputes meant less family energy available for surviving in the new world in which they found themselves.

Saúl's parents, Pedro and Velma Soto, were Mexican-origin immigrants. They had settled in a town close to the U.S.–Mexican border, and they were struggling with a multitude of problems. Work in construction was scarce for Pedro. Velma had injured her back in a work-related accident and needed surgery. Pedro's father, who was blind and crippled, lived with them; and Aydé, Velma's daughter from a previous relationship, was blooming into adolescence and creating problems within the household.

The year that Saúl entered first grade had been an especially hard one for the family. Pedro's son from his first marriage, who had lived with them for several years, returned to his mother's home in California and died there of leukemia. Velma's father also died. The entire family went back to Mexico for the funeral and was gone for almost three weeks.

Through all this, the three younger children, Juan Pedro (7), Saúl (6), and Melania (2), were watched over carefully by Velma. She worried about the seven-year-old, who often had seizures. She talked to Saúl about his fighting. She carefully monitored the children's comings and goings and agonized when they were late from school. Some days she could barely walk because she was in great pain, but she kept going. She looked after her father-in-law, got the children ready for school, and frequently drove two hours to the Mexican border to buy cheaper flour, cornmeal, and beans.

When we asked Velma and Pedro if education and schooling were important for their children, they both said yes immediately. They had had little schooling in Mexico, and they wanted their children to have more. They knew little about the American school system and how it worked, but they had taken the children to the neighborhood school, and had enrolled them in the programs the Spanish-speaking office worker had suggested. Every day when the children returned from school, Velma would ask them how they had behaved in school. She believed firmly that if they were going to learn anything at all, they had to learn to behave first.

Neither Velma nor Pedro, and least of all Saúl, were prepared for Saúl's retention at the end of first grade. *"No pasé"* (I didn't pass), Saúl said to us tearfully. His seven-year-old brother had ridiculed him for being dumb, and even his cousin Amapola, whom he always beat at everything, had laughed at him.

Velma was angry. She had spoken to the teacher only once that year through an interpreter. She had tried to explain that she had not gone to school before in response to her notes because she had a bad back and many family problems. But the teacher had not been sympathetic. In fact, in remembering that interaction, Velma recalled that the teacher had laughed at her. She wasn't sure whether the teacher had laughed *with* her or *at* her, but she had been both surprised and offended. In trying to make sense of why Saúl had been held back, Velma struggled with her own anger and confusion.

In many ways, we were also confused and upset by Saúl's retention. We first observed Saúl in school during his kindergarten year. He was enrolled in a "bilingual" kindergarten class that was taught by an English-dominant Mexican-American teacher and a Spanish-dominant aide.[1] All of the explanations about the activities to be carried out in class were conducted in English, and the teacher addressed the children only in this language. The aide provided Spanish explanations when needed by the few children who could not yet speak English. In general, however, English was the language of the classroom, and Spanish was used very little. Still, allowances were made for children who might not yet understand everything that was said. The aide could always be asked questions in Spanish, and even the teacher understood the children when they used this language.[2]

In the kindergarten classroom, Saúl appeared to do as well as the other children. He followed directions well, and when kept away from a particularly active classmate, he finished his work as expected. The end-of-the-year interview with his teacher and the aide did not reflect concern about his performance or about his ability in any way. At school, Saúl was neither troublesome nor unruly.

The following year Saúl entered the regular monolingual English-language program. In this program, children were assumed to be ready to learn exclusively in and through English. No special consideration was given to children who came from non-English-speaking backgrounds.

It is not clear to us why Saúl was placed in the regular or nonbilingual program, but apparently the school was under the impression that the parents had actively made this choice. In our conversations with the family, however, we learned that neither parent understood the difference between the bilingual program that, in theory, used Spanish for initial instruction, and the regular monolingual English program that used *only* English for all instruction. Velma did not remember having chosen one program over the other.

In terms of his English language development, Saúl seemed to us to be progressing well. By the middle of the kindergarten year, Saúl had begun to speak English at home both to his seven-year-old brother and to his half-brother, who was then living with them. Classroom observations during kindergarten and first grade also suggested that even though he was pulled out for ESL (English as a Second Language) help during the entire first-grade year, he was holding his own.

It became apparent at the end of that first-grade year, however, that all was not well. The teacher, Mrs. Lockley, recommended that Saúl be retained in grade. She felt that he was behind in reading and that he had not made enough progress.

Mrs. Lockley was neither unkind nor insensitive. She was a tiny, blonde, Anglo woman who at first glance appeared to be only a few years beyond her teens. Actually, she was in her mid-thirties, the mother of two school-age children, and a very experienced teacher. She had deliberately chosen to teach at Lincoln School, a school that primarily served Mexican-origin students, and she had high expectations for her students.

After Saúl was retained, Mrs. Lockley agreed to talk to us at the end of the school year. She was aware of our study and had allowed one of the members of the research team to visit her classroom during the entire year.

According to Mrs. Lockley, Saúl was "doing great in English." Overall, she viewed Saúl as having come a long way during his year in first grade. She commented that at the beginning he would hardly talk to her at all and that now, at the end of the year, he was even getting into little arguments with his peers. She saw this as great progress.

Mrs. Lockley did not consider Saúl to be a behavior problem and seemed surprised by our questions about Saúl's behavior that were based on information we had obtained from Velma. On the other hand, Mrs. Lockley admitted that she had had little contact with the family. She had seen Velma only twice, once when she had asked her to come in and sign the retention slip for Saúl and once in the middle of the year. She also had obtained little information about the family from Saúl. As opposed to the ESL aide who worked with Saúl and had been given many details about the family's comings and goings, Mrs. Lockley had not heard about the deaths in the family or about the reasons for Saúl's absence from school for a period of time.

She described her interaction with Velma at the time that she came in to sign the retention slip as unpleasant. She felt that Velma had been defensive. Through the interpreter (another teacher) that she had drafted for the job, Mrs. Lockley understood that Velma did not want to give her consent.

When questioned further and asked to describe Saúl's progress in the subject areas, for example in reading and math, Mrs. Lockley responded somewhat vaguely. She said that he was low average in math and very very low in reading. According to Mrs. Lockley, Saúl was part of a group of three children that she believed had not made much progress. She described his limitations and lack of progress by describing those of the entire group.

She did recall, however, that when they were doing any writing at all, Saúl was very dependent on her. He would ask for assistance frequently. She had also noticed that he seldom participated in music or art activities and that story reading seemed to bore him. At first, she had suspected that he was not understanding the story because of language limitations, but later she decided that he simply wasn't paying attention.

For Mrs. Lockley, part of Saúl's problem was the "fact" that the parents were not "involved" in his education. She pointed to her lack of communication with Velma as evidence of both disinterest and lack of involvement. She had sent notes home with Saúl that were never responded to. Velma would simply not come to the school to talk to her. Still, Mrs. Lockley felt somewhat guilty about the situation, although she felt that she had given the family ample warning of the forthcoming retention.

As it turned out, Saúl did not repeat first grade. At our insistence and with the principal's blessing, he attended summer school the year after first grade and attempted second grade the next year. During the summer, as we worked with him on his reading, he was still angry. He had wanted to spend June and July at his grandparents' farm in Mexico, riding their old mare and wading in the creek. He was quite sure that working on his reading would make no difference. Since he was dumb, he told us, we all knew that it was useless for him to spend the summer reading.

The next year, the last year of our study, Saúl was a somewhat different little boy. He became best friends with a youngster who had been retained in second grade, he spoke a lot less English, and he wasn't quite as sure as he had been before that he could win all the games and all the races that he and his cousins played.

Velma talked to us a great deal about the retention. She tried to make sense of the papers the boys were bringing home, and she even enrolled the children in a mail-order book club in the mistaken belief that she was applying for a library card. She asked for help in making sense of the children's report cards, which were all in English, and she tried to understand why American teachers kept children after school. She did not, however, become more "involved" at school in ways in which the teacher could see or understand. It was thus easy for Mrs. Lockley and the other teachers to conclude that the Soto family, like so many Mexican families, simply did not "care" about their children's education.

This book is about Mexican families. It is a book about Mexican parents, and especially about Mexican mothers and their children. It is a book about values and beliefs, dreams and struggles, newly discovered expectations and serious misunderstandings. It is also a book about unfair perceptions and well-intentioned efforts to reform families so that their children can succeed in school.

It is my purpose here to examine what appears to be a disinterest in education by Mexican parents. By bringing to life the everyday worlds of 10 newly arrived Mexican immigrant families, I hope to propose alternative interpretations for behaviors that schools and school personnel interpret as indifference.

In the chapters that follow, I will describe first-generation Mexican families as they go about the business of surviving and learning to succeed in a new world. I will talk about family strengths and about the strategies family networks use both for surviving and for giving life meaning. I will describe 10 mothers in great detail and attempt to paint a picture of how they viewed themselves as parents as they tried to adjust to a new life and to prepare their children to become competent adults.

In this book, I will argue that Mexican working-class parents bring to the United States goals, life plans, and experiences that do not help them make sense of what schools expect of their children. At the same time, schools expect a "standard" family, a family whose "blueprints for living"[3] are based on particular notions of achievement. They have little understanding about other ways of looking at the world and about other definitions of success. I will further argue that in order to understand how school failure comes to be constructed in the United States for and by newly arrived groups, one must have an understanding of the worlds from which these individuals come.

For Mexican-origin children in the United States, the fact is that school success has been elusive. Indeed, to this day, Mexican-origin children continue to fail in American schools in large numbers. By most available measures (e.g., dropout rates, standardized test scores, college enrollment), it is still the case that educational institutions are not meeting the needs of Mexican-origin students.

In the community in which I lived and worked for a period of 14 years, this was a cause of great concern. In 1983, when this study began, I had spent almost 11 years working in a community located near the U.S.–Mexican border. As a professor at a local university, I had worked closely with students who were the sons and daughters of first-, second-, and third-generation Mexican immigrants. I had documented their learning of English and their use of Spanish, and I had learned much about English/Spanish bilingualism in general. I had carried out fieldwork in the nearby towns and valleys. I had looked at language loss, language maintenance, and gender differences in language use. I knew a lot about the community, its people, and their languages.

As time went on, however, I began to focus my research on other, more pressing issues. For a period of years, for example, I studied courtrooms and the challenges encountered by monolingual Spanish speakers in the courtroom setting. The passing of the bilingual education legislation in the state took me in yet another direction. I carried out research in schools and tried to determine what kinds of Spanish language proficiencies were needed by bilingual teachers. As I became more involved with schools and with language within institutions, I found myself caring less about the study of language phenomena as such than about the ways in which Mexican-origin individuals used their two languages in order to survive.

By the time this study began, I had carried out two large studies focused on the education of Mexican-origin children. As I have pointed out above, however, the proposal that led to the funding of the study did not focus on misunderstandings between families and schools. It was not particularly concerned with parents' dreams, beliefs, and aspirations or about schools' expectations about such beliefs and aspirations. I naively still thought that difficulties experienced by non-English-speaking children had primarily to do with language. The study, therefore, was designed to follow 10 children as they started school in a community close to the Mexican border (which I call here Las Fuentes) over a 3-year period. We planned to observe these children both at home and at school and to come to a better understanding of the process of becoming bilingual. We wanted to understand how schools could best build on the experiences children had in communities in which two languages were used by most adult individuals.

During the three years (1983–1986) in which we studied the children and the families, many things happened. First of all, I came to know the families well. I saw their strength, their pain, and their determination. I saw happiness, and I saw confusion. I saw sadness, and I saw hope. I also began to understand why it might be that these families and their children would not become models of immigrant achievement in a single generation. I began to see and to compare the differences between the values held by these new immigrants and those of the American mainstream society that surrounded them.

I also came to know the children. I saw them at home. I noted their enthusiasm at entering school, and I saw the sadness in Saúl's eyes when he was not promoted, when he began to believe that he really was slow and not at all like the other children in his classroom.

And yet, Saúl was learning English. The teacher had told us he was making good progress in English. I had recordings and analyses of his developing proficiency. We knew he interacted frequently with fluent-English-speaking cousins, that he watched television in this language, and that he even fought with his siblings in English. This was true of the other children in the study also. Yet, during the course of the study, four of these children were held back in either first or second grade. Teacher interviews clearly established that the children were not retained because of language.[4] What the interviews did not establish is why these little ones appeared to the teachers to be out of step and behind their peers.

In the light of what had been our assumptions, it was difficult to make sense of what happened to the children. For me, the project, as is often the case in ethnographic research, shifted gears. I began to reexamine the family and child data that we had gathered up to that point and to try to identify other factors that might be influencing the way children were being perceived by their teachers. This refocusing of the investigation, then, caused me to carefully analyze the ways in which children were being prepared by their parents to function within the family, in the outside community, and in the school setting. I invited the interpretation of the mothers, engaged them in long conversations, and, in essence, attempted to identify specific behaviors, attitudes, and characteristics that might account for the perception by teachers of these children as "not quite ready for the next grade."

As might be expected, the reexamination and reformulation of the central questions guiding the research project also changed its theoretical focus. While initially I had predicted that this research would contribute significantly to our understanding of the process of acquiring language and literacy in a bilingual environment, subsequently it became clear that I was seeking instead to understand and explain how multiple factors, including culture and class, contribute to the academic "failure" of Mexican-origin children.

In this book, I attempt to describe aspects of the domestic and work

lives of these 10 newly arrived Mexican families. By presenting details about
their everyday lives and by including their own perspectives about their experiences, I try to show the courage and the determination of these men and
women and their children as they struggled to survive in a very alien world.
In essence, the picture of the families that I present here is one of hardworking people who were dedicated to raising their children to become good
human beings. Because of who they were and where they came from, their
dreams and aspirations for their children were modest from an American
perspective. Indeed, when talking about their dreams, most parents spoke of
honest and hardworking sons, virtuous daughters, close families, and having
todo lo necesario (the basic necessities of life). They did not think in terms of
job titles, prestige, or power. What they wanted was for their children to
grow up right, to find ways of making an honest living, to marry someone
who cared about them, and to find a way of settling somewhere close to the
people they loved. These were families where people worked hard, where
both fathers and mothers often had several jobs, where children labored bent
over in the fields next to their parents under a blindingly hot sun. These
were people who hoped for a better life, but who believed that achieving
that better life involved small things, perhaps getting paid a bit more than
they had been paid in Mexico or having access to regular employment. They
still wanted all the "good" things they had enjoyed in Mexico, like respect
from their children, like the pleasure of growing old around them, like the
happiness of spending free time around a large extended family. They were
traditional people who were a product of the "third world" and who brought
with them, in LeVine and White's terms (1986), their own models of the
"good" life.

In coming to the United States, however, what these families discovered
or would soon discover is that old codes of conduct and personal survival
strategies often do not work. Goals that they believed in and hoped to
achieve were often thought to be meaningless by the society surrounding
them. They came face to face, instead, with the industrialized "first world"
in which, as LeVine and White (1986) argue, educational development is
conceived as "a universal form of progress consistent with all human aspirations regardless of ideology or culture" (p. 18). In the case of "working-
class" Mexican immigrants, their beliefs about life and its meanings—useful
as they might have been in a "developing" country like Mexico—placed
their children in jeopardy in the eyes of American schools.

In order to talk about the "distances that must be traveled" by newly
arrived Mexican immigrants, this book is divided into nine chapters. In
Chapter 1, I will present the major theories that have been proposed to
account for the failure of nonmainstream children in schools. I will then
examine these theories as they have been applied to Mexican-origin chil-

dren. In Chapter 2, I will describe the setting in which the study took place and present brief profiles of the 10 families. In Chapters 3 through 6, I will describe the lives of the 10 mothers in some detail, discuss how the 10 families came across the border to the United States, how they survived in their new world, and how they went about raising their children. In Chapter 7, I will describe some of the children's experiences in the school context and provide a description of the confusions and misunderstandings that parents experienced when interacting with school personnel. I will discuss the educational histories of the parents, their understandings of schools and teachers, and their views about education in general. In the final two chapters of the book, I will examine the values and beliefs the parents brought with them from Mexico and discuss these beliefs in the context of the new emphasis on parent involvement.

THE TWO WORLDS: GAINING ENTRY

The families selected for study were all originally from the borderlands areas of Mexico. They were *Mexican immigrant* families, as opposed to Mexican-American families (families in which the parents are native-born citizens of this country). Selection of families for the study was made using personal networks and the assistance of the city's "barrio" school. In selecting them, we looked for parents who were Mexican-born, who used Spanish at home, who had been in the town of Las Fuentes for at least a year, who planned to remain in the area for the foreseeable future, and who had a four- or five-year-old child.

We initially contacted, by telephone or in person, all families who were referred to us by any source, in order to determine their suitability for the study and their willingness to participate. Since at the beginning of the study our focus was the acquisition of English by four- and five-year-old children, we described the project as being concerned with observing how the child talked at home and at school; with listening to him/her speak English with siblings, relatives, and friends; and with working with him/her as he/she learned to read. We presented ourselves as two *profesoras*[5] who were interested in finding out why some Mexican children did very well in school and others did not.

In spite of our efforts to communicate the fact that our purpose was to *study* their children and the entire family, the true meaning of carrying out research was not ever fully understood by any of the families. In some cases, questions about the purpose of our work were asked many months after approval had been given, and in others, our roles were recast to fit an existing category. For some families, for example, we were social workers who were part of a project such as Migrant Aid. For other families, our role was transformed into that of *maestras* (teachers) who were closely linked to the school and whose purpose it was to teach their children English.

While the process of gaining entry was not particularly difficult, the building of trust and rapport with the children and their families took a number of months, and in some cases, even years. Observations were of two types: three-day observations and single-day observations. Single-day observations involved visits of one day's duration; three-day observations involved visits to the family on three consecutive days, usually including either a Friday or a Sunday. These two different kinds of family visits allowed us to view family interaction under a variety of circumstances.

The early visits were both awkward and strained. We began by eliciting a family history and a description of the focal child's characteristics and language development. We requested the presence of both parents but often found that numerous other members of the family had been invited to participate also. In several cases, it was clear that we were being looked over and discussed with some interest. The fact that all visits and conversations were tape-recorded also contributed to the awkwardness of the interaction. In general, our first attempts to obtain information about the household were responded to with great caution. As time went on, however, interaction with adult members of the household became less awkward, more friendly, and in several cases quite close.

As far as possible, school visitations—focusing on each of the focal children— took place during the three-day or one-day observation periods described above. We observed focal children in classrooms, during special pullout program activities, in the lunchroom, and in the play yard. Additionally, we scheduled extensive interviews with teachers at different points during the three years in order to tap their evaluation of the children and their perceptions about the development of their academic skills.

During the first year of the study, I visited households accompanied by a research assistant who carefully observed household goings and comings while I interacted with the children. After playing with the children, I would then engage the mother and/or other adults in conversation. During this time, my research assistant would observe the behavior of the children as they played around the house. In later years, these interactions became more informal. I spent time in kitchens as the mothers cooked. I videotaped birthday parties, *quinceañeras* (celebrations of girls' fifteenth birthdays), and weddings. I accompanied mothers on errands, gave them rides to different places, and acted as their advocate in carrying out transactions. I could normally drop in unannounced and be greeted warmly by the children as well as the adult members of the family.

In general, conversations with the parents—actually informal interviews—were focused on a topic or topics (e.g., child discipline, household schedule, sibling rivalry) that I was trying to explore, but were also allowed to follow leads and topics introduced by adult family members. I answered whatever questions were asked of me. However, since I was aware that, unlike the pattern for getting acquainted in U.S. society, Mexicans do not ask a series of questions at the beginning of a relationship, I deliberately contributed personal information as I might have with other persons with whom I wished to become friends.[6] I talked about my children, about my family who lived on the Mexican side of the border, and about my father, who was sick, and I contributed other details about my home and background.

To a great degree, there was much that I had in common with the mothers who were part of the study. Since I had been raised in Mexico close to the U.S. border, I knew the area and its surrounding communities well. Like the families I was studying, I had experienced sadness in leaving Mexico, in knowing that I would not go back. I had also raised children in this country. Like the mothers I was studying, I too had had questions and doubts about how strict to be and about how much of my own upbringing I could impose on my "American" children. Also like the mothers in the study, I had family in Mexico whom I visited often. Like most of them, I was a native speaker of northern Mexican Spanish.

In other ways, it was apparent that I was quite different, and while I neither hid nor advertised these differences, I suspect that they were in some ways obvious. As opposed to the families that I studied, my own background had been comfortable. My family was and is part of what in the Mexican world is known as *las clases acomodadas* (people of means) and not of *las clases humildes* (people of humble origins), as were the 10 families in the study. My father was a cardiologist who practiced medicine in a Mexican border city and was himself the son of another physician. He was part of a professional class and, like other men of his background and generation, believed in pushing his children to achieve in school. He believed in education because he, and his father before him, had both achieved their status and economic position in society by completing a lengthy education.

My family, then, was part of a stable middle class that had never left Mexico. They lived (and still live) on the Mexican side of the border and enjoy both worlds, never having had to make a choice between the two. Of all of my family, I am the only one who, as an adult, made the decision to live and stay in the United States, a decision that was more circumstantial than voluntary and one that in many ways is still painful.

As might be expected by those who know Mexico and its class structure, as a child and young person, I had little contact with persons like the families and children in my study. Except for those times that I accompanied my mother to engage a new servant or to carry out some mission of mercy, I had not ever spent time among poor "working-class" families. Poor people were around us everywhere—in the streets, at church where we all packed in to hear mass on Sunday, and in cardboard shacks that came up overnight in the surrounding hills—but I had been sheltered and protected from the realities of that world. What I knew of it came from overhearing servants talk, and especially from my *nana* (a woman who lived in our household from the time I was born to the time I was 18), who came from a village in the state of Jalisco.

As an adult, I also had few opportunities to really come to know the Mexican "working-class" world. At the time that the study began, I had spent more years in the United States than I had in Mexico. By that time, I had stopped thinking of myself as a Mexicana and saw myself as Mexican-American or Chicana. It was a political identification and one that was deeply felt. By 1983 I had been engaged in the study of Spanish-speaking persons of Mexican origin in the United States for a very significant part of my lifetime.

As will be clear to those who have concerns about insider or outsider biases, my background provided me with a mixed profile. What I studied was both strange and familiar. Because of my cultural background, I would argue that I understood and was aware of many meanings that others (especially those less fluent in the language) might never have seen or heard. On the other hand, because of my class background, there was much that was both "strange" and unfamiliar.

In interacting with the families in the study, and particularly with the mothers, I tried simply to present myself as who I was then: a divorced woman with a grown son away at school and a daughter at home. For the most part, my involvement with the families called upon my resources as someone who knew the American world and how to use the system well and who simultaneously could be called upon to broker services on the Mexican side of the border. By the end of the second year of the study, my relationship with each of the 10 women in the study had become quite comfortable. They felt free to call me at home to ask for guidance, and their children came to view me as a sort of honorary *madrina* (godmother).[7] This means that I came and went without making appointments in advance and that the children were pleased and excited to see me. It also meant that our conversations became more intimate, and in some cases, the women shared with me their troubles and problems.

In 1986, as the study ended, I moved away from the borderlands—from that familiar "third country" that I had called home for many years. In the alien surroundings of my new place of residence, I missed the desert and the horizon and the sunsets. I also missed the families. For three years, my life had centered around *bautizos* (christenings), first communions, birthday parties, and *tamaladas* (festive occasions during which tamales are served). I visited one family or another several times a week. Many of the women and their children had become like a part of my own extended family. I became involved in their everyday dramas, and what happened to them mattered to me deeply. I had been allowed to enter their worlds, and by being allowed inside, I was invited to recapture a part of Mexico that I had almost forgotten and to remember both its strengths and its beauty. More importantly, however, across many types of differences, several women in the study and I became good friends. Indeed, one woman, Rosario Castro, and I became quite close. When I left, she along with her husband and her children helped me pack and move. I had a sense that she, more than anyone else—my family included—understood the fundamental cost of the choices I was making.

I began writing this book in 1987. During that first year, Rosario and I kept in touch. We wrote and spoke on the phone, and I learned about the family's brief move to California, about her daughter's graduation, and about her health and well-being. I, on the other hand, talked about being lonely, about missing the desert, and about looking forward to going home. In one of her letters, Rosario spoke about the importance of our friendship to her and about the *cariño* (fondness) that she felt for me. I was both moved and touched by her words and by the sense of the distance that I myself had traveled.

During the period that I have been attempting to write this book, the struggle has involved finding a voice with which to write *con respeto y cariño* (respectfully and in friendship). The families and the children that I studied are, to me, not just examples of Mexican immigrants, but people whom I came to know and care for. I started out seeing them and relating to them as people who were part of my study, and somewhere along the three-year period of frequent contact, I stepped over the line, and they became part of an extended network of very special friends.

As might be expected, then, in writing about the families and their children, I have changed all names and all information that might specifically identify them. As I talk about their lives, I do so with the deepest and most sincere respect and with the hope that this book will provide important insights about the circumstances in which newly arrived Mexican immigrants live their lives. If reading about the lives of these 10 families and about the school experiences of their children helps policymakers and practitioners to examine their existing assumptions about Mexican families and to question the implementation of large-scale education programs designed to help these families become less Mexican and more "mainstream," I will have repaid my debt to these very special people.

SCHOOL FAILURE: EXPLANATIONS AND INTERVENTIONS

Mexican-origin children have not fared well in American schools. Their problems have been documented by many researchers (e.g., Arias, 1986; Bean & Tienda, 1987; Carter, 1970; Carter & Segura, 1979; Duran, 1983; Keller et al., 1991; Matute-Bianchi, 1986; Orfield, 1986; Olivas, 1986; Orum, 1986; U.S. Commission on Civil Rights, 1972a, b, c; 1973; 1974; Valencia, 1991a, 1991b). Many attempts have been made both to explain the reasons for the poor school performance of this particular group of children and to intervene in meaningful ways in their educational experiences. Within the last 20 years, for example, much attention has been given, by both the research and the policy communities, to the study of factors that appear to contribute to the school failure of Mexican-background students. In general, research on the condition of education for Mexican-origin students has focused on issues such as segregation, attrition, school finance, language and bilingual education, and testing.

EXPLANATIONS OF SCHOOL FAILURE

Mexican-origin individuals are, in terms of their school performance, a part of a much larger population that includes the disadvantaged, the at-risk, and the underprivileged. A discussion of the school failure of Mexican-origin students must, therefore, be framed by a broader discussion that examines why other children who share similar backgrounds have also failed. It is important to first outline the causes of school failure among all children whom the educational establishment does not serve well and then to examine how the specific status of the Mexican-origin population might contribute in unique ways to this group's lack of educational success and achievement.

15

In general, explanations of poor academic achievement by non-mainstream children can be grouped into a number of categories. The three categories used by Bond (1981) are (1) the genetic argument, (2) the cultural argument, and (3) the class analysis argument.

The Genetic Argument

In the United States, the genetic argument—the view that certain groups are genetically more able than others (Eysenck, 1971; Herrnstein, 1973; Jensen, 1969)—had been out of favor for a number of years. Revisited recently by Herrnstein and Murray (1994), the genetic argument holds that academic talent is largely inherited and that society rewards these genetically inherited abilities. Supporters for this position argue that, given unequal innate capabilities, children of different ethnic or racial groups perform differently in school.

Strong views about the relationship between heredity and intelligence—which are largely based on the analysis of group performance on IQ tests—have been criticized by a number of scholars. Such scholars question the premises underlying psychometric testing (Figueroa, 1983, 1989; Gould, 1981; Kamin, 1977; Morrison, 1977; Schwartz, 1977; White, 1977; Zacharias, 1977), and specifically challenge the entire notion of IQ, a notion that is based exclusively on psychometric procedures and practices. A number of individuals (e.g., McClelland, 1974) have pointed out that IQ tests do not measure important features of intelligence. Others (e.g., Samuda, 1975) argue that efforts to produce culture-free tests have been disappointing. Still others (Roth, 1974) present evidence that procedures and practices in test administration may negatively affect the performance of minority children.

It is important to note that the genetic argument has failed to convince scholars within the research community who themselves may accept the assumptions underlying ability testing. Some individuals (Goldberg, 1974a, b; Kamin, 1974), for example, have challenged specific aspects of research carried out by Jensen, one of the most prominent proponents of the genetic argument. Both Goldberg and Kamin question Jensen's findings based on available twin studies. Additionally, a number of scholars (e.g., Lewontin, Rose, & Kamin, 1984) have attacked the entire concept of race. They argue not only that from a biological perspective "race" is a fuzzy concept, but also that studies focusing on adoption across racial and class lines failed to separate the genetic from the social. More recently, a number of scholars (e.g., Sternberg, 1982, 1985; Sternberg & Detterman, 1986) have attempted to move "beyond IQ" and have endeavored to examine conceptions of intelligence from a variety of different perspectives.

The Cultural Argument

As opposed to the genetic argument, the cultural explanation is currently still drawn upon by many researchers and practitioners. In its strongest form, proponents of this position (e.g., Lewis, 1966) argue that poor children are trapped in a "culture of poverty" and locked into a cycle of failure that is, in essence, self-perpetuating. Those who subscribe to this position maintain that children succeed in school only if their many deficiencies are corrected and if they are taught to behave in more traditionally mainstream ways in specially designed intervention programs.

The less extreme forms of the cultural argument do not see poor children as directly playing a role in perpetuating their own circumstances. They nevertheless consider children who historically performed poorly in school to be either culturally deprived (Bereiter & Englemann, 1966; Deutsch et al., 1967; Hess & Shipman, 1965; Hunt, 1961; McCandless, 1952) or culturally different and therefore mismatched with schools and school culture (Baratz & Baratz, 1970). Language in particular has been used as a primary example of the ways in which children are mismatched with schools and school personnel (Au & Mason, 1981; Bernstein, 1977; Drucker, 1971; Erickson & Mohatt, 1982; Heath, 1983; Michaels & Collins, 1984; Philips, 1982).

Although the line between theories of cultural difference and cultural deprivation is a fine one, it can generally be said that advocates of the cultural difference or mismatch perspective ordinarily attribute value to the backgrounds of nonmainstream children. They do not speak of deprivation, but hold, instead, that rich and rule-governed as these children's experiences may be, they are not what educational institutions value and expect. Examples of work carried out from this perspective are those on Black English (Labov, 1973) and on children's socialization for literacy in the Appalachian region of the United States (Heath, 1983).

Closely related to the research on differences between mainstream and disadvantaged children is research on parents and their ability to "support" their children's education. This work has primarily focused on parental involvement in education, parental attitudes toward schools and education, and maternal teaching styles. In general, this research takes the perspective that at-risk children do poorly in school because of their parents' beliefs and behaviors. Non-mainstream parents either do not have the "right" attitudes toward the value of education; or they do not prepare their children well for school; or they are not sufficiently involved in their children's education. During the 1960s and early 1970s, much of this research focused on Black American families. Descriptions of the supposedly inadequate home environments of Black children were used by well-meaning social scientists to refute the arguments made by geneticists about the causes of school failure.

In a review of the several streams of research on the achievement of Black children, for example, Baratz and Baratz (1970) discussed the findings of this research. Black children were found by some researchers (e.g., Hunt, 1961) to suffer from too little stimulation, while other researchers found them to be victims of too much stimulation (Deutsch, Katz, & Jensen, 1968). Others defined the problem as rooted in the inadequacy of parenting skills by Black mothers (Hess et al., 1968) and advocated compensatory programs that would teach Black women how to become "good" parents from the perspective of the majority society.

While perhaps less popular with theorists, cultural difference arguments continue to undergird a variety of practices currently being implemented in schools and communities around the country.

The Class Analysis Argument

The final explanation of school failure involves the analysis of the role of education in maintaining class differences, that is, in maintaining the power differential between groups. Proponents of this view argue that non-mainstream children do poorly in school because of the class structure of capitalist society. They argue that educational institutions function to reproduce the structure of production and that schools serve as sorting mechanisms rather than as true avenues for movement between classes. For these theorists, it is not accidental that the children of the middle classes are primarily sorted into the "right" streams or tracks in school and given access to particular kinds of knowledge (e.g., technology). The role of schools is to legitimize inequality under the pretense of serving all children and encouraging them to reach their full potential. The genius of the system resides in the fact that although the cards are clearly stacked against them, students come to believe that they are in fact given an opportunity to succeed. They leave school firmly convinced that they could have done better, perhaps achieved as much as their middle-class peers, if only they had tried harder or worked more. They are then ready to accept low-paying working-class jobs, and the working class is thus reproduced.

Explanations of school failure from this particular perspective, however, are more complex than I have outlined above. Essentially, as Giroux (1983) has argued, there are three different theories or models of reproduction: the economic-reproductive model represented by the work of Bowles and Gintis (1976), Althusser (1969), and Althusser and Brewster (1971); the cultural reproductive model represented by the work of Bourdieu and Passeron (1977, 1979, and Bourdieu, 1977); and the hegemonic-state reproductive model represented by the work of Dale and Macdonald (1980), David (1980), and Sarup (1982) and based largely on the work of Gramsci (1971).

The economic-reproductive model focuses on the relations between the economy and schooling and argues that schools reproduce labor skills as well as relations of production. The cultural reproductive model, on the other hand, attempts to link culture, class, and domination and argues that culture is itself the medium through which the ruling class maintains its position in society. Schools validate the culture of the ruling class and at the same time fail to legitimize the forms of knowledge brought to school by groups not in power. Finally, the hegemonic-state reproductive model focuses on the role of the state in organizing the reproductive functions of educational institutions.

A particular concern for a number of theorists has been the role of human agency in explaining societal reproduction. A number of individuals—although willing to agree that macro-level factors lead to a reproduction of class relations and that schools play an important role in such reproduction—seek to understand exactly how individual members of society in particular institutions actually bring about such reproduction. These scholars hypothesize that the relationship between schooling and the perpetuation of class status is re-created at the interpersonal level in the school setting and that students actively contribute to the perpetuation of their situation by viewing mainstream students and the life choices valued by this group as worthy of contempt. "Working-class" students thus band with others of their same background and present an oppositional stance to that of the "good" or successful student. This "resistance," however, rather than allowing them to break out of the "working-class" cycle, results in the replication and re-production of their class status. This particular trend in the investigation of the ways in which schools reproduce class membership is an attempt to understand the contents of the "black box," that is, to understand what actually goes on in educational institutions in order to bring about "failure" for certain groups of individuals. Work in this tradition is represented by the investigations carried out in Great Britain by McRobbie and McCabe (1981), Robins and Cohen (1978), and Willis (1977).

UNDERSTANDING SCHOOL FAILURE

From a theoretical perspective, the understanding of the difficulties surrounding the education of non-mainstream children must of necessity involve, as Persell (1977) argued, the integration of four levels of analysis: the societal, the institutional, the interpersonal, and the interpsychic. According to Persell, an adequate theory of educational inequality must take into account the distribution of power within a particular society and the ideology that supports that distribution. It must then link these macro-concerns to both existing ideologies about education and the nature of educational institutions. As Cortes (1986) maintains, moreover, such a theory must also take into account the educational process itself. It must consider factors such as the knowledge, skills, and attitudes of teachers, administrators, and counselors and individual student qualities and background, as well as instruction and the instructional context.

Unfortunately, as the discussion above suggests, to date examinations and explorations of school failure by non-mainstream students in school settings have been explored primarily from a single perspective.

School Failure and the Education of Immigrants

Current discussions of differential achievement by "new" American immigrants (e.g., Asians and Latinos) have tended to suggest that the difficulties encountered in schools by these newcomers were surmounted easily by the immigrant groups that arrived in this country during earlier historical periods. Vehement arguments against special compensatory programs such as bilingual education, for example, are frequently couched in the supposition that non-English speakers who entered the United States in the early part of the century managed to succeed in school without special attention given to their language or cultural differences.[1]

A review of the work carried out on the educational experiences of those immigrants who came into this country in the mid-19th century as well as in the early 20th century, however, presents a very different picture. It is evident that school failure or lack of school success was common and that Italian, Irish, Polish, and many Jewish children left school early and did not enter high school. Recent work on New York public schools (Berrol, 1982), for example, points out that until the 1950s, immigrant and even first-generation children in New York City received a very limited amount of formal education. This was the case not only for the "ignorant" Irish, but also for children (e.g., Jewish children) whose parents have consistently valued formal education. Indeed, the picture that emerges from the work of most researchers who have focused on the education of turn-of-the-century immigrants (e.g., Berrol, 1982; Bodnar, 1982; Fass, 1988; Handlin, 1982; LaGumina, 1982; Mathews, 1966; Olneck & Lazerson, 1988; Perlmann, 1988; Weiss, 1982; Williams, 1938/1969) is one that does not support idealistic views about the power of education to help all children succeed. Instead, what emerges is a sense that between 1840 and 1940, immigrants, rather than immediately availing themselves of the "opportunities" offered by educational institutions, made choices for their children that were framed by their views about education in general, their economic position, and the success or failure experienced by their children in school.

As has been the case in the examination of school failure in general, numerous explanations have been offered to account for the differences in academic and economic achievement of the various ethnic groups represented among turn-of-the-century immigrants. In particular, much attention has been given to accounting for the differences between generally "successful" groups such as the Jews and generally "unsuccessful" groups such as the Italians, the Irish, and the Slavs. As Perlmann (1988) points out, however, most of these explanations have had a long and ugly history in American intellectual life. As was the case in the late 1960s and early 1970s, for example, there was much concern in the early 20th century about genetic differences. Indeed, interest in ethnic differences reflected a profound suspicion of new immigrants that took on what Fass (1988) has characterized as a "racist slant." For many individuals who wrote during the early part of this century and even as late as the 1930s, differences in economic achievements (and educational achievements) by new immigrants were considered to be the result of inborn "race traits." As Fass (1988) argues, however, race was confused with what we now would consider to be culture, and many discussions about race focused on the habits and values of immigrant families. According to Fass, the eager acceptance of IQ testing in this country after World War I occurred in response to educators' concerns about the "retardation" of large numbers of pupils. IQ testing supposedly provided a means for ranking individuals according to their innate and unchanging talent and for ordering a hierarchy of groups. It offered a "scientific" rationale for existing views about inherited endowment and provided educators with justification for creating different "opportunities" for different students.

For early-20th-century immigrants, the genetic argument was used not only to account for differences in school performance, but to argue for the development of differentiated curricula suited to the particular talents of the less able members of the population. As a result, children with lower IQs (largely children of foreign parentage who were also poor) were placed in vocational or commercial programs. According to Fass (1988), in New York City high schools, "as early as 1911–12, about one third of the population was enrolled in commercial tracks or in the two special commercial high schools." Moreover, "educators did not believe that the new masses were smart enough to benefit from traditional academic subjects" (p. 67).

The cultural difference or deficit argument has also figured prominently in discussions about educational attainment among immigrant/ethnic groups in the United States. As Perlmann (1988) points out, variations in the attainment levels of different ethnic groups have been attributed in large part to their premigration histories. Much attention has been given both to the occupational skills, resulting from the positions they occupied in their countries of origin, and to the cultural attributes (attitudes, habits, values, and beliefs) that newcomers brought with them. A number of scholars, for example, have argued that certain groups (e.g., Italians) did not improve their lot as rapidly as others because their cultural background did not allow them to take advantage of the opportunities offered to them by the educational system. These scholars generally maintain that other groups (e.g., the Jews) did indeed bring with them views and attitudes about education that were congruent with the focus on the importance of schooling present in this country. Dinnerstein (1982), for example, argues that the cultural heritage of the Jews (what he considers to be "their high regard for learning") was vital to their achieving social mobility through education. Agreeing with this general view of cultural deficit, LaGumina (1982) stresses that Italians did not enjoy similar rapid mobility through education because southern Italian peasants who immigrated to the United States were conservative, fatalistic, and family-oriented. A parallel argument is made by Sowell (1981) and others about the Irish and their cultural orientation. Miller (1985, cited in Perlmann, 1988) views the traditional Irish peasant culture as communally dependent and fatalistic, and Irish people as "feckless, child-like, and irresponsible" (p. 53).

For those individuals who support the cultural background explanations of differences in school attainment, the issues are straightforward. Certain groups of immigrants did not bring with them life experiences and cultural values that would have allowed or encouraged them to take advantage of the opportunities offered to them by American educational institutions. These immigrant parents failed because cultural "differences" prevented them from expecting their children to persevere and to succeed in school.

Scholars who take this perspective do not generally ask questions about the ways in which children of different groups were treated in schools, about whether the curriculum responded or failed to respond to these children's needs, or about the ways in which extreme poverty might have impacted on families' decisions to withdraw their children from school. The root of the problem is seen to reside in the shortcomings of the immigrants themselves.

Other scholars offer a different perspective. Steinberg (1981), in particular, argues that cultural explanations of differences in attainment are based on a "New Darwinism" in which cultural superiority and inferiority have replaced biological measures of superiority. For New Darwinists, he maintains, there are certain cultural traits associated with attainment and achievement (e.g., frugality, temperance, industry, perseverance, ingenuity), while others (e.g., familism, fatalism) are associated with limited success and social mobility. Steinberg contends that Horatio Alger stories about success and hard work are based primarily on New Darwinism and glorify the effect of tenacity and hard work without taking into account the many other factors that impact on people's lives. Specifically, such myths discount the importance of the structural locations in which new immigrants find themselves in their new society.[2]

More recently, Perlmann (1988), in his work on ethnic differences in schooling among the Irish, Italians, Jews, and Blacks in Providence, Rhode Island, between 1880 and 1935, has presented evidence that supports the argument that differences in attainment among ethnic groups are the results of social processes that have long histories. He contends that an understanding of such differences involves "determining the specific manner in which these general factors—the pre-migration heritage, discrimination, and the place of the migrants in the new class structure—operated, and interacted, in the history of a given ethnic group" (p. 6). From the data that he examined, Perlmann concluded that "neither culture nor discrimination nor class origins in the American city can alone provide a credible summary" (p. 219). He further argues that there is not a single consistently primary factor or a single generalization that will account for differences in individual ethnic histories.

In sum, explorations of differences in school success among the various immigrant groups that entered this country between 1840 and 1940 have in general terms attempted to account for the inequality of their educational outcomes by using the same three arguments used to explain the educational failure of non-mainstream children in general. The genetic argument coupled with the cultural difference argument appears to have been used most frequently. However, it also appears that the cultural argument, with its perspective on desirable cultural traits and characteristics, was the most influential. To date, beliefs about desirable individual and family characteristics continue to be reflected in both research and practice.

Recent Immigrants, Minorities, and School Achievement

In present-day American society, the success or lack of success experienced by turn-of-the-century immigrants is often contrasted with that experienced by African-Americans as well as with that experienced by Latinos. While there are some parallels between the position occupied by African-Americans in this country with the positions occupied by both Latinos and earlier "problem" immigrant groups, there are also many significant differences.

A few scholars have attempted to understand these differences by focusing on the economic-reproductive effects of societal arrangements and taking into account the responses of oppressed or exploited populations to these societal arrangements. Ogbu (1978, 1983, 1987a, b), for example, has sought to identify important distinctions between different groups of present-day "minorities" in the United States. He discusses *immigrant minorities* and *caste minorities* and shows that there is a clear difference, for example, between newly arrived Korean immigrants (an immigrant minority) and Black Americans (a caste minority), who have suffered generations of discrimination and racial prejudice. He argues that immigrant minorities frequently achieve success in ways that caste minorities do not, because they are both not conscious of the limits the majority society would place upon them, and content to do slightly better than their co-nationals who remained at home. Caste minorities, on the other hand, are quite aware of the reality in which they live, of the jobs they will never get, and of the kinds of lack of success they will experience. Arguing that caste minorities develop folk theories of success based on the options available to them in that society, Ogbu suggests that these individuals justifiably reject education because they also reject the common view that it can provide them with true alternatives.

For Ogbu, the question of why different groups of non-mainstream children succeed while others fail is answered within the tradition of the class analysis argument and in particular from the economic-reproductive perspective. For Ogbu and for theorists who work in this tradition, pre-migration factors are of less importance than the discrimination that is experienced by different groups in this society, their particular location within the class structure, and their awareness or perception of the permanency of that location.

THE MEXICAN-ORIGIN POPULATION

The Mexican-origin population of the United States, as opposed to other recently arrived immigrant groups, includes individuals who have been here for generations and who see themselves as the original settlers of parts of the United States as well as individuals who have arrived here relatively recently as both legal and illegal immigrants. Generalizations about the Mexican-origin population with regard to educational success or failure are difficult to make because there are important and significant differences (generational, regional, experiential, linguistic) among the various groups that make up the Mexican-origin population.

There is evidence to suggest, however, that a large majority of Mexican persons who emigrate to the United States do not come from the groups that have obtained high levels of education. There are problems, however, in generalizing about the class origins of both early and recent Mexican immigrants. According to Bean and Tienda (1987), Jasso and Rosenzweig (1990), Portes et al. (1978), and Portes and Bach (1985), Mexican-origin immigrants are poor and have low levels of educational attainment. However, Durand and Massey (1992) have argued that generalizations about

Mexican migration to the United States are inconsistent and contradictory. They maintain that case studies (e.g., Cornelius, 1976a, b, 1978; Dinerman, 1982; Massey et al., 1987; Mines, 1981, 1984; Mines & Massey, 1985; Reichert & Massey, 1979, 1980) of Mexican "sending" communities (communities from which large numbers of Mexican nationals have emigrated) have yielded very different views about a number of questions. Among other topics, these studies present contradictory evidence about the class composition of U.S. migration. Durand and Massey (1992) argue that a few community factors, including age of the migration stream, the geographic, political, and economic position of the community within Mexico, and the distribution and quality of agricultural land, affect the class composition of migration. The authors stress the difficulties surrounding attempts at generalization, and they suggest that such generalizations can only be made when a number of communities are studied using a common analytical framework. What this means is that educational researchers must use caution in interpreting findings about Mexican immigrants and persons of Mexican background.

As might be expected, a number of researchers have attempted to be sensitive to intragroup differences when working with Mexican-origin populations in educational settings. Matute-Bianchi (1991), for example, proposes five different categories for students: (1) "recent Mexican immigrants," who have arrived in the United States within the last three to five years; (2) "Mexican-oriented" students, who are bilingual but retain a *Mexicano* identity and reject the more Americanized Mexican-origin students; (3) "Mexican-American" students, who are U.S.-born and highly acculturated; (4) "Chicanos," who are U.S.-born, generally second generation, and frequently alienated from mainstream society; and (5) "Cholos," who dress in a distinct style and are perceived by others to be gang-affiliated.

Consistently clear differentiations between members of these several categories are difficult to make, and because of this, the study of the causes of school failure for the different segments of this population becomes complex. The Mexican-American group does not fit neatly into the categories proposed by a number of researchers. For example, the Mexican-origin population cannot be classified adequately using Ogbu's (1978, 1983, 1987a, b) two categories, *immigrant* and *caste* minorities. The problem is that there are simultaneously both *immigrant* minorities and *caste* minorities within this single population. The former group includes those individuals who have recently entered the United States and cyclical immigrants who have worked in this country for years at a time, but who return to Mexico for extended periods. The latter group could include children of recently arrived *Mexicanos* whether U.S.-born or not, as well as first-, second-, third-, fourth-, and fifth-generation residents of several regions of the country. In several areas (e.g., Texas), persons of Mexican origin were already residing in the area when the area was annexed by the United States. While these individuals were not indigenous to the areas, they were certainly more "indigenous," for example, than persons who have arrived in the area within the last 20 years.

In this book, I take the position that the distinction between Mexican-origin persons who can still be categorized as immigrants and those persons who must be considered "hyphenated Americans" (Mexican-Americans/Chicanos/Cholos) has to do with a number of factors. Those persons who can be categorized as "immigrants" from Mexico (whether born in this country or not) still have what can be termed an "immigrant mentality," that is, they are oriented toward the home country, identify with Mexico, and measure their success (as Ogbu has suggested) using Mexican nationals in Mexico as their reference group. Mexican-Americans or Chicanos, on the other hand, no longer look to Mexico for identification. Their ties with Mexico have weakened and they see their lives as being carried out exclusively in this country. In general, these persons consider themselves to be different from white Americans as well as from Mexican nationals. More importantly, however, members of this group have often experienced discrimination in this country as members of a low-status and stigmatized minority. They have frequently developed an "ethnic consciousness" and have a sense of sharing the same low status as other Mexican-origin people. Mexican immigrants are immigrant minorities, while Mexican-Americans/Chicanos are caste minorities. This latter group is conscious of discrimination and prejudice by the majority group directed at Mexican-origin people *in particular* rather than at new immigrants or at outsiders in general.

What I am suggesting is that the development of an awareness of being both different and unacceptable to the majority society is a key factor in the shift in identification from immigrant to caste minority by Mexican-Americans/Chicanos. I would argue that Mexican immigrant individuals can be considered full members of the caste minority group in the United States when they:

1. become conscious that they are no longer like Mexican nationals who have remained in Mexico,
2. feel little identification with these Mexican nationals,
3. self-identify as "Americans,"
4. become aware that as persons of Mexican origin they have a low status among the majority society, and
5. realize the permanent limitations they will encounter as members of this group.

Mexican-Origin Students and Explanations of School Failure

According to a number of researchers (e.g., Arias, 1986; Duran, 1983; Fligstein & Fernandez, 1988; Meier & Stewart, 1991; Rumberger, 1991), Mexican-origin students have experienced a long history of educational problems, including below-grade enrollment, high attrition rates, high rates of illiteracy, and underrepresentation in higher education. As might be expected, a coherent theory that takes into account the many factors that impact on the poor school achievement of Mexican-origin students has not been proposed. However, a number of factors have been identified as influencing the school achievement of Mexican-origin children. These include: family income, family characteristics, and language background (Macías, 1988; Nielsen & Fernandez, 1981; U.S. Department of Education, 1987); teacher/student interaction (Buriel, 1983; So, 1987; Tobias, Cole, Zinbrin, & Bodlakova, 1982; U.S. Commission on Civil Rights, 1972b); school and class composition (i.e., segregation and tracking) (Espinosa & Ochoa, 1986; Fernández & Guskin, 1981; Haro, 1977; Oakes, 1985; Orfield, 1986; Orum, 1985; Valencia, 1984); and school financing (Dominguez, 1977; Fairchild, 1984).

As will be noted, of the factors that have been identified as influencing the school achievement of Mexican-origin students, one factor (family income) can be said to be indicative of the family's location in the social structure. Two factors (school composition and school financing) can be identified as involving the school or institutional context, and two other factors (family characteristics and language background) can be considered to refer to a set of "cultural traits" not unlike those discussed by the literature on immigrants written in the early part of this century.

Not surprisingly—given that the cultural difference explanation of school failure is still drawn upon—much attention has been paid by researchers and practitioners to both language differences and family characteristics. Although most researchers working on the language problems of Mexican-origin children do not see themselves as working primarily within the deficit/difference paradigm, language issues have come to dominate the debate surrounding the education of today's "new" immigrants. The literature that has concentrated on language background issues as they relate to Mexican-origin children is immense and encompasses the study of a number of different areas, including the investigation of the process of second-language acquisition, the sociolinguistic study of language use in Mexican-American communities, the study of the relationship between teacher behaviors and second-language acquisition, the instructional use of two languages (e.g., bilingual education, two-way immersion), and the effects of various types of language intervention programs on Mexican-origin children.[3]

As compared to the literature on language background, the study of family characteristics as they relate to the education of Mexican-origin children has, in general, attempted to discover whether and to what degree these characteristics are like or unlike those found in mainstream American families. One important trend in this research (e.g., Laosa, 1978; McGowan & Johnson, 1984) has been the study of socialization practices within Chicano families. Interestingly enough, in spite of clear evidence that research conducted in this country on child development and on "desirable" socialization practices is biased (Laosa, 1984b; Ogbu, 1985), recent implementation efforts focusing on parent involvement include family education components that are directly based on a deficit-difference paradigm. I will return to this point below.

In addition to the study of socialization practices, research on family characteristics has included work on the relationship between family constellation (size and sibling structure) and children's development, and on the relationship between single-parent families and children's development and scholastic performance (Henderson & Merritt, 1968; Laosa, 1984a; Le-Corgne & Laosa, 1976; Valencia, Henderson, & Rankin, 1985).

In comparison to the work that has been carried out from the deficit-difference paradigm, much less work has been carried out from the class analysis perspective on the causes of the low school attainment in the Mexican-origin population. Increasingly, however, broad examinations of the educational experiences of this population are being written that include attention to the power relationships between the dominant majority population and the Mexican or Chicano minority. These analyses (Meier & Stewart, 1991; San Miguel, 1987) take the perspective that policies resulting in segregation practices and in unequal school financing reflect the structural location of the Mexican-origin population.

Work in the tradition of the economic-reproduction model has been carried out by Ogbu and Matute-Bianchi (1986), Matute-Bianchi (1986, 1991), and Foley (1990). This work has been concerned with trying to understand differences in performance by Mexican-origin students of different generational backgrounds and has included an attempt to link factors such as premigration educational experiences, attitudes toward education, attitudes toward the majority group, and the like with academic achievement. Foley (1990), in particular, examined high school students' behaviors in school against a parallel study of discrimination and prejudice present in a Texas border city. For these researchers, societal arrangements themselves as reflected in teacher–student and student–student interactions in the classroom result in their reproduction.

In sum, research carried out on the causes of school failure in Mexican-origin students has followed the principal trends present in the research on non-mainstream populations in general. Less attention has been given to examining the genetic argument among this population, although interest in testing and test bias has been high.[4] For the most part, the research on this population can be categorized as falling within the cultural deficit-difference paradigm in that it attempts to explain low scholastic achievement by focusing on differences brought to school by the children themselves. What is evident is that single-factor explanations of school failure among the children of first-generation Mexican immigrants are inadequate and cannot account for the complexity of the experience. To attribute to language factors alone, for example, what is inextricably linked to elements such as children's non-mainstream behavior, teacher perceptions, and assumptions made by the schools about parents and by parent about schools, is simplistic. In order to account for the academic failure of Mexican-origin students from, for example, the perspective of theories of reproduction, researchers are faced with the challenge of having to account for the elements that lead to this reproduction using a binational framework.

FIXING THE PROBLEM: EDUCATIONAL INTERVENTIONS

In spite of the complexity of the problem of school failure for non-mainstream children, those concerned about its remediation have focused on attempting to change particular aspects of the institutional and instructional contexts in the hope that such changes will bring about increased school success. While aware of the structural factors that frame the problem, these researchers and practitioners represent the tension that Carnoy and Levin (1985) have described as existing between "the unequal hierarchies associated with the capitalist workplace" and "the democratic values and expectations associated with equality of access to citizen rights and opportunities" (p. 4).

In comparison to theorists who have sought to explain the nature and circumstances of educational failure, practitioners and policymakers have focused on breaking the cycle of low educational achievement or bringing about change in schools and in school outcomes. It is interesting to note, however, that programs that have endeavored to alter or reverse educational outcomes for poor, disadvantaged, or at-risk children have reflected the thinking of theorists who have worked within the deficit-difference paradigm. Many of these theorists have tended to address single micro-level factors such as English language fluency, standardness of spoken English, or the blend and mix of students of different racial groups within a given school. These research and theoretical foci, in turn, have led to the implementation of programs that offer narrow solutions to far broader problems (e.g., bilingual education programs, desegregation programs, Head Start) and that have been marginally successful. Ironically, even though the theories that held that problems experienced by at-risk children were their own "fault" or responsibility have been called into question, program implementation still responds to this fundamental view. With few exceptions, programs aimed at at-risk children are designed to address key shortcomings or "deficits" in these students in order to assist them in succeeding in the school environment.

It is not surprising that researchers working within the class analysis paradigm argue that such programs leave existing institutions largely untouched and that these institutions continue to reflect the power realities of the larger society. For that reason, they point out, compensatory programs have failed to meet the expectations of those policymakers and practitioners who sincerely hoped that correcting or compensating for key factors would bring about significant changes in total educational outcomes.

In the case of Mexican-origin students, the absence of a sound underlying perspective that brings together explanations with interventions is particularly evident. Not only is there a lack of a coherent theory about macro-level factors that can adequately explain the failure and success of these children in American schools, but there is also a lack of coherence among the many theories that have focused on micro-level variables. In general, the work of both policymakers and practitioners involved in the education of Mexican-origin children also reveals a very practical and problem-oriented focus. The focus for such individuals has been finding solutions, establishing policies, funding programs that will address the needs of these children, and implementing promising programs in spite of heavy local and national political fire.

While from the perspectives of class analyses of schooling and society the educational problems of Mexican-origin children cannot be alleviated without a major change in the societal structure that impacts on every level of students' lives, from the perspective of many policymakers and practitioners, what is needed is the right kinds of instructional solutions, the right kinds of school programs in order to bring about meaningful, if not lasting, change. Single and partial solutions, then, often take on extraordinary meaning, and these interventions become the focus of intense debate. The politics of bilingual education (a solution designed to focus on children's inability to profit from instruction carried out exclusively in English), for example, have been particularly acrimonious. Many practitioners, parents, and policymakers are convinced that good bilingual education programs *by themselves* will impact significantly on educational outcomes.[5]

The fact is that current educational outcomes—high drop-out rates, grade delay, low test scores, and low college enrollments by Mexican-origin students—demand solutions. Whatever the realities of the structures of inequality in this country may be, practitioners feel a strong pressure to find ways of helping their students to succeed in school.

THE CONCEPT OF FAMILY INTERVENTION

In this book, I am concerned primarily with those examples of educational intervention that focus on families and their young children. I will argue throughout this book that this focus is problematic, and I will point out that this particular approach to equalizing educational outcomes is based directly on the deficit-difference paradigm.

In the section that follows, I will discuss a recently popular educational intervention perspective that has focused specifically on parents and families. This strategy, currently known as *parent involvement,* is considered by some researchers (e.g., Becker & Epstein,1982; Bennett, 1986; Diaz-Soto, 1988; Epstein, 1982, 1985, 1986b, 1991; Epstein & Dauber, 1991; Henderson, 1987; Simich-Dudgeon, 1986; Walberg, 1984) to result in various kinds of positive benefits for both parents and children. As I will point out below, this strategy is currently being implemented around the country, and its use is being advocated by both policymakers and practitioners.

The position I will take here is that, like many of the family intervention programs that came before it, parent involvement is an attempt to find small solutions to what are extremely complex problems. I am concerned that this "new" movement—because it is not based on sound knowledge about the characteristics of the families with which it is concerned—will fail to take into account the impact of such programs on the families themselves.

In order to provide a context for this position, which I will elaborate further in later chapters, I will discuss current thinking about parent education and provide a brief review of the literature that has focused on this notion.

Parent Education Programs for Mexican-Origin Families

Within the past decade, there has been a renewed interest in the impact of families and homes on children's education. Concern about parent "involvement" in children's learning has been expressed by educators, legislators, and religious leaders. The generally held view, as the publication *What Works* (U.S. Department of Education, 1987) made evident, is that schools depend directly on parents for assistance in educating children, and that without parental help the schools cannot carry out their work as effectively. The tone and direction of this publication reflects the thinking underlying many current attempts to solve what is perceived to be a serious problem. The section on the home within *What Works* (p. 5) makes the following statement:

Curriculum of the Home

Research: Findings: Parents are their children's first and most influential teachers. What parents do to help their children learn is more important to academic success than how well-off the family is.

Comment: Parents can do many things at home to help their children succeed in school. Unfortunately, recent evidence indicates that many parents are doing much less than they might. For example, American mothers on average spend less than half an hour a day talking, explaining, or reading with their children. Fathers spend less than 15 minutes.

They can create a "curriculum of the home" that teaches their children what matters. They do this through their daily conversations, household routines, attention to school matters, and affectionate concern for their children's progress.

Conversation is important. Children learn to read, reason, and understand things better when their parents:
• read, talk, and listen to them,
• tell them stories, play games, share hobbies, and
• discuss news, TV programs, and special events.

In order to enrich the "curriculum of the home," some parents:
• provide books, supplies, and a special place for studying,
• observe routine for meals, bedtime, and homework, and
• monitor the amount of time spent watching TV and doing after-school jobs.

Parents stay aware of their children's lives at school when they:
• discuss school events,
• help children meet deadlines, and
• talk with their children about school problems and successes.

Research on both gifted and disadvantaged children shows that home efforts can greatly improve student achievement. For example, when parents of disadvantaged children take the steps listed above, their children can do as well at school as the children of more affluent families.

At first glance, this statement appears to be straightforward and unproblematic. For middle-class practitioners, for middle-class parents, and for those who are familiar with middle-class standards and practices and who aspire to be middle class, there is not much to quarrel with in this set of recommendations. Of course parents should spend time with their children. Of course they should talk to them and engage them in conversations.

There are many activities on this list, however, that poor and newly arrived immigrant parents do not engage in. Moreover, there are assumptions in this seemingly innocuous statement about how families should live their lives. As I will endeavor to make clear in the descriptions of the 10 families that I will present here, for various important reasons, some families do not observe routines or discuss school events, or even tell their children stories. They cannot provide books or supplies, and they do not have hobbies. Many parents do not know how to read. Many others work late. Most have little understanding about school deadlines or about how to "monitor" their children's homework.

What is evident, however—given the above position about the role of families in education—is that many educators and policymakers believe that attention must be directed at educating or changing what I term here "nonstandard" families, that is, families that are non-mainstream in background or orientation (e.g., nonwhite, non-English-speaking, non-middle-class). This concern about nonstandard families and the widely held belief that these families—for the good of their children—must be helped to be more like middle-class families has led to a strong movement in favor of family intervention or family education programs.

In the case of Hispanic families, and in particular in the case of Mexican-origin families, the perception that these families must be brought into the mainstream is particularly strong. For example, while in office, the former Education Secretary, Lauro Cavazos, strongly criticized Hispanic families (Suro, 1990). Arguing that neither the language barrier nor economic difficulties completely explain the problems of Hispanic students, he stated that Hispanic parents deserve much of the blame for the high dropout rate among their children. According to Cavazos, Hispanics have stopped placing a high value on education. They have not acknowledged the problem, and they have not cared that youngsters have dropped out of school. For Cavazos, then, the first vital step in improving education for Hispanics involves, not obtaining increased funding for programs at every level, but obtaining a commitment from Hispanic parents that they will work to educate their children.

Inflammatory as Cavazos's remarks were, they simply echoed what has been generally believed by many American educators to be true: Hispanic parents are neither committed to nor involved in their children's education. These educators—because they have neither the experience nor the information that might help them make sense of the lives of people different from themselves—feel both angry and indignant at the seeming indifference of Mexican-origin parents.

Not surprisingly, many well-meaning educators have decided to intervene and to try to interrupt the pattern of failure. And like many educators, social workers, and policymakers in the past, they have decided to implement programs that have as their purpose teaching Mexican-origin mothers how to help their children succeed in school. As a result, many kinds of programs have been established around the country.[6] Most focus on mothers, and most hope to teach what middle-class professionals believe are valuable parenting skills: for example, how to prepare nutritional meals, how parents should talk to their children, how little ones should and should not be disciplined, and how everyday household objects and activities can be used to teach children valuable school-related skills.

In one well-known and well-funded program established in the Southwest, for example, 2,000 low-income Mexican-origin families are being served under an umbrella of subprograms. In the parent-child education segment, mothers are visited at home and taken to receive instruction at a central program office while their children from birth to two years are cared for by others in a pleasant and well-designed child care center. They learn how to be "better" parents while they make toys for their children. They network with other parents, and they are encouraged to go to school, to learn English, and to aim for better jobs for themselves and for their children.

In another program established on the West Coast, the focus is home literacy in Spanish. Program organizers teach parents to read to their children and to encourage their writing of stories. Parents begin to write, too, and they take great pride in their children's stories. The program brings parents together to share their children's efforts and to support their "involvement" in their children's education. The aim of the organizers is to build parents' self-esteem and confidence, to develop their literacy skills, and to break the cycle of school failure for their children.

Initially, even without empirical evidence of their effectiveness, few would want to fault such programs. Indeed, as historians of education (e.g., Schlossman, 1976, 1978, 1983, 1986) have made clear, the tendency to solve perceived problems affecting families in this country by "educating" parents goes back to the turn of the century. As Schlossman (1986) has pointed out, the family-in-crisis motif is perennial and has led to a tendency "to see parent education as a solution for deeply rooted social problems" (p. 39).

A Brief Overview of Changing Goals and Purposes of Parent and Family Education

In this country parent education has been known by very different names and has had many goals. Movements to implement parent education programs have responded to varying perceptions about the existence of different problems and have been influenced by a wide variety of values or ideals about what should be. As Florin and Dokecki (1983) and Dokecki and

Moroney (1983) have pointed out, an overview of the changing goals and purposes of parent and family education reveals that concern about families has periodically shifted its focus between "mainstream" and "troubled" families. From 1600 through 1800, for example, educational programs aimed at families sought to instill moral values and to combat immorality and corruption. From 1850 to 1880 and again from 1900 to 1920, the goal of parent education programs was to socialize new immigrants to this society's dominant values. During certain periods (e.g., 1880–1900 and 1920–1940), parent education programs were aimed at the middle class and were mainly concerned with political corruption and moral responsibility. Beginning in the late 1950s, in an attempt to redress social inequalities, parent education programs were directed at the disenfranchised urban poor. The goals of such programs included the equalization of opportunities, the promotion of school success, and the early cognitive development of at-risk children. In the 1980s, in part as a result of the activities of the Barbara Bush Foundation for Family Literacy (1989), funding was made available to parent education programs that focused on developing the literacy skills of both parents and children.

According to Dokecki and Moroney (1983, pp. 56–59), the knowledge bases and theoretical/philosophical underpinnings as well as the specific purposes of parent education programs have shifted in important ways. Beginning in the early part of this century, for example, practices were directly influenced by theories about child development. According to Schlossman's (1983) overview of the first three decades of the 20th century, the nascent science of child development had a "tremendous popular appeal." In particular, "scientific" support for parent education was helped along by the efforts of foundation funding. Schlossman (1983) carefully documents how the Laura Spelman Rockefeller Memorial enlisted university researchers in the cause of child development research, in the publication of *Parents Magazine,* and in the cause of instructing women on how best to raise their children. Similarly, Laosa (1984b) traces the close relationship between these activities and the establishment of several government agencies: the National Institute of Mental Health in 1946, the National Institute of Child Health and Human Development in 1963, and the Office of Child Development in 1969. He comments that during the 1960s the public concern about children in particular led to an expansion of support for research in child development as well as to an expansion of funding for children's programming. Belief in the importance of education as well as in the need to equalize opportunities for the children of poor and immigrant families led to the implementation of compensatory programs. Early childhood intervention, according to Laosa (1984b), "was seen as having an unlimited potential not only for breaking the cycle of poverty, but also as a possibility for forging revolutionary changes in the entire educational system" (p. 54). However, as Laosa also points out, "professional knowledge and scientific expertise often greatly exceeded the available supply [of reliable data]." Sheldon White (1968, p. 204, cited in Laosa, 1984b, p. 54), for example, stated that "Placed in the uncomfortable role of experts without expertise, we are all in the business of trying to supply educated guesses about the nature of children's cognitive development."

During the 1960s and 1970s, that is, during the period in which the deficit-difference paradigm was widely supported, research on child development was designed to inform policies and practices that might improve educational opportunities for disadvantaged children. However, as Ogbu (1982) has argued, the underlying assumption of this research (e.g., Bloom, Davis, & Hess, 1965; Hunt, 1969; White et al., 1973) was that poverty, unemployment, and low attainment were caused by the inadequate child-rearing practices of the poor themselves. Criticizing the process-product research paradigm, Ogbu (1982) contended that these studies were designed to show "causal relationships between family processes, especially parent-child interaction on the one hand and childrearing outcomes—generally the language cognitive, motivation and social competencies—on the other" (p. 253). For the most part, these studies compared particular kinds of skills and competencies found in minority parents with those found among middle-class white parents.

The problems with this particular orientation are more evident today than they were when this research was first conducted. Nevertheless, the view that there exists a universal model of human development and a set of particular competencies that all children should acquire if reared adequately still influences both policy and practice. Evidence from cross-cultural research on child socialization has had little impact on the notion that, as Ogbu (1981) maintains, sets up "white middle-class childrearing practices and competencies as the standard upon which all others are measured." Even though this research documents the fact that children around the world are socialized to develop those skills and competencies that are necessary for them to live as competent adults in their particular societies, childrearing strategies of minority populations have not generally been seen from that perspective. The socialization practices of these populations are seen as deficient or limited, rather than as based directly on the family and community's experience in providing their children with the competencies they will need in order to survive.

There is evidence, moreover, that in this country, notions about maternal competence and appropriate care for young children have changed dramatically during the last 85 years. Indeed, as Wrigley (1989) has demonstrated, the increasing emphasis on the cognitive stimulation of young children is not only recent but also rooted in the social context of the times.

Her analysis of 1,017 articles drawn from the literature directed at parents written between 1900 and 1985 revealed that between 1900 and 1910, experts were concerned about hygiene, regular routines for baby management, and babies' physical care. Between 1900 and 1935, many articles argued that stimulation harmed babies and recommended leaving children strictly alone. By the 1930s, when child development had become a nascent science, experts began to be concerned about children's social and emotional development. Finally, in the 1960s, as poor children were targeted for special compensatory programs, interest in stimulating children's intellectual growth increased sharply. As a result, Wrigley (1989) argues, "middle-class families soon became interested in stimulating their young children's learning" (p. 65). By 1980, what Wrigley (1989) terms "better babies" were children "who were geared to perform academic feats at an unusually early age" (p. 71). She argues that because education has become even more important in "sorting people into different occupations and class locations," parents must strive to foster in their children those competencies and skills that they will need in order to enter high-prestige professions.

Unfortunately for those who have worked to equalize opportunities for disadvantaged children by involving their parents in parent education, what emerges from the scholarship on parent education programs in general—especially those that were designed as part of an effort to equalize opportunities—is that there are no clear answers or formulas for providing early educational advantages for disadvantaged children. Research carried out on the effectiveness of many programs designed to provide an early start for nonmainstream children is contradictory. Different reviews of the literature (e.g., Boger et al., 1986; Bronfenbrenner, 1974; Goodson & Hess, 1975; Lazar, 1988; Lazar et al., 1977) provide different interpretations of the findings. Florin and Dokecki (1983), for example, present the findings of evaluations of parent education programs and begin by pointing out that the cross-study comparison of projects is exceedingly difficult. Using only studies that had a true or quasi-experimental design, they concluded that "as a group, parent education programs have demonstrated moderate to high immediate IQ gains in program children" (p. 41). They emphasize, however, that these gains gradually decrease over time but do persist into the elementary school years. They also report that evidence from objective measures of school achievement, special education placement, and grade retention is also not altogether consistent. They point out that even though results of evaluations focusing on both child and parent outcomes demonstrate a number of positive effects, "unbridled enthusiasm" should be tempered because of the possibility of biases in self-selected program samples, effects produced by non-treatment variables, and the lack of representation of the programs included in evaluation comparisons.

The Parent Involvement Movement

The currently popular term for family intervention/parent education programs appears to be *parent involvement.* Parent involvement in schools is being strongly advocated by both researchers and practitioners. Claims about the positive effects of such involvement (Becker & Epstein, 1982; Bennett, 1986; Clark, 1988; Diaz-Soto, 1988; Epstein, 1982, 1985, 1986a, 1991; Epstein & Dauber, 1991; Henderson, 1987; Simich-Dudgeon, 1986; Walberg, 1984) maintain that parent involvement results in raising student achievement among low-income and minority youngsters, developing parents' abilities to help their children, fomenting positive attitudes by children and parents toward teachers and schools, reducing absenteeism and dropout rates, and increasing home–school communication. McLaughlin and Shields (1987) suggest, however, that the involvement of disadvantaged parents may not have achieved what educators had hoped.

According to the NEA publication *Schools and Families: Issues and Actions,* the four currently popular parent involvement models are: (1) parents as volunteers, (2) parents as receivers of information about the school, (3) parents working at the school, and (4) parents working with their own children at home. Recent research, however, suggests that teachers' views about parent involvement seem to center around the notion that parents should receive training so that they can adequately work with their children at home. Olsen et al. (1994), for example, documented in their study of reform efforts in 32 schools in California that the "prevalent belief was that for teachers to do their job at school parents need to do their job at home" (p. 95). Teachers primarily wanted parents to support their children's school work. They had less interest in parents' becoming genuinely involved in restructuring efforts and only valued their ability to help out as volunteers, as advocates of the school, and or as fundraisers. Moreover, teachers generally expressed negative views about parents and thought of them as uneducated, poor, and dysfunctional.

Similarly, Lareau (1989) found in her research on parental involvement that there are important contrasts in home–school relationships between white middle-class and white working-class parents that raise questions about both the effectiveness of involvement and the degree to which teachers welcome such involvement. Lareau argues that rather than a question of degree or amount of involvement, it is the middle-class parents' ability to mobilize their cultural capital that accounts for differences in achievement between their children and the children of working-class whites. Even though white working-class mothers were found by Lareau to have high aspirations for their children, and even though they spend time working with their children, they do not have the resources available to middle-class mothers. They often do not know how to respond when their youngsters complain that their attempts at helping them are "all wrong," and they do not have friends who are members of the teaching profession. When talking to their children's teachers, working-class mothers often feel insecure and apprehensive.

According to Lareau's view of the middle-class "home advantage," children from this background succeed in school because their parents have power (social and occupational status), competence (knowledge about schools and school learning), education, income and material resources, a vision of the interconnectedness of home and work, and networks of individuals who have information about schools and school practices.

Working-class mothers' involvement is never quite satisfactory. Working-class parents must, therefore, depend much more on both teachers and schools. They cannot serve in the role of co-teachers as the schools would hope that they could. Lamentably, because of this, their home–school relationships will fall short of what school personnel have currently concluded is desirable for *all* families. Indeed, if teachers use the middle-class family as a standard, teachers will generally assume that all parents who are "committed to their children's education" will engage in the same kinds of activities and behaviors. They will often surmise quite erroneously that parents who do not do so are unsupportive of their children's academic performance.

Parental involvement, then, may not quite be what its supporters would hope. Relationships between parents and schools do, in fact, reflect the structural locations of these individuals in the wider society. Simply bringing parents to schools will not change the racist or classist responses that teachers may have toward them and their behaviors. Parenting classes alone will not equalize outcomes.

THE VIEW FROM INSIDE TEN FAMILIES

In the chapters that follow, my objective is to bring into focus the everyday lives of 10 women whose energies were primarily involved with the survival of their families and who viewed themselves as successes or failures in terms of their ability to contribute to that survival. By showing how these 10 families lived, what they thought about, believed in and aspired to, I hope to raise serious questions about current family education programs that seek to teach immigrant adults how to parent. What my data will show is that Mexican parents do indeed know how to parent, but that because their parenting styles are the product of their class, culture, and experiences, they are unlike those of the American model of the "standard" family.

As will be clear in my description of the parents and their children, I am not arguing here that their patterns of living and of socializing their children are unique or different from those found among people in many parts of the world. Instead, it is my contention that the Mexican-origin families that I followed are similar in many ways to the turn-of-the-century immigrants who were considered to be familistic, fatalistic, and otherwise unacceptable by the mainstream members of the population.

It is my position also that a view from inside the families may help to put into perspective old cultural-deficit theories in new clothing. By inviting readers to come to know 19 adults and 12 children, I want to offer a basis for examining and weighing carefully efforts ultimately designed to change stable, successful, and functioning households. By presenting the lives of 10 families, I hope to offer insights about how their lives and the lives of other people like them might be altered by well-intentioned intervention movements designed to help non-mainstream children to succeed in school. Very specifically, I contend that to date, we still lack the kinds of knowledge that Bronfenbrenner (1979) referred to when he wrote:

> I shall presume to speak for the profession in pointing out what we do know and what we don't. We know a great deal about children's behavior and development, and quite a bit about what can and does happen inside of families—parent child interaction, family dynamics, and all that. But we know precious little about the circumstances under which families live, how these circumstances affect their lives, and what might happen if the circumstances were altered. . . . Before we can engage in parent education of the kinds here proposed, we have to learn a good deal more than we know at present about the actual experience of families in different segments of our society. (p. 220)

CHAPTER 2

THE SETTING AND THE FAMILIES

THE BORDERLANDS

The United States and Mexico share a border that is almost 2,000 miles long. A total of six northern Mexican states (Baja California, Sonora, Chihuahua, Coahuila, Nuevo León, and Tamaulipas) are adjacent to four southwestern American states (California, Arizona, New Mexico, and Texas). The border region includes a total of 34 Mexican counties that are adjacent to 25 counties located in the United States.

The town where this study took place is located in one of the Southwestern states bordering Mexico. This is an area of the country known as the U.S.–Mexico borderlands, a region that spans both the United States and Mexico.

The families that took part in this study settled within this boundary zone, that is, they settled in a town within 100 miles of the border cities of Ciudad Juárez, Chihuahua, and El Paso, Texas. These families, although living in the United States, continued to be residents of the greater border area itself. They frequently traveled between the Mexican state of Chihuahua and the adjoining American states to the north. For some families, traveling between countries was limited to occasional grocery-shopping expeditions to Ciudad Juárez, but for other families—especially for those whose members were legal residents of the United States—being borderlands residents meant that they had access to the best of both countries. They could maintain ties to Mexico; at the same time, they could live and work in a setting that provided them with important opportunities not available to them in their country of origin.

Together, the border cities of Ciudad Juárez[1] and El Paso, Texas, comprise a large metropolitan area with a population of close to two million. Of the Mexican *fronteras* or border cities, Ciudad Juárez is considered to be the most populous. Within the last two decades, Juárez as well as the other Mexican border cities has experienced a dramatic increase in population. Large numbers of residents of the cities and villages in the interior of Mexico have migrated to the border, drawn by an industrialization program that has encouraged the building of "offshore" American-owned factories. These factories have generally employed young female workers in the assembly of products that are then shipped back to the United States.[2]

The proximity of the United States and the possibility of crossing the border to work at much higher wages has also continued to be a strong pull for many residents of the Mexican interior. In addition to the lure of possible employment in the *maquilas* or border factories, migration by whole families to the Mexican border often takes place in response to the fact that the head of the family has already crossed over into the United States. The move to the border by the family makes it possible for the male parent to see his wife and children more frequently than he would if they were to continue to reside in central or southern Mexico. In many cases, the move to the border is also a first step in the long journey to becoming legal residents of the United States.

LAS FUENTES

Las Fuentes is the name I have given to the city where the study itself took place. It is located in the United States in a narrow river valley within a few hours' drive of the Mexican border and the cities of El Paso, Texas, and Juárez, Mexico. Like many other towns in this border area, Las Fuentes is surrounded by desert and flanked by a high bare mountain. It is not a particularly pretty place.

In the spring and summer, the water in the Rio Grande—which farther downstream serves to mark the international boundary—flows gently through the narrow basin in which Las Fuentes is located. There are trees along its banks and very green cultivated fields that contrast with the dry high mesas and arid land beyond the valley proper.

The summer is long and very hot. The midday sun is scorching; on some days even the asphalt softens because of the burning heat. But the evenings are beautiful. The sun sets against an almost turquoise sky, and bands of orange, pink, lavender, and purple fade slowly into the darkness.

In the winter, the fields are barren and the days are cold. The riverbed is dry, its water stopped by a dam many miles upstream. Once or twice a year it snows. Schools close for a day or two. Children build snowmen and laugh as inexperienced motorists skid in the icy streets. But in a day or so, the sun shines brightly and quickly melts the ice and snow.

Winter is short, and spring begins early. It is a Southwestern spring in which there are sandstorms and days of whistling winds and dust. But finally the wind stops, new crops are planted, and once again another cycle begins.

Las Fuentes can most accurately be described as a small, semirural community located near a large urban area. It is not a large town, and there is little that attracts visitors to the city itself. The neighboring town of La Mision, however, with its Spanish-style plaza and mission church, is popular with tourists, and its many curio shops and restaurants are a source of employment for many residents of Las Fuentes. Together, Las Fuentes and La Mision have a population of about 50,000. In the 1980 census, 20,500 residents of the area identified themselves as persons of Hispanic descent.

Las Fuentes and La Mision can be roughly divided into two sections: the valley proper, which is settled primarily by farming families and farm workers and includes the town of La Mision, and the city of Las Fuentes.

The Valley

The section I call the valley here includes the town of La Mision, as well as many large and small farms. These farms have been owned by both Anglos[3] and "Hispanics"[4] for generations, and have provided employment for both documented and undocumented Mexican field hands. The largest farm in the area is an extremely successful enterprise that regularly employs and provides company housing for hundreds of families of Mexican origin who live there on a permanent basis.

The town of La Mision, because of its attraction to tourists, has undergone gentrification but takes pride in its history and "quaintness." Its residents include penniless artists, wealthy art patrons, well-to-do Southwest history buffs, old "Hispanic" families who are descendants of the founders of La Mision, and poor *Mexicano* immigrant and lower-middle-class Chicano families. La Mision School, which serves the farming valley area, offers one of the two bilingual programs available in Las Fuentes and La Mision.

The City

Las Fuentes is itself subdivided into various subsections: (1) the old downtown area and business district; (2) the east side, in which newly arrived Mexicanos, Chicanos, Blacks, and poor Anglos reside; (3) the very mixed (Anglo and Chicano) neighborhoods; and (4) the primarily Anglo neighborhoods. The east side is the poorest of all subsections and is known locally as the "Mexican" neighborhood.

General Characteristics

Because of Las Fuentes's proximity to a large urban border area that has a population of over two million, its residents move easily between the semi-rural valley setting and the urban context. Large numbers of residents of Las

Fuentes work in the border city of El Paso and commute on a daily basis. Others travel to El Paso regularly in order to shop, attend movies, concerts, and the like, or to visit the Mexican city of Juárez across the river.

In general, the residents of Las Fuentes are employed in a variety of types of work. A nearby government military and research base provides employment for many professionals in technical fields and for clerical and other staff. The state university employs technical, clerical, and janitorial support staff in addition to its teaching faculty. The farming and canning industry regularly employs unskilled workers on both a seasonal and year-round basis. Employment is also available, as it is in cities of the same size, in service occupations, in construction, in both state and city government, in retail marketing, and in the food industry.

The "Mexican" Barrio

The families involved in the study all live on the east side of Las Fuentes in an area of the city known to its residents as the "Mexican" community or "el barrio." This community is a part of the city that is bordered by the old downtown section on the west, by a mixed middle-class community on the east, by a fast-growing new business district on the south, and by mostly undeveloped desert to the north.

As compared to other sections of Las Fuentes, the barrio or east side neighborhood does not look like it is part of an ordinary American city. Instead, it closely resembles typical working-class neighborhoods in many parts of Mexico. For example, the majority of the houses are made of adobe and are built close to the street. Front doors open not on stoops or porches or front yards, but directly onto the sidewalk. When there are yards, they are very small, planted with brightly colored flowering plants, and always surrounded by walls or fences. Most houses are stuccoed or neatly white-washed, but a large number are in a state of disrepair, and the adobe can be seen under crumbling stucco. On a few of the older streets, several more stately homes are found, some surrounded by rock walls or wrought-iron fences. These were the homes of some of the original Hispanic residents of Las Fuentes.

Essentially, the east side neighborhood is a residential area; however, two streets that run north-south are part of the expanding business area of Las Fuentes. Plumbers, electricians, contractors, and other owner-operated enterprises are located on these two streets. Many of these businesses serve not the immediate community, but the entire Las Fuentes area. Small neighborhood *tienditas* (family grocery stores) are scattered throughout this section of the city. Some are very small and appear to be rapidly losing out to the quick-shop corner grocery store chains.

Very little graffiti can be found on the whitewashed walls of the houses and businesses in the neighborhood. With the exception of a small mural painted on a wall behind the public restrooms in one neighborhood park, street art is not in evidence. The graffiti found in this park was primarily in English but included many Spanish names.

All large public signs in the neighborhood, including street signs, store signs, and billboards, are found only in English, as are instructions on public telephones. The only printed material in Spanish is found in several convenience stores that serve the immediate neighborhood. This material includes two newspapers printed in Juárez and a supply of *fotonovelas*.[5]

As compared to other Mexican communities located at a greater distance from the border, which have made special efforts to create a "typically" Mexican business district, the residents of this barrio appear not to have attempted to use written Spanish in the neighborhood at all. I conjecture that for newly arrived immigrants, the very close proximity of the border provides access to the "real" thing, that is, to the genuine Mexican business community. In communities that are located at a greater distance from the border, local merchants have much to gain from importing genuine Mexican articles and food items. This was not true in Las Fuentes, where residents could easily drive to Ciudad Juárez and purchase those items at their original low cost.

Residents of the Neighborhood

In planning the research project, we had initially been concerned about not studying 10 families in isolation. In order to understand how they functioned and how they survived in the world around them, we felt it was important to study the entire east side neighborhood and to understand exactly what living there required of its residents. In order to obtain a clear picture of the community, then, we carried out two separate activities: (1) we surveyed 50 households in the community, and (2) we visited business establishments located near to or in the east side barrio.

Beginning in November 1983, we conducted a door-to-door survey of 50 households in the community and obtained detailed information about the neighborhood and its residents. Specifically, the survey sought to determine exactly what kinds of language and literacy skills would be required of newly arrived Mexican children in order for them to become competent members of the community in which they would live. In order to select the households, an aerial photograph of the community was obtained and dwellings were numbered. Fifty dwellings were selected randomly from the total number of dwellings identified. Interviews were conducted with occupants of each of the selected dwellings.

A detailed study of all business located in the community was also undertaken. The purpose of this activity was to obtain information about the language skills needed by the residents of the area from a slightly different perspective. We felt that by observing locations in which business was normally transacted in the community and by interviewing long-term employees/owners, it would be possible to discover how much English and Spanish were spoken in the community outside of the home domain, and what levels of proficiency appeared to be needed by individuals in order to carry out their everyday affairs. In carrying out this phase of the community study, we visited every business located in the community.

The majority of the interactions that we observed in the streets of the east side of Las Fuentes involved Hispanics, that is, persons who—by their dress and demeanor—could be identified as either Chicanos or newly arrived Mexicanos.[6] However, in one section of the neighborhood, interactions among the small number of Black residents in the area were frequently observed, also.

Results of the door-to-door survey revealed that residents of the area include long-term Chicano residents over the age of 50, young Chicanos who have moved back to the east side to raise their children in the original neighborhood, a few older Anglos who settled there as young people, a few younger Anglos in their mid-twenties who saw themselves as occupying temporary cheap housing, a community of African-Americans that had been in the east side for several generations, and newly arrived Mexicano immigrants. Most of the rental housing in the neighborhood was owned by Chicanos who originally lived in the area but who, over the years, have moved to better neighborhoods.[7]

Language Use in the Community

With few exceptions, English is the language of primary interaction heard in the streets and in the business areas of the community. Spanish, when it is heard, is generally spoken at a low volume and between members of the Hispanic group to each other. It is also frequently used as a secret language by Chicanos/Mexican-Americans in order to stress in-group membership or even to exclude outsiders. Most Chicanos ordinarily address strangers of both ethnic groups in English and normally refuse to speak Spanish to Anglos. *Mexicanos,* on the other hand, not wishing to call attention to themselves (especially if their legal status in the country is ambiguous), avoid speaking at all in those contexts in which speaking their only language, Spanish, could potentially provoke negative reactions.

Persons heard speaking to each other exclusively in Spanish (without code-switching into English) are normally identified as newly arrived *Mexicano* immigrants, as opposed to long-term residents or second-generation

Chicanos. Ordinarily, newly arrived immigrants are treated kindly (if distantly) by Chicanos. If it is clear that if immigrants do not speak English, Chicanos will accommodate to the use of Spanish even when it involves extreme effort. This is particularly true in business interactions.

Even among long-term residents of the community, however, observations revealed that certain Hispanics (for example, elderly women and preschool children) are frequently addressed in Spanish by others. Interviews confirmed that elderly Chicanos (in spite of having learned and used English at school) prefer to use Spanish in later years. This is especially true of women who have not worked outside the home and who have interacted primarily with members of the family.

Overall Rhythm of the East Side Neighborhood

During the daytime and evening hours in the winter and spring, there is little activity in the neighborhood. Occasionally a group of teenagers walks down the street, or a mother walks to the store with her children. Except for the busy streets that cross the neighborhood, there is little traffic in the streets of the barrio. In the summer, however, the picture is quite different. During the long evening hours, entire families take advantage of the cool sunsets and sit out on the front steps of their houses or pull chairs out to the sidewalk. Children of all ages run and play in the streets until well after dark while their elders chat with each other and observe others in the neighborhood as they come and go.

There is a sense of transience in the neighborhood, rather than a sense of community or permanence. Little history has been shared by people living next door to each other or on the same street. Families move frequently within the neighborhood to find better housing or lower rents. There is little sense of "community" or of belonging to a shared world. Most people do not know their neighbors, and most newcomers do not feel particularly welcome. Newly arrived immigrants learn to survive on their own or rely on the help of already established family networks. They expect little from the "strangers" living around them.

FAMILY PROFILES

As might be expected, there were many similarities and many differences among the families that participated in the study. Essentially, all families had in common the fact that both parents were first-generation immigrants.[8]

Figure 2.1 presents an overview of the 10 families, the place of birth of each parent, the number of children in each family, and the focal child. It is

important to point out, however, that in all cases, I have used only pseud-
onyms.

As will be noted from Figure 2.1, there were some important similarities
and differences among the families. For example:

–9 out of the 10 families were two-parent families. The only single
    parent in the group was Carmen Ornelas.
–Of the 19 parents, only Terrence Sotelo was born in the United States.
–7 of the 10 families had 4 or more children. The largest family in the
    group had 8 children and the smallest family had 2.

It is important for me to point out also that two sets of families were
related. The Pedro Soto family and the Arturo Soto family were related
through both the fathers *and* the mothers. The fathers were brothers and the
mothers were sisters. The Leyba and Castro families were also related—
Reina Leyba was the sister of Chuy Castro.

In terms of their experience and familiarity with the United States, the
10 families were of 3 main types: (1) families in which one parent had lived
in the United States for over 25 years; (2) families in which one parent came
to the United States as a child or in the early teen years; and (3) families in
which both parents came to the United States as adults.

Families with One Long-Term U.S. Resident

Three families fell into the first category, that is, families who had one
parent who had lived in the United States for over 25 years. I have presented
a brief sketch of these families in Figure 2.2.

The Pedro Soto Family. The Pedro Soto family had been in Las
Fuentes for approximately nine years. Pedro was in his mid-fifties and his
wife, Velma, was in her mid-thirties. They had been married for a little over
8 years. At the beginning of the study, the members of the household included Pedro and Velma, Aydé (Velma's daughter from a previous relationship), the couple's three children (Juan Pedro, Saúl, and Melania), Carlos
(Pedro's son from a previous marriage), and Gerardo Soto (Pedro's blind
father). Various members of Velma's family (sisters, nieces, and her mother)
also spent periods of time in the household.

Pedro first crossed the border when he was in his late teens. He worked
in the United States illegally for a period of time, but was finally able to
obtain his legal resident status. His first wife was a *Mexicana* whom he had
met while in the United States. They married in this country and raised a

FIGURE 2.1
Family Profiles

Family/Parents' Names	Place of Birth	Children (age at beginning of study)	Focal Child
Soto, Pedro	Saucillo, Chihuahua	Aydé (12) Juan Pedro (7) Saúl (5)	Saúl
Soto, Velma	Valle de Zaragoza, Chihuahua	Melania (1)	
Soto, Arturo	Saucillo, Chihuahua	Lorena (17) Virgilio (14) Corina (11)	Amapola & Jasmín
Soto, Amelia	Valle de Zaragoza, Chihuahua	Amapola (5) Jasmín (4)	
Sotelo, Terrence	Big Spring, Texas	Sara (11) Lola (9) Terry Jr. (7)	Pamela & Keith
Sotelo, Isela	Juárez, Chihuahua	Pamela (5) Keith (4) Ada (3) Abby (1) Vanessa (born during study)	
Leyba, Héctor	Namiquipa, Chihuahua	Maya (8) Josué (5) Chepe (1)	Josué
Leyba, Reina	Namiquipa, Chihuahua		
Castro, Chuy	Namiquipa, Chihuahua	Miguel (15) Rebeca (13) Elena (12)	Lucila
Castro, Rosario	Namiquipa, Chihuahua	Oscar (11) Susana (7) Lucila (4)	
Gómez, Federico	Camargo, Chihuahua	Federico Jr (4) Ernesto (3 mos)	Federico Jr.
Gómez, Eulalia	Nuevo Casas Grandes, Chihuahua		

FIGURE 2.1
continued

Family/Parents' Name	Place of Birth	Children (age at beginning of study)	Focal Child
Tinajero, Javier	La Cuchilla, Michoacán	Rolando (8) Alejandro (7) Marica (5)	Marica
Tinajero, Socorro	Juan Aldama, Zacatecas	Emma Alicia (1)	
Ramírez, Joaquín	Rio Bravo, Tamaulipas	Ricardo (9) Rosana (7) Joel (5)	Joel
Ramírez, María Elena	Rio Bravo, Tamaulipas	Ramiro (8 mos)	
Cerda, Ernesto	Guanajuato, Gto.	Victoria (5) Elisa (4)	Victoria
Cerda, Gloria	Torreón, Coahuila	Donna (2)	
Ornelas, Carmen	Juárez, Chihuahua	Julio (7) Carmensita (5) Cynthia (4) Nena (3) José (2) Anelena (newborn) Octavio (born during the study)	Cynthia

family of several children. Carlos, the youngest child of that union, was 18 at the time the study began.

Pedro worked at a number of different jobs and lived for a long period of time in California, working primarily in construction. It was in California that he became a member of a carpenter's union, a membership of which he was quite proud. Pedro was also proud of the fact that he could communicate in English.

At some point in his early to mid-forties, Pedro and his first wife were divorced. The divorce seems to have affected Pedro deeply, and he returned to his village in Chihuahua for frequent visits and also spent time with other relatives in Ciudad Juárez. During this period, he began to court his brother's sister-in-law, Velma, who was a single parent of a little girl. The couple married, and Pedro returned to the United States with his new wife and her child. They finally settled in Las Fuentes because Velma disliked California

FIGURE 2.2
Family Residence in the United States

Families with One Long-Term U.S. Resident			
Family	*Parent*	*Time in U.S.*	*U.S. Citizen*
Soto	Pedro	38 years	no
Tinajero	Javier	25 years	no
Sotelo	Terrence	50 years (estimate)	yes
Families in Which One Member Came to the U.S. in Early Youth			
Family	*Parent*	*Time in U.S.*	*U.S. Citizen*
Cerda	Gloria	Arrived at 12	no
Gómez	Eulalia	Arrived at 12	no
Families in Which Both Parents Came to the U.S. as Adults			
Family	*Parent*	*Time in U.S.*	*U.S. Citizen*
Ornelas	Carmen	5 years	illegal
Soto	Arturo	15 years	legal
	Amelia	5 years	legal
Castro	Chuy	11 years	legal
	Rosario	4 years	legal
Leyba	Héctor	4 years	legal
	Reina	4 years	legal
Ramírez	Joaquín	11 years	legal
	María Elena	11 years	legal

and New Mexico, two states where the couple lived for several years. Las Fuentes seemed ideal to Velma because it was close to the border and because her sister Amelia and Pedro's brother Arturo also lived there.

At the time of the study, Pedro was semiretired and worked only occasionally. His energies were devoted to building a two-bedroom cement-block house for the family. The land on which the house was being built was bought with money saved up by Pedro during the previous 20 years.

The Tinajero Family. At the beginning of the study, the Tinajero family had been in Las Fuentes for only a few months. They lived in a small apartment in an apartment building located in one of the worst sections of the east side neighborhood. Members of the household included Javier (in his late forties), his wife, Socorro (in her early thirties), their four children (Rolando, Alejandro, Marica, and Emma Alicia), and Socorro's mother, Doña Carmen.[9]

Like Pedro Soto, Javier Tinajero immigrated to the United States in his early youth. He spent most of his time in the Denver, Colorado area, where he had relatives and where he was quickly given a job working in a Mexican restaurant. He remained in the United States illegally for a number of years until he was able to obtain legal resident status. It appears that he was helped in this endeavor by his first wife, who was a U.S.-born Chicana.

Javier remained in the Denver area for almost 20 years. During that time he raised a family, worked in relatives' restaurants, and finally opened a restaurant of his own. His business failure, coupled with problems with his wife and her family, led to a bitter divorce. Like Pedro Soto, Javier left Denver, returned to the Mexican border, and found a new wife. This time he married a young, hard-working *Mexicana* who was then employed as a hotel housekeeper. After about five years of moving from place to place and working at many different jobs, the couple settled in Las Fuentes, where Javier opened a very small Mexican restaurant.

At the time the study ended, the Tinajeros were slowly making it. They had bought a house and had brought Socorro's sister and her husband from Mexico to work with them in the restaurant. Javier's previous experience in this country and in the restaurant business was the family's most important resource.

The Sotelo Family. Of the 10 families in the study, the Sotelo family was the poorest. During the 3-year period in which the families were followed, a total of 10 people (2 adults and 8 children) lived in a series of rented 1- or 2-bedroom houses in the east side neighborhood. Terrence Sotelo Sr. (the only American-born citizen in the study) was an unemployed mechanic in his mid-fifties. The family lived from a small check from the Veterans Administration, from another monthly check the origin of which was unknown to Mrs. Sotelo, and from public assistance in the form of food stamps.

Like Javier Tinajero and Pedro Soto, Terrence Sotelo went through a divorce and a time of loneliness and despair. At the time that he met his second wife, Isela, in Juárez, he was in a wheelchair as a result of an automobile accident. Even though he had some doubts about his ability to father children, he married Isela after she became pregnant with Terry Jr.

Isela Sotelo, a woman of about 30, although married to an American citizen, entered the United States illegally, as did Sara and Lola, her two children from a previous relationship. Although the remaining six children were born in this country and were American citizens, no attempt had been made by Terrence to establish legal residence for Isela.

Families in Which One Member Came to the United States in Early Youth

The second category of families I identified were families in which one of the two parents came to the United States in late childhood or early teens (see Figure 2.2).

The Cerda Family. Like the Sotelo family, the Cerda family lived in a series of three different houses during the period of the study. For a stretch of time, they also moved in with Gloria Cerda's mother. The Cerda household included Ernesto Cerda and his wife, Gloria; Victoria and Elisa, who were Gloria's children from her first marriage; Donna, who was Ernesto and Gloria's child; and Gloria's father, who was in his sixties.

Ernesto was a newly arrived Mexicano of about 25 who came from the interior of Mexico. He spoke no English but generally worked as a janitor and in general housecleaning and service. When janitorial work was not available, he worked in the fields picking whatever crop was in season. He had been in Las Fuentes only a short time when he met and married Gloria. He was here illegally.

Gloria, who was 24 at the time the study began, had been in Las Fuentes since the age of 12. She was brought to the area by her mother, who by then had worked in the area cleaning houses for a number of years. When she arrived in Las Fuentes, Gloria was sent to school, but because of her limited schooling in Mexico and her lack of knowledge of English, school was never a comfortable place. She dropped out after the ninth grade.

After 12 years in the country, however, Gloria spoke English well. She knew how a number of systems work (e.g., how to send children to school outside their neighborhood), and, unlike other *Mexicanas,* had the courage to get out of an unhappy first marriage. She appeared to move comfortably between the Chicano and the *Mexicano* worlds.

The Gómez Family. Of the 10 families in the study, the Gómez family came the closest to the middle-class standard family. Federico Gómez worked for the physical plant service of a large local institution as a house painter, and Eulalia worked evenings and weekends as a waitress at her brother's restaurant. The couple lived in a two-bedroom house that they were buying and slowly remodeling. They had two children, Federico Jr. and Ernesto.

Like Gloria Cerda, Eulalia Gómez also came to Las Fuentes from Mexico illegally at the age of 12. She was brought to the area by one of her brothers to help with child care. Unlike Gloria, however, Eulalia did not spend several years in an American school. It appears that she attempted seventh grade and soon dropped out to return to Mexico for a period of time. When she came back to the area, she never enrolled in school again. Up to the time that the study ended, Eulalia said that she spoke and understood little English.

Unlike Ernesto Cerda, however, Federico Gómez had several advantages. As the son of a U.S.-born citizen who returned to Mexico, he was able to enter the country legally. When he arrived in Las Fuentes, he had a network of relatives in the area who were able to help him. He was also better prepared than other immigrants. Federico had completed *secundaria*[10] in Mexico and had worked with his father on his farm. Working at planting appealed to him and he began mowing lawns and cleaning yards. He soon developed a loyal group of customers. After some years, he was able to obtain a more permanent job with the assistance of other family members. He nevertheless continued to operate his yard maintenance service in his spare time.

Compared to the other families in the study, the Gómez family enjoyed a much higher standard of living. Household furnishings, children's toys, and even the ownership of a large used car and a pickup truck reflected that standard. As compared to Gloria Cerda, for example, Eulalia's 12 years' experience cleaning houses had given her a clear idea of what she wanted for herself and for her children. It was clear that she and her husband shared the same dream and the same views about how to make their dream possible.

Families in Which Both Parents Came to the United States as Adults

I placed 5 of the 10 families in this category. In each case, both parents came to the United States as adults. The male parent, however, came over first and spent several years by himself in the country.

The Ornelas Family. Carmen Ornelas had been in Las Fuentes for about 5 years. At the beginning of the study, she was a woman in her late twenties or early thirties who was the single parent of 6 children. By the end of the third year of the study, she was a single parent of 7 children.

Carmen was a native of Juárez. She was raised on the border by her grandmother because her mother worked illegally in El Paso as a domestic servant in order to support them all. She was familiar with the U.S. side of the border and had crossed frequently into El Paso as both a child and a young woman. She had never resided in the United States, however, until she moved to Las Fuentes.

Carmen and her family lived in a two-bedroom duplex on a busy street in the east side neighborhood. She had no relatives in the city, nor did she visit her relatives in Juárez frequently. Her illegal status in the United States and her fear of getting caught prevented her from crossing the border often.

Carmen did not drive and did not speak English. This is an interesting fact because of her long-term residence in Juárez. Most residents in the area acquire at least a basic command of English. Her lack of English skills is also of note because of all the parents in the study, she was the individual who had the most formal education. She had completed *secundaria*[11] in Mexico and had then graduated from an *"escuela de comercio,"* a two-year secretarial program.

Because of her inability to drive and her nonexistent English skills, Carmen appeared to depend on one neighbor for dealing with the outside world and on her current male partner for transportation. Apparently, she also received some assistance from the fathers of the different children.

The Soto Family. Arturo and Amelia Soto were the brother and sister of Pedro and Velma Soto, who have been discussed above. Arturo (age 42) worked as a farm hand on a local farm. Amelia (age 40) did not work outside the home during the three years of the study.

Arturo had been in the United States approximately 15 years. He had worked in the Las Fuentes area for most of that period, and he had moved his family from his village in Chihuahua to Juárez, where he could visit on weekends. After about 10 years of employment on the same farm, Arturo was assisted in entering the country legally by his employer. Sometime later, he was able to obtain legal resident status for his family as well.

Of the 10 families, the Arturo Soto family was the only one that lived outside the east side neighborhood. During the period of the study, they lived on the farm where Arturo worked, in an old adobe four-bedroom house that had been the main farmhouse at one time. The household consisted of Arturo and Amelia, their five children, and their niece, Cristina. As was the case in the Pedro Soto household, a number of different relatives spent long periods of time visiting.

The Castro Family. Like Arturo Soto, Chuy Castro (age 35) also spent a period of about 11 years working illegally in the United States and traveling back and forth between Las Fuentes and a village in Chihuahua. After he obtained legal status, his family moved to the border, and he visited Juárez every other week.

Compared to other men in the study, Chuy had the advantage of having several brothers in Las Fuentes who helped him to obtain regular work in construction, an occupation that was far more lucrative than farm labor. All of the brothers were here legally. This was because their mother had been born in the United States. Even though Doña Pepa had lived in Mexico most of her life, she was able to reenter the country when she was in her fifties and bring in with her some of her adult children.

For Chuy, the decision to remain in the United States and to move his family to Las Fuentes took place, however, only after most of his brothers and sisters had moved to the area. Initially, his wife Rosario (age 30) and their children entered the country illegally. Some years later, they were able to obtain legal resident status.

During the time of the study, the Castro family lived in a four-bedroom house in a low-rent project. The household included Chuy, Rosario, and their six children.

The Leyba Family. At the time the study began, Héctor Leyba (age 29) and his wife Reina (age 28) had been in the United States for four years. Reina, who was the sister of Chuy Castro, was helped to enter the country by her mother (the U.S. citizen described above) and by her brothers and sisters who were already in the area. These relatives also helped Héctor to obtain work in construction and Reina to obtain work in a local factory. Various members of the family also helped them by taking care of the children while the couple worked.

Except for the two women who worked in family restaurants, Reina Leyba was the only woman in the 10 families who worked steadily year-round. The Leybas had three children, Maya, Josué, and Chepe.

The Ramírez Family. The Ramírez family was the only family of the 10 who did not have ties to the state of Chihuahua. Both Joaquín (30) and María Elena (26) were from the U.S.–Mexico border area adjacent to the state of Tamaulipas. The couple had crossed the border illegally before they married and set up house in the Texas valley. They had moved to Las Fuentes because Joaquín's father and sister were in the area. Since Joaquín's father had remarried a U.S.-born Chicana, he was able to help the couple obtain legal residence.

During the period of the study, the Ramírez family also lived in several different houses. The composition of the household varied, but essentially it included Joaquín and María Elena and their four children, María Elena's sister and her two children, and a brother of Joaquín's. María Elena's mother had also moved to the area and lived in the east side neighborhood with a man she had met in Las Fuentes.

Joaquín worked as a farm laborer and generally followed the crops in a three-state area. He normally traveled with his father and other relatives and stayed "in the field" for two and three months at a time. María Elena was not employed during the time of the study, but she had occasionally worked in local canneries.

MAKING THE DECISION TO LEAVE MEXICO

Pedro and Velma, Héctor and Reina, Javier and Socorro, and all the other adults in the study had much in common with each other. They had come to the United States, as did other groups of immigrants in the past, looking for opportunities and hoping to live better lives. In recalling why they had made the decision to leave Mexico, all of them mentioned being able to earn a better living for their families and being able to give their children more than they themselves had had. For some of the women, like Velma Soto, Isela Sotelo, and Socorro Tinajero, the decision to leave involved following the man they had married. For others, like Gloria Cerda and Eulalia Gómez, the decision was made for them by other adults. For all of them, whether they had family networks in the area or not, deciding to leave Mexico and everything that was ordinary and familiar took courage. In some cases, they made the decision slowly, a little at a time, in order to lessen both the pain and the fear.

Life in Las Fuentes, no matter how close to the border, was different from living in Mexico, whether in Ciudad Juárez or in their own villages. The houses were different, the stores were different, and the language was different. Ultimately, they and their families would become different, too.

In the chapter that follows, I will describe why it was that the adults often deceived themselves into thinking that they were not really changing their lives significantly by coming across into the United States. I will describe their familiarity with the U.S. side of the border, their assumptions about what life would be like here, and the uncertainties faced by all of them in becoming legal residents of this country.

CHAPTER 3

COMING ACROSS

ENTERING THE UNITED STATES

Hundreds of thousands of immigrants have entered this country since the beginning of this century. For people who were born in this country, however, it is often difficult to imagine what it was like for early immigrants to leave their countries and to arrive in the United States. The reopening of Ellis Island in 1990, however, brought to life for the American people the moment of arrival in the United States of many of these individuals. Using old pictures and moving recollections of a number of now fully established former immigrants, the media sought to paint a picture of the determination, hopes, and dreams of those who arrived in New York, saw the Statue of Liberty, and prayed that they would be allowed to remain in this land of opportunity. For these Ellis Island immigrants, the process of coming to the United States during the early part of this century involved a decision to leave the home country, a long and often difficult journey, and a definite moment of arrival and entry into the United States. What is clear from the Ellis Island Museum archives is that for these early immigrants, there was a precise moment in which the home country was left behind, and a precise moment in which they entered the United States. Many documents of the period offer evidence of the fact that many of these individuals could later recall the exact dates of these events, their feelings at the moment of departure or arrival, and even the detailed circumstances of the processing routine. In many ways, arrival and processing at Ellis Island had the effect of a legal ceremony or ritual that forever after changed the lives of these "new" Americans.

In contrast to the Ellis Island experience, for the 10 families who participated in this study, there was no legal ceremony and no ritual at the moment of arrival. For these largely borderlands people, their coming across to *live* in the United States (rather than to buy goods or work temporarily) was not the result of a long and difficult journey. Most had spent time in the United States on numerous occasions, and most had relatives here. "Coming across" involved simply crossing at a legal entry point by using their own or a relative's local border crossing card[1] or entering illegally elsewhere along the 2,000-mile border.

As opposed to Ellis Island immigrants, all the adults in the 10 families did not say goodbye to their country of origin. They did not see themselves as leaving, never to return. The acts of leaving and of crossing the border were in themselves not particularly unsettling events or even occasions that deserved to be remembered clearly.

In examining the differences between these two groups of immigrants, it is important to emphasize that the reaction of the 10 *Mexicano* families to the experience of entering the United States was not the result of indifference or lack of enthusiasm. Instead, it was the result of superficial familiarity with the U.S. side of the border and of an initial ignorance about how life in this country would be different from life on the Mexican side of the river.

With two exceptions (the Ramírez family), one or both parents in all 10 families had spent a period of time living on the the border, in Juárez. They had moved from villages and small towns in rural areas of the state of Chihuahua, or other Mexican states, to Juárez, the largest city in that northern border state. They had learned how to survive in a large urban area that is crowded, poor, and generally unkind to new arrivals. The U.S.–Mexican border, therefore, was a familiar place to them. They knew it through relatives, through tales told about crossings and returns, and through numerous reports of schemes and plans to cross into the United States that had either failed or succeeded.

Contact with the American side of the border was seen as ordinary and normal. Even though "*el otro lado*" (the other side) might have been romanticized from a distant village, once in the area, it became almost a part of everyday life. For example, all the women in the study who lived in Juárez for even a short period of time crossed frequently into the United States, especially into the city of El Paso. For residents of Juárez who have secured local border crossing cards, crossing into El Paso from Juárez involves simply walking or riding across the bridge, showing the card, and entering U.S. territory. On weekdays, the lines at the bridge are long, and cars are lined up for blocks as thousands of Juárez residents enter El Paso to shop, to work,[2] or to go to school. Heavy traffic between the two cities is normal, and the interdependencies between the two economies are well documented.

For the women and children, the move from the villages to the border was the first step in bringing the family together after years of absence and periodic visits. Once on the border, the experience of having crossed or having attempted to cross the border legally or illegally became a familiar one. In some cases the illegality was low-risk and simply involved borrowing someone else's border crossing card or green card in order to go shopping in El Paso for several hours. In other cases it involved walking across the river at night or early morning and spending weeks or months working as domestic servants in El Paso homes. It was even the case that a few of the women spent periods of several months with their husbands who were already in the United States, leaving their children behind with relatives in Juárez. These long stays usually took place in anticipation of a permanent move and often involved looking for housing, examining available options, and simply getting to know the place where they would bring their children.

The experience for the men was somewhat more traumatic. For most of them, crossing into the United States involved leaving their towns in rural Mexico when they were in their late teens or early twenties and entering the United States illegally. Some men had connections and leads that helped them cross the river and relatives who helped to find them work. Others made it on their own, to the border area, to Juárez, and then across the shallow muddy waters. None of the men spent much time living or working on the Mexican side of the border. They crossed as soon as they could and persevered in crossing and recrossing when caught. For the most part, all of the men in the study had spent years in the United States before they moved their families to Juárez.

Again, in contrast to the Ellis Island immigrants, most of the *Mexicanos* in the study entered the country illegally or helped their families to do so. Whatever trauma was associated with coming across, then, had to do with the fear of getting caught and with the fear of having to go back. In every case, the illegal status of one or more family members made them feel vulnerable. For years at a time, they lived with the knowledge that at any moment they or members of their family, including their children, could be arrested by the border patrol and sent back to Mexico. The fact of being illegal made them easy targets for exploitation and for blackmail by angry neighbors and even resentful relatives.

THE ILLEGAL PERIOD

Of the 18 Mexican-born adults in the study, only 3 entered the country legally from the beginning. The remaining 15 adults spent a period of time in the United States as undocumented or illegal aliens. Being undocumented, therefore, was part of the history of each of the families. It was generally taken for granted, for example, that men came over first, that it would take them time to become established in the country, and that having found a way of supporting their families, they would send for them and bring them across. Few of the wives had clear knowledge of what the process had been for their husbands. The details of their crossing over and their hiding and being caught were not dwelt on. What was important was that their husbands had been able to cross over and stay. If a man had been able to find a job and work so well that his *patrones* still wanted him back after he was caught and sent back to Mexico, this was a source of pride. It meant that his abilities had been recognized and his hard work valued.

When Amelia Soto talked about her husband, Arturo, and his employers, for example, she was quick to point out that the *viejitos* (the old farmer and his wife) had come to depend so much on Arturo that they would wait for him until he could cross over again whenever he was caught. They had had many farmhands, she would boast, but never one as dependable as Arturo. These Americans were very amused, she added, at how good Arturo became at avoiding the border patrol checkpoints on the highway[3] after many years of sneaking back to their farm.

Not all of the men had to establish themselves with total strangers. Some of them were not quite on their own; they came at the invitation of members of the family who were already here and who were willing to help them find out if they, too, could make it in the United States. Chuy Castro, for example, came over to work with his brothers. They helped him to learn the construction trade, housed him, and hid him during the time he was in the country illegally. For his wife Rosario, however, this did not detract from the value of his effort. Had he not been able to make it in the country, had he not been a good worker, she said to her children often, he would not have been able to send for the family.

In general, then, there was a sense among most of the families that they had gotten here because the men worked hard. They knew of others who had not made it, who were not tough enough, perhaps, or who were lazy and wanted it easy.

This sense of success and satisfaction at being in the country does not mean, however, that the period of being here illegally was not difficult. It was especially difficult for the women and their children. Once here, if they had set up a household and brought with them some of their family treasures, moving quickly and hiding was not easy. As long as they were living with relatives, they could still come and go. But once they had rented a place, bought furniture, and put children in school, it wasn't quite as simple. What made the situation even more frightening was the little understanding they had of how the system worked. There were rumors and tales and more tales, all of which were false, about things that had happened, about how a mother was caught and kept locked up until she revealed where all her children were, about how schools turned in undocumented children, and even about how children born in this country could lose their citizenship if their mother married an illegal alien.

Gloria Cerda's mother, for example, who had come to the United States to work in her early youth and finally married a U.S. citizen, valued her legal status immensely. When Gloria divorced a citizen and married a young undocumented Mexican, her mother lived in fear that her two grandchildren, who were U.S.-born and a product of the first marriage, would be deported. She urged Gloria to leave her new husband in order to protect her children.

The length of the illegal period varied greatly from family to family. Some women and children obtained legal status within a very short period. Others were still here illegally after a period of more than eight years' residence. Often children from previous marriages remained undocumented for many years. Moreover, even when every member of the immediate family had acquired legal status, if they were sheltering relatives who were still undocumented, they were still afraid and uncertain.

The issue of legal status, then, was a central one for most of the families. Many individuals had had family members arrested and deported. Many had been informed on by neighbors, and some had even been turned in by employers after they had completed a job. Because of this, they were necessarily cautious. Our first attempts, for example, to elicit family histories resulted in guarded, bare-bones narratives. It was only years later that I understood how suspicious of our true motives the families had been.

Normally, families kept to themselves. Children played only with siblings and cousins, and very little information was given out to strangers. "*No quiero que sepan mis cosas*" (I don't want them to know my business), said Reina Leyba when explaining why she didn't let her children play with the neighbors' children. "*A los niños les sacan todo*" (You can get everything out of children).

For us, the most revealing example of how privately the families lived their lives in the light of fear and uncertainty was the fact that two years after the Ramírez family had moved next door to the Ornelas family, the children (several of whom were in the same classrooms) did not play with one another at all. The children of each family played only in their own yards and with their siblings or visiting cousins. It was only after I told Carmen Ornelas and María Elena Ramírez that the other children were part of the study that the women began to nod at one another and to allow their children to play in each other's yards. However, none of the children were allowed inside each other's houses.

The illegal period, then, even though it became almost "normal," did have its costs. During the time they were undocumented, every member of the family was vulnerable. Because of this vulnerability, these individuals lived their lives looking over their shoulders. They were suspicious, and they were fearful. Even as they learned how to function in a new world, they had to move in that new world carefully. They tried to blend into the neighborhood and to go unnoticed by strangers. Children were cautioned not to give out information, and adults were frequently urged not to complain even in the face of unfair treatment by employers.

In spite of these fears and these tensions, people did not appear to dwell constantly on the dangers. They were cautious, and they trusted few outsiders. And yet, within the families, they simply lived their lives. There were no sober or tragic moods surrounding their everyday interactions. Children laughed as they played. Babies were born. New possessions were purchased, and through it all, there was a simple acceptance of the reality surrounding them.

ARREGLANDO (BECOMING LEGAL)

The term *arreglar* is used by many Mexicans when referring to the process of legalizing their residence in the United States. The expressions *estoy arreglando* or *todavía no he arreglado* simply mean, "I'm getting my legal papers" or "I haven't gotten my legal papers yet." Although literally "*arreglar*" means to fix or to repair, there is no connotation of "fixing" or carrying out the process by some illegal means.

In general, few of the individuals in this study could explain how it was that they or members of their family had obtained legal status. Because they had no experience with bureaucracies, they had vague notions about what the process of becoming legal involved. Many had been helped by relatives. Some had hired lawyers. Some, like Eulalia Gómez and Rosario Castro, simply knew that because their mother-in-law had been born in the United States, all of the children and their families had been able to get papers eventually.

The stories told by several of the women, however, about how they got here and what the process entailed for them reveal a great deal about how these individuals, especially the women—who were originally from rural Mexico and who had little contact with lawyers, documents, and visas— attempted to make sense of the new world that they had entered.

Rosario Castro, for example, spoke about her experience in crossing the border illegally to join her husband, Chuy. She began her story lightly, almost poking fun at the fact that they had been caught.

ROSARIO: *Nosotros no nos vinimos arreglados. Yo pasé por el río. Por cierto que la primera vez nos agarraron. Lucila y yo pasamos.*

We didn't come in legally. I came in by the river. Actually, they caught us the first time. Lucila and I crossed.

G.V.: *¿De veras? ¿Cómo las agarraron?*

Really? How did they catch you?

¿Qué les hicieron?

What did they do to you?

ROSARIO: *No nomás nos agarró la migra y nos encerró. Ay[4] nos tuvieron seis o siete horas. Pero esa noche me volví a meter. No nos agarraron. Chuy fue por mí. Aquí estaba en Las Fuentes.*

Well the migra (the border patrol) just caught us and locked us up. They had us there six or seven hours. But that night I came in again. They didn't catch us. Chuy went to get me. He was here in Las Fuentes.

She then continued in a more serious tone:

Hacía mucho que nos queríanos venir. Antes de que naciera Lucila. Yo quería que naciera aquí. Chuy desde 79 había metido ya sus papeles. Y nada que nos avisaban. Nos vinimos a Juárez yo y los niños y Chuy iba y venía cada dos semanas.

We had been wanting to come for a long time. Before Lucila was born. I wanted her to be born here. Chuy had put in his papers (applied for legal status) in 1979. And they didn't let us know anything. The children and I came to Juárez and Chuy went back and forth every two weeks.

According to Rosario, when Chuy's father realized how hard it was for the family, he advised them to come over anyway while their application was being processed. But because Chuy thought that it would be dangerous, they went to see a lawyer.

Ya ese abogado Jorge no está aquí porque lo agarraron en algo chueco, pero él nos dijo que nos pasáramos todos y que de aquí hiciéramos la aplicación de quedarnos. Pos eso hicimos, pero nomás nos quisieron dar el permiso por un mes. Nos dio miedo porque tuvimos que echar mentiras de cuánto teníanos aquí.

That lawyer, Jorge, is not here anymore because they caught him doing something crooked, but he told us to come across and to put in an application for a permit to stay from here. Well, we did that, but they just gave us a permit for one month. We got scared because we had to lie about how long we had been here.

Rosario remembered that she had been particularly worried. She imagined coming in with all the children, pulling them out of the school where she had managed to get them enrolled in Juárez, only to be thrown out within a month. Because she considered the one-month permit worthless, Chuy then went to his older brother for advice. Aurelio, who had been in the country nearly 20 years, advised Chuy to get another lawyer. As a result of that advice, Chuy went down to El Paso to the border patrol's "*corralon*" (the big corral), where the Immigration and Naturalization Service (INS) detains persons who are caught in the United States illegally until they are returned to Mexico. There he found another lawyer who agreed to take care of things for the whole family for $1,000.

Rosario recalled:

Yo tenía mucho miedo ese día que lo fueran a agarrar ay y no lo dejaran salir. Pero ni le preguntaron nada los de la migra. Lo que sí sé es que sí nos arregló un permiso ese abogado por año y medio para todos. Nos vinimos a los files a ganar dinero para pagarle sus mil dólares. (Entonces sí había mucho trabajo no como ahora.) Y trabajamos todos, yo y Miguel y Rebeca y hasta Oscar. Y luego ya nos dieron el permiso y nos tuvimos que volver a ir a Juárez y entrar ya arreglados.

I was very scared that day that they would catch him there and not let him leave. But the migra didn't even ask him anything. What I do know is that the lawyer did get us a permit for a year and a half for all of us. We came to work in the fields to make money to pay him his thousand dollars. (At that time there was a lot of work, not like now.) And we all worked, me, Miguel and Rebeca, and even Oscar. And then they gave us the permit and we had to go back to Juárez and come in legally.

For Rosario, getting in legally mainly involved money and finding the right lawyer who knew the right people. When asked to speculate about why she thought it took so much money, she explained that a lot of people had to be paid to make things easy.

Es como cuando lo agarran a uno en Juárez quesque porque va uno muy fuerte. Le da uno cinco dólares y todo se arregla.

It's like getting stopped by a policeman for supposedly going too fast in Juárez, you give him five dollars and everything is fine.

Isela Sotelo was under the same impression, although she also had only inexact notions about what the process involved. Her situation, however, was much more precarious than Rosario's because her husband Terrence (a U.S.-born citizen) often threatened her with deportation. After Terry Jr. was born, Isela married Terrence. She entered the United States using her border crossing card and brought Sara and Lola, her children from a previous relationship. Seven years later, she and Terrence had six children, all of whom had been born in the United States and were American citizens. Isela and her daughters, however, were still in the country as undocumented aliens.

As compared with Rosario Castro's story about becoming legal, Isela's story, rather than recalled, unfolded during the period of the study. We were consulted on a number of issues and asked for help. Isela worried a great deal about her status, especially because of Sara and Lola. By talking to us she tried to make sense of what she had been told by Terrence and to determine whether or not he was telling her the truth.

Isela constantly tried to make sense of contradictory information. But without relatives in the area, and without access to her own family in Juárez, she was clearly at a disadvantage and largely dependent on her husband's knowledge of the United States.

Unfortunately for Isela, during the third year of the study, circumstances forced her to press forward to obtain her own legal status in the country as well as that of Lola and Sara. Her children, unlike those of the other families, got into frequent fights with other neighborhood children, and as a result, a neighbor who was a third-generation Chicana called the border patrol and reported her belief that the entire family was in the country illegally.

Isela talked about the arrival of the border patrol cars and about the officers and their questions. She had been very frightened and had expected that they would arrest her and the two girls immediately. The little ones, seeing how frightened their mother was, began to cry. She assumed that they had not taken her because the children were crying and because she had showed them a check stub from the money Terrence received from the Veterans Administration. She knew that this proved he was a citizen.

Soon after that, according to Isela, Terrence contacted his relatives in El Paso and began to put the process of getting her papers in motion. Isela went to have pictures taken. Sara and Lola stayed close to the house and away from the neighborhood children, and I (whose status as a *maestra* was thought to be important) was asked to write a letter saying that she was a woman of good conduct whom I knew to have six children ages seven and under who were born in this country. For a few weeks it appeared that everything would work out well. Terrence had seen a lawyer in El Paso who had given them advice.

A few weeks later, Isela seemed less optimistic. She had found out that the process required what were to her large amounts of money. She explained the procedure to me, as follows:

Porque tiene uno que pagar 260 para que le entreguen la mica.[5] *Pero como yo tengo que tener primero el pasaporte mexicano para ir a los . . . rayos x. No, pri-*	Because one has to pay 260 so they give you the card. But since I have to first have my Mexican passport to go to x-ray. No, first, right now be-

mero, 'horita antes que nada ya debo de tener un pasaporte mexicano. Ya cuando vaya a rayos x, ya llevo el pasaporte mexicano y los rayos x y me voy a la imigración de los americanos que está en Juárez y ay es donde me van a dar la mica.

Pero 'horita los rayos x dicen que cobran 30 dólares, y el pasaporte mexicano me va' costar 20. Y 20 me costó el certificado de matrimonio y lo los retratos que llevan como un teip como con sello. Y algunas recomendaciones.

Tiene uno que tener gasolina, hacer gastos, y que va, siempre ya estando allá, le van a retrasar adentro de la oficina de imigración. Porque le van a volver a hacer rayos x, que son 5 dólares, que son 10 dólares. Tiene que ir uno preparado.

fore anything else, I should have a Mexican passport. When I go to x-ray, I already have the Mexican passport and the x-rays and I go to the American immigration that's in Juárez and that's where they're going to give me the card. But right now, x-rays they say they charge 30 dollars, and the Mexican passport is going to cost me 20. And I paid 20 for the marriage certificate and then the pictures that have like a tape with a seal. And some recommendations.

You have to have gas, spend money, and then once you are over there, they're going to delay things in the immigration office. Because they are going to take x-rays again, (and say) it's five dollars, it's ten dollars. You have to go prepared.

For Isela, becoming legal was a matter of spending money and of being prepared for unexpected expenses. She anticipated both delays and having to grease a few palms in the process. In spite of the costs, Isela was still hopeful. She had been holding onto the family's income tax refund.

Tenemos lo del incom tex. Ya lo tenemos listo. No queremos gastarlo. Pa tenerlo listo pa terminar.

We have the income tax (money). We have it ready. We don't want to spend it. So we have it ready to get it done.

She was still hopeful also that Sara and Lola would obtain legal status soon. When I inquired whether the children would also be getting their *micas* that summer, she responded:

Yo, nomás. Pero cuando nos dan una aplicación ay nos preguntan cuánta familia tenemos y cuántos son de aquí y cuantos no y ay le pusimos que yo y mis dos chavalas, las dos grandes. Yo pienso que o, en este tiempo, ta no teníanos los

Just me. But when they give us an application there they ask us how many there are in the family and how many are from here and how many are not and we said on there that me and my two girls, the big

registros de adopción y los mandamos
traer y cuando yo vaya les voy a decir.

ones. I think that, oh, at this time
we didn't have the adoption registra-
tions yet and we sent for them and
when I go I'm going to tell them.

For Isela, then, knowledge about becoming legal was largely derived from information she received from her husband. To this information she added bits and pieces of other facts drawn from conversations she had with us, with her husband's occasional employer, and with a legal aid attorney she consulted on another matter. What she tried to do was to get enough information to challenge her husband's claims and to force him to move the process forward. Isela, for all of her seeming powerlessness, believed that as the mother of six American citizens under the age of seven, she would not be thrown out of the country. What she worried about was Sara, a precocious and flirtatious girl. She wanted to make sure that both her older children would be protected and would have access to both medical care and food stamps. As will be seen in the chapter that follows, Isela was remarkably resourceful; however, when the study ended, she was still in this country illegally.

Arreglando or becoming legal was a process that in and of itself consumed enormous amounts of family energy and substantial family resources. As can be seen in the cases of Isela and Rosario, for the families in the study, the process of becoming legal was thought to be both complicated and expensive. Most individuals were convinced, moreover, that being able to obtain alien resident status required a large element of luck. There was no understanding that the procedure was governed by a set of rules and regulations. Attempts to inform several of the men and the women about those regulations, about their rights in general and their right of appeal if denied, were not understood or were simply disbelieved.[6] My opinion, for example, if it contradicted what I term the "family collective wisdom," was heard and, I believe, appreciated; but ultimately, it did not have the value of what members of the family had themselves learned through their own experiences.

Having crossed over, each of the families was determined not to go back. Becoming legal was important. It gave them permission to stay. It gave them access to services and freedom from fear of deportation. Most of all, it made it possible for them to redirect their energies to other goals and other needs.

MAINTAINING LINKS TO MEXICO

For most of the families, grief or nostalgia about leaving "home" surrounded not the act of crossing into the U.S., but the act of leaving their small towns and villages for the first time. Moving from these villages to urban Juárez was, especially for the women, the most difficult part of their journey.

Once inside the United States, many individuals struggled to maintain contact with the part of the world that they knew and loved. For some, maintaining contact involved making frequent trips back to rural Chihuahua several times during the year. They sought to share with their children some of what the village or the "*rancho*" (the farm) meant to them, and they, therefore, made a special effort to have the children spend time there during the summer months. Family talk was often filled with recollections of good times spent in the village and with family back in Mexico. Favorite animals were remembered, as were favorite places and favorite foods.

Velma Soto, for example, struggled with her sense of sadness at having left the *rancho* and tried, much more than did her sister Amelia, to make the ten-hour drive there several times a month. She was particularly close to her father, and until he died in the third year of the study, she saw it as her duty to visit him frequently. For Velma, moving to the United States to live had not been particularly traumatic. What she wanted was to be within a few hour's drive of relatives in Juárez and to be able to return to the *rancho* frequently. The fact that she and her immediate family were in another country did not appear to be particularly problematic to her as long as they were in a part of the United States where she was still close to the people that were important to her. In many ways, Velma wanted the best of two worlds for both herself and her children.

Other families in the study were less nostalgic about their original homes. It may have involved rationalization or it might have had to do with the fact that for them, it was difficult to return. These families, however, spoke about their towns and villages and compared them unfavorably with Las Fuentes and with what they had in their new homes.

For María Elena Ramírez, for example, and other individuals like her, maintaining contact involved bringing members of their extended families into the United States to join them. María Elena, who still had four sisters living in Mexico, had managed to bring her mother, Doña Ester, and one of her sisters and her children to Las Fuentes. Doña Ester, who was in her early fifties, lived next door during the first year of the study and a few blocks away during the latter two years. María Elena was pleased that after years of a bad marriage to a stepfather who was now dead, her mother had found a good man to take care of her. She reported that her sisters in Mexico resented the fact that Doña Ester was there with her, but she responded, "*Pero no le hace falta nada. Tiene todo.*" (But she doesn't need anything. She has everything).

Now that her sister Cristina was with them also, María Elena was even more content. She no longer felt as alone as she used to. It mattered little that the house was crowded and that Cristina's children fought constantly with her own. She did not even mind the fact that there was less of everything to go around. "*Donde comen unos, comen otros*" she said (Where some eat, others can too).

During the three years of the study, only the Cerda, Sotelo, and Ornelas families did not maintain ties to Mexico by either visiting frequently or bringing family over. Every other family housed visiting relatives for long periods of time. Some of these relatives, such as Velma and Amelia Soto's mother, for example, spent several months of each year in Las Fuentes and then returned to Mexico to spend time with her other children. Other relatives came to stay, often at the urging of the family. In the Tinajero family's case, for example, in order for Socorro and Javier to make a success of the little restaurant that they started, they needed dependable child care. Socorro's mother, then, was asked to come and stay. Similarly, since more workers were needed at the restaurant, Socorro's sister, her husband, and their children were encouraged to come across and try living in the United States. For a period of time, a total of 13 people (2 families, each with 4 children, and an elderly woman) shared a three-bedroom, one-bathroom house.

For most of the families, however, the ideal stage to be reached was the stage when the family was reunited on this side of the border, when all of the important extended family that could move had been brought across. For the Castro clan (which included Reina Leyba and her family), this was almost a reality. Only one brother and one sister, out of a family of nine, remained behind. For Eulalia Gómez and her husband, the ideal stage had already been reached. "*No nos queda nadie allá*," Eulalia reported (We have no one left over there). "*No hay a que volver.*" (There is nothing to go back to).

COMING TO STAY

In spite of initial sadness when leaving their villages, in deciding to leave Mexico and become residents of the United States, the only real sense of loss for most individuals involved leaving members of the family[7] behind. For these *Mexicanos*, happiness consisted of being close to family and of not having to spend an entire lifetime far away from loved ones. As was the case for the Ellis Island immigrants, however, the journey to the United States also represented a better life, a life for which sacrifices had been made and would continue to be made for many years. In spite of this awareness, few individuals were aware of how very far indeed they had traveled and of how much farther away from Mexico they and their children would venture. Even when imagining better lives, their experiences had not prepared them to envision the profound and fundamental changes that living in the United States would bring them. They had no real sense of what this country was like. They had no way of contrasting it with what Mexico had been to them or of understanding that they had moved from the "Third" to the "First World." They expected simply to live their lives as they had lived them before. They had no concept of the demands that the "First World" would ultimately make of them.

CHAPTER 4

THE TEN WOMEN

The descriptions of the families that I am presenting in this book primarily reflect the experiences of the 10 women in the study as well as the interpretations of some of these experiences as recounted to me in conversation. In the course of the three years of the study, it was the women who were my principal informants. It was they who shared with me details about hardships and views about what was really important in their lives. It was they who, in the midst of making tamales or struggling to make sense of their children's experiences in this country, talked to me about their feelings, their dreams, and their frustrations.

In this chapter, I will describe and present each of them as individuals who were separate from and yet closely linked to both their husbands and their children. In offering a more detailed view of who they were, how they got to this country, and how they were using their resources in order to survive in a very different world, I hope to make real to the reader the perspectives from which I was allowed to see their world.

ISELA SOTELO

Isela Sotelo was 35. She was the 8th of 14 children and the first daughter born to a mother who had moved from rural Mexico to the Juárez border. Isela's source family included seven brothers and six sisters, all of whom were still in the Juárez area. Isela lived with her family only until she was 15. She then began to work as a live-in domestic servant for a middle-class Juárez family.

When Isela was 22, her first child was born. Two years later, she had a second child by the same man. It is unclear whether she ever married him. What is clear is that she was unhappy in the relationship, that her partner was unfaithful, and that he beat her frequently. Of this relationship, Isela said:

Si alguien toma y cumple, pos no le hace. Pero si no cumple y le pega a uno	If somebody drinks and still carries out his obligations, then it doesn't

. . . Siempre no aguanté porque era muy golpeador.

matter. But if he doesn't and he hits you . . . Anyway, I couldn't put up with it because he was a beater.

Isela, however, was a survivor. At around the age of 25 she met Terrence Franklin Sotelo, a man 24 years her senior. He had been injured in an automobile accident and was confined to a wheelchair at the time they met. Half-Anglo and half-Chicano, Terrence was a divorced ex-serviceman from Big Spring, Texas, who felt alone and down on his luck, and was happy for the company she provided. They began to live together first in Juárez and then across the border in El Paso, Texas.

Within a year, Isela became pregnant. Because of his recent injury, Terrence did not believe the child was his. He was convinced that he was now unable to father children. In spite of this, Isela was allowed to keep the baby. Fortunately, Terry (known to the family as Junior) resembled Terrence Senior a great deal. His fair coloring and green eyes and the fact that he closely resembled Terrence's older children when they were babies made his paternity evident to Terrence. Isela and Terrence were married soon thereafter.

At the time the study began, Terrence and Isela had been together for over 8 years. They had lived in El Paso, Texas, Anthony, Texas, Odessa, Texas, and finally in Las Fuentes. They now had a total of eight children. The family included the children from Isela's previous relationship, Sara (11) and Lola (9), Terry (Junior) (7), Pamela (5), Keith (4), Ada (3), and Abby (1). Vanessa was born during the second year of the study.

Life was not easy for Isela. She was disconnected from her family, and she had no support network in Las Fuentes. She and her two older children were in the country illegally, and because of this, they visited Juárez infrequently. Terrence spent most of his days at a friend's used car lot, but he was not employed regularly. At the lot, he sometimes repaired cars for his friend. Isela claimed that Terrence was an excellent mechanic and that he was often rewarded with a day's use of a car. This was a particularly welcome reward because Las Fuentes is a city that has little public transportation.

The family lived on a monthly check of $122 from the Veterans Administration, a "green" check in the amount of $116, and public assistance in the form of $335 in food stamps issued in the name of Isela's six U.S.-born children. Isela did not know why Terrence received the VA and the "green" checks, but had requested that they be issued in her name in order to prevent Terrence from drinking and spending the money as soon as it arrived. When Isela talked about this, she mentioned it matter-of-factly. She was resigned to the fact that her husband had certain faults, but she was also determined to survive.

Pero sabe que él, él tiene la tomada, pero si él hace por no tomar, pues no toma. Pero si hay un problema, él se va luego, luego a la tomada. Le digo yo que no, pues eso lo pone peor, y luego cuando se pone nervioso, hasta yo la llevo. Pues ande, a veces, pues yo voy luego, luego y le digo, me quejo. Vale más que usted no haga nada.	But you know what, he's a drinker, but if he tries not to drink, he doesn't drink. But if there's a problem, he starts drinking right away. I tell him not to, but that makes him worse, and then when he gets nervous, he even takes it out on me. Sometimes even I'll tell him right away, I'll file a complaint. You'd better not do anything.

Although Isela did not speak English (i.e., she could only understand and respond to selected words and phrases), it was she who was responsible for negotiating the system. Terrence was familiar with the different agencies, but his responsibility was limited to pointing Isela in the right direction. In spite of her own limitations, Isela defended Terrence and commented that he was much too nervous and could not stand in line or wait for long periods. His knowledge about how the system worked, however, made it possible for her to obtain both services and information from a variety of agencies. It made it possible, in fact, for Isela to protect herself and her children from Terrence.

At the time of the study, Isela had applied for housing assistance and had consulted a legal aid attorney to deal with an initial denial of her application. It was through these efforts that she soon learned that she could request Terrence's check in her own name.

Le dije a Gloria lo que estaba pasando y ella me ayudó y me dijo, "sabe qué, voy a hablar con la trabajadora para decir que ponga el cheque a su nombre," y me dijo, nomás procure algo de identificación. De pronto arreglé una identificación.	I told Gloria [the social worker assigned to her case] what was happening and she helped me and said, "You know what, I'm going to talk to the worker to tell her to put the check in your name," and she said just make sure to have some identification. Right away I got myself identification.

Normally Isela walked long distances to carry out important tasks such as washing clothes, buying groceries, and going to government offices. Depending on the time of year and the day, she might take three or four children with her. When necessary, Sara, her oldest daughter, was brought along to interpret.

Isela did not thoroughly understand how things worked in the United States. She was aware that some of her children "*tienen tarjeta*" (have a card), which entitled them to certain services; but she had no idea why some children were covered and others were not, or even what kind of services were available.

Isela was a fighter. When a neighborhood gang of Chicano boys began to annoy and threaten her children, she both called the police and took on the boys herself. She was particularly vigilant of her oldest daughter Sara's whereabouts and behavior. Her concern included Terrence Senior's actions toward Sara as well as Sara's increasingly evident interest in young neighborhood males.

In the last three years, two of the Sotelo children had been involved in serious accidents. At the age of three, Keith was run over in the driveway by his father, and during the first year of the study, Lola was hit by a truck that ran up on the sidewalk as she was walking home from the grocery store. Both accidents involved hospitalizations and fear about the children being permanently injured. Lola, for example, was out of school for a three-month period. Even though Lola was well at the time that the study ended, the task of getting the private insurance agency of the responsible party to pay medical bills was ongoing.

Between husband, children, and the outside world, there were few moments in the day when Isela was not busy. During part of the day she washed clothes because she wanted her children to change every day. When she could not walk to the laundromat, she washed by hand in a washtub and hung clothes outside. She cooked three meals, cleaned the crowded two-bedroom house, hugged a child here and scolded a child there, and monitored her husband, checking up on his whereabouts and feeling out his moods. Predictably, Isela seemed tired. She looked old beyond her years but was neither angry nor bitter. She was a good-humored, optimistic person who was deeply committed to her children and who, in spite of many difficulties, was learning to survive in her new world.

VELMA SOTO

Velma was a large-boned, heavyset, dark-skinned woman in her middle to late thirties. She had large brooding brown eyes, high cheekbones, and thick lips. Her hair was worn shoulder-length and appeared to be dyed a dark-reddish brown. When she went out, she wore red lipstick and blue eye shadow, but normally wore no makeup around the house.

Velma's source family included a total of seven brothers and sisters. One sister and one brother remained at the *rancho* in Mexico. Two sisters and another brother lived in nearby Juárez. Only Velma and Amelia were in the United States on a permanent basis. Velma's mother, Eleuteria, who divorced her husband sometime after her last child was married, spent her time visiting all her daughters. Her permanent place of residence was Juárez, but she also visited Velma and Amelia for two or three months at a time. Since she entered the United States illegally when she visited, the family considered it safer for her to remain a long period of time rather than cross back and forth frequently.

Few details were offered by Velma about her adolescence or early twenties. This may be due to the fact that she felt some shame about having had an *hija natural* (a child born out of wedlock). It appeared, however, that she left *el rancho* and spent some time working in Juárez. On one occasion she shared the fact that she had worked in a local expensive private hospital as a cleaning woman and confessed that she had hoped to stay and train as a nurse at the same institution. No additional information was ever offered about why she chose not to pursue this interest.

During the time she lived in Juárez, Velma had not attempted to cross over to El Paso to work there before her marriage to Pablo. As a resident of Juárez, however, she obtained a local border crossing card, which permitted her to cross over and shop in the United States. She found that she used it only to visit her sister Amelia, who by then had moved to Las Fuentes.

While naturally alert and energetic, because of the medication she was taking, Velma frequently appeared groggy. It was not unusual to find her napping in the middle of the day or else complaining about the pain in her back and the resulting pain in her leg. From the way she held her body and walked across the room on especially bad days, I got the impression that she was moving in spite of very great pain and discomfort. On those days, I was also aware that she grimaced as she changed position even slightly.

Not surprisingly, Velma was bitter about her accident and her resulting injury. She claimed that the incident that resulted in her disability was the fault of the canning company for which she worked, since several large crates had fallen on her as she carried out her routine tasks. Following the advice of coworkers, she secured the services of a young Anglo attorney who specialized in worker's compensation cases. She was optimistic that the company would settle and give her enough money to compensate for her not being able to work again.

Her relationship with me grew closer over time, so that she came to ask my opinion on matters ranging from arguments with neighbors to her pending lawsuit against the cannery. I often played the role of translator and read documents sent by her English-monolingual attorney. As she learned more about my life, she also felt free to offer advice about my children and my family. It was during such intimate conversations that, by talking at length about her husband, her sister Amelia, and her doubts, fears, and sorrows, she revealed more about herself to me.

After her father's death, for example, Velma spent a long time remembering him, talking about dreams in which he seemed years younger, and showing me faded black-and-white snapshots taken at family gatherings, weddings, and the like. These conversations were usually initiated when she asked about my own father's poor health and about my mother. It was clear, however, that she wanted to talk about her father and her sense of loss. She appeared to be confused about her strong feelings of sorrow in comparison to the more controlled responses of other members of the family.

Velma's view of herself was that she was both strong and resourceful. She was impatient when, because of her back injury or because of her lack of understanding of how the system worked, she could not get things that she wanted for her family. Few things stopped her, however, and when confronted with problems and setbacks, Velma would soon concoct a new plan or scheme and enlist the help of her sister, her children, her husband, and anyone around who might be willing to help.

AMELIA SOTO

Amelia Ramos de Soto was a timid, slightly overweight woman of about 36 or 37. Her left eye crossed slightly, and she tended to depend on other family members, particularly her sister Velma, for dealing with the outside world.

Amelia had been married for over 18 years. Her husband, Arturo, was raised in the same area of Chihuahua. Initially, the couple wanted to stay in their village to raise their family there. It soon became clear, however, that they could not make an adequate living from working with Amelia's parents on the farm. Like many other men in the town, therefore, Arturo began to make a yearly trip across the border in order to make ends meet.

At the beginning, Amelia remained in the village with her children. Arturo sent money and visited his family whenever he could. Since this area is at least a seven-hour drive from the El Paso–Juárez border, however, Arturo did not visit very frequently.

After about three years, then, Amelia moved to Juárez with her two-year-old daughter, Lorena, and remained there for 10 years. Her children Virgilio (14 at the beginning of the study), Corina (11 at the beginning of the study) and Amapola (6 at the beginning of the study) were born in Juárez. Fortunately for Amelia, her sisters Velma, Edwina, and Ana had moved to Juárez also. By the time Amapola was born, Eleuteria Ramos (Velma and Amelia's mother) had separated from her husband and had moved to the border also.

Arturo continued to work in the United States and visit Juárez on a biweekly basis. He was fortunate in finding stable work on a farm in Las Fuentes as a general all-around farm and ranch hand. It was his "*patrones*" (the boss and his wife) who helped him obtain legal status and later pushed him to send for his wife and children. At the time the study began, the entire family had been in Las Fuentes legally for five years. Their youngest child, Jasmín, had been born in an old farmhouse where the family was allowed to live rent-free.

In comparison to the small houses and apartments in the east side Mexican neighborhood of Las Fuentes where the other nine families in the study lived, Amelia and Arturo's house was quite large. It was located in the valley very close to the river and away from town. It may have at one time been the main house on the property. In 1983, the stucco had peeled and the adobe underneath could be seen clearly. The house was surrounded by cultivated land, corrals, and a dirt yard. Inside, the house was cool and dark and had large rooms with low ceilings.

Amelia was not employed during the three years of the study. For a time, she worked in local canneries, but because this job required that she leave Amapola and Jasmín in a rural community center, she explored other kinds of work. We were told that for a time she worked for a janitorial service during the late evening hours so that the children could be cared for by Arturo.

Because of the location of the house, Amelia felt somewhat isolated from the rest of the world. There were no stores within walking distance of the house, and her children had to ride a bus to schools located from 5 to 10 miles away. She considered this to be especially confusing for the younger two girls, particularly for Jasmín when she began morning kindergarten at the age of 5.

In many ways, Amelia's days depended on her sister Velma. Since Amelia did not drive, she relied on her teenage daughter, Lorena, or on Velma to drive her to the grocery store and the laundromat. Because she rarely shopped for food in the Las Fuentes area and preferred to shop at the market in Juárez, both women drove to the Mexican border several times a week. They considered the two hours spent on the road a small price to pay for the amount of money they saved.

In the second year of the study, Amelia came to regret her frequent visits to Juárez. Her daughter, then 18, became involved with a young man who lived close to her grandmother's house in Juárez. It suddenly became serious when Lorena became pregnant and decided to drop out of high school in order to get married. Initially Amelia was quite angry at her daughter for getting pregnant and at her husband for being in favor of the marriage. While she could not articulate why high school graduation was critical, she had come to believe that "finishing school" was very important in the United

States. Since Lorena was in her senior year, Amelia made every effort to convince her daughter not to drop out. Much as she disliked her new son-in-law, she was willing to have them both live in the house so that Lorena could finish out the year. Lorena, however, had no interest in returning. She was in love and living in a place where she had spent 10 years of her life. Juárez was home in a way that Las Fuentes would never be.

For a long time, Amelia missed Lorena deeply. Slowly, however, the family became used to her absence and Amelia once again became caught up in the everyday business of living and caring for her family. Corina began to make more demands for her attention. Virgilio needed to be prodded to work after school and in the summer, and Amapola and Jasmín both fought often with Velma's children. For a time also, it appeared to Amelia that Arturo was having an affair. She was troubled about his many mysterious trips to Juárez and the sudden disappearance of his paycheck.

Amelia, however, did not consider herself to be unhappy. Indeed, she did not appear to view her life in these terms. "*La vida no es fácil*" (life is not easy), she said often, and even comparing herself with Velma (a comparison both sisters carried out constantly), she would say: "*Siempre yo creo que no me ha ido tan tan mal*" (I don't think I've had it so very bad after all).

REINA LEYBA

Reina Castro de Leyba was a slightly plump, cheerful woman in her late twenties who loved to talk and was generally full of fun and mischief. She was one of the youngest of a family of 11 children, 9 of whom were in the United States. During the period of the study, four sisters and three brothers lived in the Las Fuentes area. Reina's mother also lived in Las Fuentes.

The exodus from a small town in the state of Chihuahua to Juárez and then to Las Fuentes was first undertaken by Reina's oldest brother, Agustin. During the years that followed, other brothers and sisters followed, bringing their families with them. Most of them spent long periods in the United States during the time that their alien resident status was being processed. Reina's mother, Doña Pepa Castro, was born in El Paso and was an American citizen. Because of this, legal entry was possible for the entire family. Both Doña Pepa and her late husband also moved to Las Fuentes to enjoy the company of their grown children and grandchildren. They remained in the area and felt that they had little to return to in their small town.

In essence, for the Castro family in all of its many branches, Las Fuentes had become home. This was where they had close relatives, where they were building new lives, and where they fully expected that their children would grow up. Doña Pepa, the grandmother, was very much the focus of family activities, and her house was a refuge for grandchildren, sons, daughters, and all of their spouses. *El rancho*[1] in Mexico, where two other grown children remained, was part of an idealized memory and a place where children frequently went to spend part of the summer.

Reina was the mother of three children. At the beginning of the study, Maya was 8, Josué was 5, and Chepe was 1. She and her husband, Héctor, had lived in Las Fuentes for a period of one year.

Reina felt lucky to be working at a local factory in spite of the fact that she worked the three-to-eleven shift. She was hopeful that when she obtained more seniority, she would be able to work at a different time of day. She was bothered by the fact that she was not home in the evenings with her husband and children; she spent every one of her breaks calling home to make certain that everything was in order. She even paid a neighbor to pick up her two older children immediately after school so that she could see them before she went to work. Often she was frustrated by the fact that Maya was sometimes kept after school by a teacher. Of this, she said:

. . . *porque yo estoy pagando pa que me los traiga un señor y me los lleve a la escuela. Y me los deja, después de la clase a Maya. Dije yo pos si la deja por algo la deja. Siempre pos a mí, pos es que yo me voy con el pendiente, que la niña no llega, y tengo que estar hablando. Por eso yo quiero que lleguen ellos antes de irme, por eso le estoy pagando a él, porque solamente así apenas llegan. La del apuro soy yo a ver si llegaron bien, usté sabe. A ver cómo llegaron.*

. . . because I'm paying for a man to bring them from school and to take them there. And she [the teacher] keeps them after school, keeps Maya. I said, well, if she keeps her, it must be for a reason. It's just that I leave with that uncertainty, that my little girl doesn't get home, and I've got to be calling. Because of that I want them to get here before I leave, that's why I'm paying him, because only that way will they barely get here. I'm the one in a hurry to see if they got here okay, you know, to see how they arrived [from school].

Reina's child care arrangements were complex. She could generally depend on a niece to watch the children immediately after school until her husband arrived home from work. However, during school holidays or spring break, she had to send the children to her mother's or to another relative's house. Even when her child care arrangements worked, Reina had mixed feelings about leaving her children with her husband on a daily basis. She commented that he often took them out when they should be doing homework and kept them up much too late. Also, instead of taking on household tasks such as warming up food or washing dishes, he made Maya do the work. For Reina, this was unacceptable because she saw her daughter as too young to be forced to carry out adult tasks.

Reina was both a cheerful and an optimistic person. During the course of the study, she and her family moved twice, once to a small apartment and finally to their own new house. The first move was both difficult and upsetting, especially because she underwent major surgery soon after that time. Moreover, Reina's long working hours created tensions for the family and for the marriage. The second move took them out into the desert where Héctor, with the help of Reina's brothers, had built a cement-block house. When asked to comment on their lives, however, the Leybas said that they did not regret having cut corners and skimped and saved in order to be where they were. For them, building a house—even in the desert and without running water—was the first step in "making it" in their new world.

ROSARIO CASTRO

Rosario Castro was Reina Leyba's sister-in-law. Rosario's husband, Chuy, was one of Reina's older brothers. Unlike Reina, however, Rosario was neither plump nor generally cheerful. Instead, she was a painfully thin woman in her mid-thirties who looked at least 10 years older. At the time the study began, Rosario and Chuy had been married for 18 years and had 6 children: Miguel, 15, Rebeca, 13, Elena, 12, Oscar, 11, Susana, 7, and Lucila, 4.

Rosario and her children had been in the United States legally for four years. Before that time, Chuy had spent some years in this country by himself, but since Rosario and the children were still in their hometown in the section of the state known as the Chihuahua sierra, he would also spend time there whenever he could. After several years, Rosario moved to the border in the hope that she and the children would be able to see more of Chuy and eventually cross into the United States themselves. Before they decided to settle in the United States permanently, she and the children would spend periods in the Las Fuentes area with Chuy's mother, Doña Pepa.

As compared to Doña Pepa's other sons, Chuy was somewhat of a black sheep. He drank heavily and was often unable to work. On weekends, the problem was particularly severe. It is interesting to note that during the entire three years of the study Rosario mentioned Chuy's drinking only twice. Whatever information we obtained about the situation was provided by other members of the family. Indeed, whenever the family talked about Rosario and her children, they would inevitably refer to "poor Rosario" and Chuy's drinking. Rosario, on the other hand, appeared to be both very proud and very loyal. Even though she sought my help on many occasions in dealing with other problems, she never once complained about her husband or his drinking.

Despite her thinness (a look that her chubbier in-laws described as scrawny), Rosario did not appear to be either weak or easily frightened. I got the sense of a woman of tremendous strength, a woman who kept the family going and was determined that in spite of the hardships, her children would have time for both music and laughter. She was variously described by her in-laws as a woman " *de mucho carácter*" (of great strength of character), "*de armas tomar*" (a fighter), and one who at the worst moments would always find a way out.

Rosario was from the same area of Chihuahua as her husband and the entire Castro family. She said little about her early life except for the fact that she left home quite early. After her father died, she was sent to live with an aunt because her mother began to live with another man. She recalled that her aunt made her go to work and that she began to clean houses when she was still in her early teens.

Her wedding to Chuy was apparently a happy occasion. A small snapshot in the family album that she showed us proudly portrayed a slightly fuller Rosario dressed in a long white dress and veil. Both she and Chuy were standing in front of an adobe house, he looking somewhat awkward in a too-small suit. The dress was beautiful, she told us with a nostalgic look, and added that it had been lent to her by a relative. "*No estaba gorda*" (I wasn't pregnant), she added, "*y por esto me vestí de blanco*" (that's why I dressed in white).

Since the time of her marriage, Rosario had continued to work hard. She had continued to clean houses and looked upon this work as the most reliable. She had also worked in the harvest fields picking chili and lettuce and in local canneries. For a brief period, she was hired to work in the same clothing manufacturing plant where her sister-in-law Reina was employed. Because of problems at home, however, she was not able to work the three-to-eleven shift.

Rosario's greatest worry was her own health. She had serious recurring problems and needed an emergency D&C. However, the family had no medical insurance and Rosario tried not to worry her husband or her children. After much discussion and after consulting a gynecologist in Juárez and investigating the cost of having the procedure done in a Mexican hospital, both Rosario and Chuy decided to wait. They were both hopeful that Rosario's condition would somehow improve by itself.

Seeing Rosario with her children, one could almost believe that she might actually will herself into good health. She clearly enjoyed their noisy interaction and spent long periods of time talking to them about how they must behave and why. She carefully policed Miguel's and Rebeca's school attendance and worried that they would fall in with the wrong crowd. She often made unexpected appearances at their schools to make certain that they were indeed there. Her daughter Rebeca's attempts at playing hooky were met with great wrath. Rosario was determined that they would both graduate from high school. To this goal, she dedicated an enormous amount of energy.

Life was not easy for Rosario. Because of Chuy, it appeared that she could not plan too far ahead. It was often the case, for example, that a paycheck was spent at the bar and not on food. Rosario's job was to hold things together, to make certain that the little ones didn't fight, that Miguel (her oldest son) did not take to drink himself, that Rebeca didn't get pregnant, and that the rent was still somehow paid. In spite of this, the Castro household was not a somber place. Music was always playing loudly. The children liked to sing and were encouraged to do so, and there was always a family gathering and cousins of all shapes and sizes to play with.

"*Nos ha ido bien*" (things have gone well for us), said Rosario when asked to tell us how things had gone for her and the family, "*en este país todo es más fácil*" (in this country everything is easier).

GLORIA CERDA

Gloria Cerda was a large, dark-skinned woman in her mid-twenties. She was a pleasant, talkative woman who smiled frequently. She was currently in her second marriage and was the mother of three children. Two of these children (Victoria, 5, and Elisa, 4) were products of her first marriage to a U.S.-born and -raised Chicano. Donna (2) was the daughter of her husband of two years, Ernesto Cerda. Ernesto was a recent immigrant from Guanajuato, Mexico, who entered the United States a year before he married Gloria.

Gloria, on the other hand, came to the United States and to the Las Fuentes area when she was around 12 years old. For some years before that, she and three of her brothers lived with their father in Juárez. Their mother, Cuca, worked as a domestic servant in Las Fuentes and spent little time with them. She did, however, send money to keep the family going.

Gloria remembers this period as a difficult one. It was she who carried out most of the cooking and the cleaning for her father and brothers. She especially resented having to wash clothes for them using only a scrub board and tub. "*Se me conjelaban las manos cuando salía a tender*" (my hands would freeze when I went out to hang out the wash), she recalls, "*pero nadie me ayudaba*" (but no one would help me).

Gloria's mother, Cuca, was also bitter about this period. She considered her former husband (they had been divorced for over 15 years) to be a weak and worthless man. In recalling her life then, she said angrily:

Lo único que tenía que hacer era estar a cargo de los muchachos, pero ni eso sabía hacer. Todo se le iba en gastar lo poco que yo le mandaba . . . . Yo si hubiera podido me hubiera traído a mis muchachitos luego luego. Pero hasta que no me divorcié y me casé con un ciudadano no pude hacerlo.	The only thing he had to do was to be in charge of the children, but he didn't even know how to do that. All he did was spend the little that I sent. . . . If I had been able to, I would have brought over my little ones right away, but I couldn't do it until I got divorced and married a [U.S.] citizen.

Gloria, however, was somewhat more forgiving of her father's shortcomings. She had provided a home for him for several years, although he was now in an advanced state of alcoholism and seldom worked. In spite of his many problems, Gloria felt that she could not abandon him.

Of all of the women in the study, Gloria appeared to have the most knowledge about the American school system and about life in the United States. When she arrived in Las Fuentes, because she spoke no English and had had no previous schooling in Mexico, she was put into a third grade classroom. After some months she was moved up to fifth grade because of her age and size. School, however, was never an especially happy experience for Gloria, and not surprisingly, she dropped out after the ninth grade.

At the time that the study began, Gloria was living in the middle of the east side of Las Fuentes, in the Mexican barrio. She and her husband, the three children, her father, and a baby that they were caring for at the time shared a one-bedroom apartment attached to a larger house that was then occupied by the landlord. Gloria was unemployed, but was keeping the children of a sister-in-law who had been hospitalized. She kept the three-month-old baby at night and the other two children (2 and 4) during the hours that their father worked.

During the three years of the study, Gloria and Ernesto moved three times. Once during an especially hard period when Ernesto lost his job with a janitorial service company, the family (except for Gloria's father) moved in with Doña Cuca, Gloria's mother. Now a widow, Doña Cuca was left a house by her second husband. This house, located on one of the busiest streets in the neighborhood, had become a refuge for Gloria and her brothers, stepbrothers, and stepsisters as well as for all of their children.

Gloria's ideal was to live as close to her mother as she could and to spend part of each day chatting with her and with other members of the family. Over the years, she had come to know the system well, and she had been able to obtain many different services for her family. On occasion, however, depending on Ernesto's situation, Gloria worked outside the home in the fields or as a chambermaid in one of the local motels.

As compared with the other mothers who were a part of this study, Gloria spoke English quite well. She was able to make herself understood in all normal, everyday activities, and she could also argue and persuade using this language. Even though Spanish was the language of interaction in her immediate as well as her extended family, Gloria often spoke to her children in English. It was common for her to issue commands and directives in this language, such as, "Sit down, Elisa," or "Don't fight." Even the youngest child appeared to understand these directives quite well.

Also as compared with the other mothers, Gloria made a decision not to send her oldest child, Victoria, to the "barrio" school. Instead, she picked a school in the adjoining area, gave a false address, and sent Vicky there. When questioned, however, about the reasons for her choice, they appeared not to be related to academic programs, teachers, or the like. Instead, Gloria confessed that she had always liked the school because it seemed so pretty. When she had just arrived from Mexico, she would often walk by and see children playing in the well-equipped playground and would wish that she could go to that school herself.

Gloria appeared to be happy with her life and did not seem to share her mother's worries about her *Mexicano* husband. For Gloria, the fact that he was a good man and treated her well was more important than his being an American citizen. For her, if the family did not have serious problems and if her children did not have to do without, life was exactly what it should be.

EULALIA GÓMEZ

Eulalia Gómez was a pretty woman of about 25. She had a lovely complexion, medium brown skin, and almost yellow eyes. Of all the mothers in the study, Eulalia came the closest to being "middle-class" in both orientation and lifestyle. It appeared, however, that this orientation was acquired after some years in the United States.

In terms of background, for example, Eulalia shared much with the other women in the study. She was born in a rural area in the state of Chihuahua and lived there until the time she was 14. One important difference, as compared to other parts of the state, was that the area of Nuevo Casas Grandes where she was from has more contact with the outside world. There is a large Mormon settlement in the area and several very large cattle ranches, and the town itself enjoys more prosperity than the towns in the sierra, which are close to the Tarahumara Indian region.

Eulalia was a product of a poor family of six children, and, like many of the other women in the study, she also suffered the consequences of her father's drinking problems. An older brother was the first to come to the United States. He settled in the Las Fuentes area and was soon followed by another brother. After some years, the two men sent for their parents and their younger sisters. Eulalia was then 14 and her two sisters were very young children. Soon afterward, her father left for California and her mother returned to Mexico with her youngest daughter. Eulalia and the other sister stayed in the United States.

Apparently, Eulalia had very little schooling in Mexico or once she arrived in Las Fuentes. She quit school after the seventh grade. Ten years later, Eulalia still claimed that she spoke very little English.

At the age of 18 Eulalia married Federico Gómez. Federico was also a newly arrived Mexican immigrant from the state of Chihuahua. He was from the city of Camargo, a town that is also mainstream in orientation and not located in the Tarahumara or Indian section of the state.

According to Eulalia, Federico completed secondary school in Camargo—an accomplishment that is unusual for working-class boys. He arrived in Las Fuentes at the age of 24. His entrance into the United States was facilitated by the fact that his mother, although she returned to live in Mexico after her marriage, was born in this country. The fact that Federico was able to remain in school for a period of eight years suggests that his family did not immediately need for him to contribute financially to the household.

Federico and Eulalia were the parents of two boys. At the beginning of the study, Federico Jr. was 4 and Ernesto was 3 months old. Eulalia had decided that she would only have two children; she commented that because her husband's family had produced only males, it was unlikely she would ever have a little girl. She felt strongly that large families made it difficult for children to get everything they needed.

For the Gómezes, making it appeared to involve having enough money to buy pretty things, to make their surroundings attractive, and to be able to travel to Mexico to visit family or other places just for fun. Their two children were very much the center of their attention, and much time and effort was devoted to both of them. They were treated as conversational partners, expected to display information on demand and to charm visitors (like ourselves) with their childish antics. Unlike the other mothers, whose energies were engaged in the struggle to survive, Eulalia had time to plan, to think, to consider alternatives, and to simply enjoy each of her two children.

CARMEN ORNELAS

Carmen Ornelas was the single parent of seven children between the ages of 10 years and 6 months. I am uncertain about her exact marital status, but it appeared that her children were the products of several different relationships. At the beginning of the study, for example, when her oldest child was seven years old, she spoke of herself as living with the father of her two youngest children, José (2) and Anelena (1). By the end of the second year of the study, however, she commented that she was now separated from this man and was quite angry at his behavior. In the third year of the study, while involved in a new relationship, she became pregnant unexpectedly. This child (Octavio) was born during the last six months of the study.

Compared to the other women in the study, Carmen seemed to be very different. The differences, however, went beyond the fact that she was both a single parent and had children out of wedlock by several different men. The differences involved her background, her experiences, and her expectations.

As opposed to many of the other women who lived in Juárez as either adults or children, Carmen did not have a difficult time there. She was an only child who was raised by her grandmother in Juárez while her mother worked across the border in El Paso and took care of other people's children. She remembered her childhood as a happy one and her grandmother as loving and kind. Her greatest treasures were her Barbie dolls.

Carmen did well in school in Juárez and finished primary school in normative time. She then completed *secundaria* and "*comercio*" (special training in secretarial and business skills). This level and amount of education is quite unusual for working-class girls in the Juárez area. I assume, then, that Carmen enjoyed the kind of lifestyle that permitted her to remain in school for a long period of time. In Carmen's case, one can conjecture that her mother's income from her work in El Paso provided her daughter with certain luxuries—among them education beyond the elementary level.

Upon completing *comercio*, Carmen worked for a bank, as a secretary and as a cashier. She commented that she was successful and liked all of her jobs. "*Pero entonces*" (but then), she added, "*me casé y encargué a éstos*" (I got married and had these [children]).

Carmen said little beyond that about her "marriage" and her own personal life. Questions about relatives or in-laws were met with either evasive answers or a change of subject. She did admit that she had former in-laws in Las Fuentes but insisted that she and her children saw them rarely.

From time to time her mother, who was still living in Juárez, would come to visit; and during the first year of the study, she and the children traveled to Juárez to see her grandmother, who still lived in the same house where Carmen was raised. During the second year, however, the grand-mother died suddenly and Carmen was deeply saddened because she could not attend the funeral in Juárez. At that time, she spoke of her children as "anchors" who kept her from doing many of the things she wanted to do.

Carmen's children were beautiful youngsters of all different colors and hues. The oldest two children, Julio and Carmensita, were both dark-skinned and somewhat chubby. Cynthia (our focal child) had very fair skin and enormous dark eyes and looked not at all like her older two siblings. Nena, the fourth child in the family, was also dark, but her skin was several shades darker than Julio's and Carmensita's and her hair suggested some Afri-can ancestry. Anelena and Jose (the two youngest until the birth of Octavio) were closer in coloring to Cynthia. Their hair was thick and straight and both had the high cheekbones and the almond-shaped eyes of their *mestizo* ancestors. Octavio's coloring was somewhere between the darker older chil-dren and Cynthia.

Because of the number of children in the household, Carmen's life was both busy and hectic. An enormous amount of her time was consumed in bathing children (a task she carried out every day), cooking, cleaning, and walking different sets of children to preschool programs. Carmen did not own a car and was dependent on others to provide transportation. Because she spoke no English, she appeared to be quite afraid of driving in the United States, although she claimed to have driven when she lived in Juárez.

The family lived in a two-bedroom duplex that had a small living room, a kitchen with a table for eating meals, one bath, and a tiny utility area. Carmen did not own a washer and dryer and either walked or was driven to a nearby laundromat. For the most part, both Carmen and her children kept to themselves.

The interior of the Ornelas residence often changed unexpectedly as new things were suddenly acquired. These acquisitions (e.g., new couches for the living room, a new stereo, framed pictures and decorative plaques for the walls) appeared to reflect the status of Carmen's relationships with differ-ent men. Because different children's toys also appeared from time to time to include very expensive items (for example, Cynthia owned two Cabbage Patch dolls and her sisters did not), we thought that such toys might have been gifts from individual children's biological fathers or purchased with money sent by them. This was only a conjecture, but there appeared to be no other logical explanation for the fact that a woman struggling to make ends meet would buy expensive toys for only one of her children. Since Cynthia did not own a winter coat and was sent to school shivering in her mother's knit shawl, we could not believe that Carmen herself would choose to buy this child toys instead of other necessities.

Surviving, for Carmen, appeared to involve strategies that were not used by the other women in the study. Her circumstances demanded that she keep food on the table, the rent paid, and her children safe and warmly dressed. Like the other mothers, she used all of the resources that she had to make it from one day to another, but she also found the time to laugh with her children, to tease them, and to hold even the noisiest and most irritable of her babies.

MARÍA ELENA RAMÍREZ

María Elena Ramírez and her husband, Joaquín, were both 28 years old. They were from a small town close to the Mexican border in the state of Tamaulipas. They had been in the Las Fuentes area for about 10 years.

María Elena was raised in a very poor family of six daughters by a man she described as a strict stepfather. She remembered her early youth as a time in which she and her sisters were allowed to do very little. Both she and Joaquín talked about their small town as being very primitive. María Elena was never sent to school and could barely read and write.

María Elena and Joaquín began "going together" when they were quite young, and, because of María Elena's stepfather's rules, they were only allowed to see each other in the presence of one of María Elena's sisters. When Joaquín left to go to work with his father in the Texas valley across the border, María Elena soon decided to join him. They lived together for a number of years before they were married. At the time the marriage took place, two of their children, Ricardo and Rosana, had already been born.

During those early years, both María Elena and Joaquín were in the United States illegally. Joaquín's father, however, had divorced his wife and married a U.S. citizen. Because of this marriage, his own status became legal, and he was able to help Joaquín and María Elena become resident aliens. At the time of the study, Joaquín's father and his new wife, as well as their two daughters, who were 12 and 11, lived in Las Fuentes.

María Elena and Joaquín had four children. Ricardo, the oldest (11 at the end of the study), was a very tall youngster who was also quite overweight. He was an excellent student who brought home straight A's on his report cards, but who hated sports and PE because he was teased cruelly by the other children about his weight. Rosana (9 at the end of the study) was a cheerful, pretty girl who very much resembled her mother. Unlike her brother, however, Rosana was held back in first grade. Our focal child, Joel, was 5 at the time the study began and at the end was nearly 8. He was also large for his age. The baby of the family, Ramiro (3 at the end of the study), was the center of attention of the entire household.

María Elena had not worked since the birth of Ramiro. Before that, she worked during the harvest season picking onions and chili. She had also worked in a local cannery. She spoke and understood very little English.

Joaquín described himself as a contract field laborer. He worked picking whatever crops need to be picked (chili, onion, lettuce) and traveled to neighboring states with his father and another group of men who together formed a team. During one season, for example, he traveled to Phoenix, and worked there for four weeks, and then left for the Denver area to work there for a two-month period.

Joaquín appeared to have learned how to use the system successfully. He believed that he had been helped by his appearance—he was over six feet tall, was light-skinned, and had reddish hair—and by the fact that he spoke English well enough to carry out negotiations with English-speaking mono-linguals. He had been able to obtain housing assistance and to collect unemployment at times in which no work was available in the region.

María Elena was used to her husband being gone. She complained that the children did not mind her as well as they did their father, but she did not hesitate to give them all a whipping when it appeared that they were getting out of hand. She depended on Rosana in those instances in which English was needed, but she also got moral support from the fact that her mother lived nearby. During the last year of the study, she particularly enjoyed having her sister and her three children (ages 15, 7, and 6) living with her also.

María Elena also derived support from the church the family attended. They were members of the Primera Iglesia Bautista (First Baptist Church) and felt very much a part of the congregation. They began to attend the church because it happened to be across the street from Joaquín's father's home (a place where they stayed when they first arrived in Las Fuentes). As time went on, however, they had made friends in the church and believed that they got a great deal out of going. María Elena particularly liked the programs available for children (e.g., Sunday school, summer bible camp). She also felt that she could go to members of the church and to the pastor for help and advice.

María Elena considered herself to be quite lucky. The family was poor, but the feeling was that they had everything they needed and even just a little bit more. They might shop at flea markets for their children's clothes and they might not have heat in the house on very cold winter days, but they were together and there was always enough "*masa*" (cornmeal dough), "*carne de puerco*" (pork), and red chili to make another batch of tamales. For María Elena, this meant a great deal.

SOCORRO TINAJERO

Socorro Tinajero was a quiet, soft-spoken woman in her late thirties who had many strengths. These strengths, however, were not immediately apparent. In any interaction with the couple, Socorro generally deferred to Javier and stayed quietly in the background. She had no doubts, however, about her own capacity or about her contributions to the family restaurant.

Socorro was proud of her husband and of the fact that he was a hard-working man. As an energetic and efficient woman herself, she found herself pitying her sister, whom they had brought in to work at the restaurant, and her lazy brother-in-law. "*Le salió muy flojo*" (He turned out to be very lazy), she commented. For Socorro, as well as for the other women in the study, finding a good husband was a matter of luck. The phrase used by Socorro, "*Le tocó muy mal esposo*" (She was dealt a very bad husband), revealed the widely held belief that life dealt out different things to different people. Some women were lucky and some were not. But in any event, they had to make do with what they had. "*A cada quien lo que le toca*" (everyone has their lot in life), Socorro said philosophically. There was no point in wishing for different children or a different husband.

Socorro's history made it clear that she had in fact tried to do the best she could with what she had. At the age of 12, she had started to work full-time for a middle-class Juárez family. Although one of her sisters had gotten pregnant—"*Julia se embarazó y no se casó con el muchacho*" (Julia got pregnant and didn't marry the boy)—Socorro had kept out of trouble. She went on to find better jobs for herself and did not get involved with anyone until she met Javier. Javier had ambition, and he had a dream, and both of these were important to Socorro.

Working at the family restaurant, Socorro was both happy and tired. Her days were long and she wished that she had more time to spend with her children. For the first time she was experiencing a deep conflict and did not know exactly how she would balance her child-raising obligations with being her husband's assistant at the restaurant.

Socorro worried a great deal about her children. She was worried about Alejandro, who had been held back in school twice, and she was concerned that her mother, although a kind and caring person, could not really anticipate problems. She could see that boys in the neighborhood were already getting into trouble and she did not trust her mother's instincts. For Socorro, the United States was different:

Aquí no es como en Juárez. Los hijos se descomponen, se hacen flojos y vagos, y   This place isn't like Juárez. Kids can go bad here, they get lazy and wan-

hay más peligros. Es importante saber	der around and there are more dan-
con quien andan.	gers. It's important to know who
	they are with.

Because Alejandro was epileptic, Socorro worried especially about his health. Marica had also begun to have trouble in school and now insisted that she did not want to go to the restaurant at all. She did not like to dry dishes or empty trash cans, and would rather stay home and play. Socorro considered her to be spoiled and undisciplined and blamed her behavior both on her teachers at school and on her mother. She was determined that all of her children would learn how to work hard.

As the study ended, Socorro was devoting a great deal of her time to learning English. She went to class, watched television in English, and tried to talk to those customers who were willing to be patient with her. She had decided that in order for the family to make it in this country, one of the adults had to speak English well, and she was determined to succeed.

THE WOMEN: AN OVERVIEW

As opposed to what is generally believed about Mexican women, the 10 women whom I came to know were neither passive nor particularly submissive. They viewed their job as keeping the family going, and their goals and objectives, therefore, were centered not on themselves as individuals but on the entire family as a functioning unit.

For many of the women, their early lives had been hard. They had grown up in poor families, and they had entered the workforce while they were still children. Most of the women felt, however, that they had been dealt good hands; that is, that they had drawn good, hard-working husbands and healthy children. A few of the women, like Isela Sotelo and Rosario Castro, lived with problems of alcohol addiction; and others, like Socorro Tinajero and Velma Soto, lived with serious illnesses in their families like epilepsy and chronic back pain. But even Socorro and Velma considered that life had treated them well.

From some perspectives, the lives of these women might seem limited. Self-fulfillment outside the family unit was largely nonexistent, and the quality of the marital relationship itself did not appear to be an important focus of concern. In many ways, for these women, things were simple: They got married, they had children, and they worked to keep the family going. Satisfaction came from helping their husbands make it, from watching their children grow and become good people, and from being close to the people they loved.

In many cases, my questions appeared to baffle them. Did they feel exploited? Did they think it was fair that they really had two jobs and their husbands had one? Did they feel powerless? Did they resent waiting on their husbands, their brothers, and their sons? I was told that women were simply not like men, that we had our role and our mission. Men were different. Things were not easier for men or harder for women. Things just were, and people lived with what was.[2]

As I think about the women in the study, words that come to mind for describing them include *spirited, brave, optimistic, determined, loyal,* and *perseverant.* These were by no means "wimpy" women. Their spirit and their determination, however, were not directed toward goals such as achieving financial independence or individual distinction, or even developing an egalitarian marriage. They were directed at living out their roles in life as they understood them. They were traditional Mexican working-class women who understood their own success to involve meeting the two goals of helping their husbands to make a living and helping their children to grow into responsible adults. Happiness involved small things, everyday satisfactions, the absence of pain, the possibility of laughter, and always the presence of family.

As the following chapter, "Surviving in a New World," will make clear, these two goals were themselves more challenging than it might first appear. Learning to survive in the United States in and of itself demanded a very large amount of these women's energy, resources, and time.

CHAPTER 5

SURVIVING IN A NEW WORLD

THE BUSINESS OF SURVIVING

Making a living, finding housing, and living from day to day demanded large amounts of energy from the adults in all 10 families. People were different. Work was different. The world that surrounded them operated in a language they did not speak. Notions of what was private and what was public were different, and there were rules and regulations governing even trivial issues. Things that had been simple at home were not simple in this country. Building a house required permits, serenades brought the police and angry phone calls from neighbors, and even standing around on street corners could be called loitering. Everything was more complex than it had been in Mexico.

For the families, it seemed that in the United States there were always unexpected complications, but each of them struggled to develop strategies for surviving. Some individuals attempted to learn a few English phrases quickly so they could transact simple business; some called upon their very young children to act as translators; and those that had access to their family's collective wisdom used it frequently. In many ways, however, each of the families broke new ground. They learned things they did not know, and they took on fights they had never expected to be involved in. However, the families were determined to make it and to succeed by working hard. Once here, these families had no intention of either giving up or going home.

MEDIATING EXPERIENCE: THE FAMILY'S COLLECTIVE WISDOM

In spite of their overall familiarity with the United States, even those individuals who had spent a lifetime crossing the border soon found out that living in this country required knowledge they did not have about simple ordinary things. They discovered also that assumptions they made about how things worked were generally wrong, that things they had taken for granted were not available, and that rules and regulations were far more difficult to circumvent here than they had been in Mexico.

For those families who had networks of extended family in place, like the Castros, the Leybas, the Gómezes, the Sotos, the Ramírezes, and the Cerdas, there was a repository of what I call the "family's collective wisdom" that was available to guide them in making a living, staying healthy, getting housing, and using existing systems.[1] Few important decisions were made in these families without wide discussion and without consulting the senior "authority" in the family (e.g., an older brother, an uncle, an aunt, or another relative who had been here many years). This individual would generally have access to other sources of information, such as former employers who knew the system well and who could be trusted.

Because of the many uncertainties faced on a daily basis by various individuals and because of the consequences of making wrong decisions, the family's collective wisdom was relied on almost totally, sometimes even in the face of evidence that its experience base might be incomplete. The strength of the family wisdom and a sense of how slowly the repository of collective experience developed became clear to me after I became very close to several of the families. In my acquired role of honorary "*madrina*" (godmother) I was often asked for advice and help. I accompanied people to court, I taught women how to get papers notarized, and I translated important letters. However, when I tried to give advice spontaneously about some problem, my opinion was related to the senior family authority, examined, discussed, and usually politely rejected.

Individual members of the family contributed to the group's repository of knowledge and information as their experiences were shared and examined. Schemes that worked were talked about and laughed about at family gatherings for a long period of time. When new problems arose, if a precedent was not obvious, much time would be given by the family to discussing the issue before a course of action was recommended. Individuals who had knowledge or information contributed that information, and finally, the family "authority" would give his or her opinion.

The strategy of collecting opinions was not limited, however, to those families whose networks were well established. Isela Sotelo, for example, questioned everyone she could about the process of becoming legal. She asked questions and told about her circumstances. When she was trying to determine how to get Terrence to adopt her older children, Isela listened very closely to the different opinions she heard. Similarly, when Velma Soto was trying to decide whether or not to have surgery for a spinal injury, she talked to neighbors, to her attorney, to our research assistants, and to us. In each case, she solicited advice and compared and contrasted views.

What became apparent to me from interacting with the women and their children was that they valued experience and based their decisions on instances of "collected" experience rather than opinion. When they questioned me, they asked not what I thought about a certain issue or problem, but rather what had I *done* about a similar situation. The assumption was generally made that I, too, had encountered similar problems or had to make similar choices. For example, the question "*¿Usté cómo le hace cuando se enferman usté y sus muchachos?*" (What do you do when you and your kids get sick?) was meant to get at whether I went back to Juárez for medical attention or saw a doctor in Las Fuentes. Whenever I was asked such questions, I responded truthfully. In this case, I responded to the medical question and said that I generally went to a doctor in Las Fuentes for ordinary things that were covered by insurance. I added that occasionally I would get a second opinion from a friend or associate of my father's in the medical community in Juárez for more serious problems. I was not asked to give reasons for my actions. My reply was interpreted exclusively from a perspective that sought to determine whether it was best to use American doctors in Las Fuentes or Mexican doctors in Juárez and summarized as follows: "*Sí, usté va aquí por la aseguranza, pero les tiene más confianza a los médicos mexicanos*" (Yes, you go here because of the insurance, but you trust Mexican doctors more).

As a survival strategy, the gathering of experiences was a sound one. For the individual, tapping the family repository of collective wisdom provided a way of dealing with the unknown and of weighing different possible actions or responses. For the family groups, the sharing of problems and the seeking of advice by different members provided insights into the kinds of problems and issues that could arise for them in the future. Lessons were extracted from mediated experience, and these lessons served as a guiding framework for dealing with the unfamiliar. A complex and multileveled information structure was built from pieces of knowledge contributed by members of the network. These pieces of "knowledge" were in many cases incomplete, distorted, or simply wrong. Within the structure, however, they made sense. They provided direction, and they allowed family members to survive intelligently in a confusing world.

MAKING A LIVING

Finding and keeping employment was the greatest challenge faced by each of the male adults. A steady job, of whatever sort, was highly valued, and leads about possible employment were passed on within the family networks. As I noted earlier, of the nine males in the study, two of them (Pedro Soto and Javier Tinajero) had come to the United States as very young men.

They had started at the bottom (one in construction and one in the restaurant business) and had worked their way up to union membership and restaurant ownership, respectively. Now, in the second phase of their lives and raising a new set of children, each of these two men worried about leaving youngsters behind unprotected. Pedro confessed that he worked twice as hard as he had as a young man, and Javier justified his long hours at the restaurant by pointing to his children.

Most of the other men (Chuy Castro, Héctor Leyba, Federico Gómez, Joaquín Ramírez) had used family networks and connections to find their first jobs in this country. They had not had to struggle by themselves. On the other hand, they knew that anything other than a first-rate performance in the workplace would result in discrediting their relatives and in putting in jeopardy not one but several jobs.

Except for Federico Gómez, whose job as a house painter led him to paint small desert scenes for pleasure, none of the men in the study expected anything more from their jobs than a steady income and the satisfaction of being considered good workers by their employers. When I asked both the men and and their wives whether they enjoyed their jobs and whether this was what they had imagined themselves doing as adults when they were children, they found the questions difficult to answer. None of the men could remember what they had imagined as children. Moreover, their perspectives on job enjoyment or job satisfaction were summed up in the comment made by Chuy Castro: "*Es trabajo*" (It's work). "*No es para divertirse uno*" (It's not about having fun). Not surprisingly, according to the adults in the study, people everywhere did not work because they liked to; they worked because they had to at whatever job was available.

Men who had worked as farm laborers in Mexico and as construction workers here did not see themselves as either one or the other exclusively or primarily. They talked about themselves as workers who for a time might work on a farm, in construction, or washing dishes. Work did not define them in any particularly permanent way.

To illustrate the types of work carried out by the adults in the study, I have summarized their occupational histories in Figure 5.1.

As can be seen in the chart, of the nine males in the study, the eight individuals who had been born and raised in Mexico all came from rural areas and had all originally worked on farms. Not surprisingly, six of these individuals entered the labor force in the United States working as farm laborers. At the time of the study, however, only two men, Arturo Soto and Joaquín Ramírez worked on farms. (Arturo had a regular job as a farmhand, and only Joaquín still followed the crops over a three-state area.) Of the remaining seven males, three worked or had worked in construction, one

Figure 5.1
Parents' Occupational History

Name	Occupational History
Soto Pedro	In Mexico: farm laborer In U.S.: farm laborer, construction worker
Velma	In Mexico: domestic servant, orderly in hospital In U.S.: domestic servant, farm laborer, cannery worker (unemployed during study)
Soto Arturo	In Mexico: farm laborer In U.S.: farm laborer
Amelia	In Mexico: worker on family farm, unemployed in Juarez In U.S.: cannery worker (unemployed during study)
Ornelas no husband present	
Carmen	In Mexico: secretary, cashier In U.S.: unemployed during study
Sotelo Terrence	In U.S.: Army mechanic, part time mechanic
Isela	In Mexico: domestic servant In U.S. before marriage: domestic servant (unemployed during study)
Leyba Héctor	In Mexico: farm laborer In U.S.: farm laborer, construction worker
Reina	In Mexico: worker on family farm In U.S.: factory worker
Castro Chuy	In Mexico: farmhand, construction worker In U.S.: farm laborer, construction worker
Rosario	In Mexico: domestic servant In U.S.: farm laborer, cannery worker, factory worker, domestic servant
Gómez Federico	In Mexico: worker on family farm In U.S.: yard maintenance worker, painter with physical plant dept. at local University
Eulalia	In U.S.: babysitter for relatives, part-time waitress in family restaurant, babysitter for sister

Figure 5.1
continued

Name	Occupational History
Tinajero Javier	In Mexico: farm laborer In U.S.: cook's helper, restaurant owner/cook, farm laborer, slaughterhouse laborer
Socorrro	In Mexico: chambermaid, housekeeper in major hotel In U.S.: farm laborer, cannery worker, husband's assistant in restaurant
Ramírez Joaquín	In Mexico: farm laborer In U.S.: farm laborer
María Elena	In Mexico: domestic servant In U.S.: farm laborer, cannery worker (occasionally) (unemployed during study)
Cerda Ernesto	In Mexico: farm laborer In U.S.: farm laborer, janitorial service
Gloria	In U.S.: farm laborer, domestic servant, motel maid, babysitter for relatives (unemployed during study)

worked in janitorial services, one had a semiskilled job as a painter, one owned his own restaurant, and one was retired and worked only occasionally as a mechanic.

Of the 10 females, 2 left Mexico as children and never worked there. Three women who spent most of their lives in Juárez worked in very different occupations: Carmen Ornelas worked as a secretary and a cashier at a bank. Isela Sotelo worked as a domestic servant, and Socorro Tinajero had started as a chambermaid at a local hotel and moved up to supervising housekeeper. The four women who had grown up in rural areas had worked on their families' or their relatives' farms.

In the United States, one of the women (Reina Leyba) had a regular, full-time job in a local clothing manufacturing plant. Two women (Eulalia Gómez and Socorro Tinajero) worked in restaurants. The other women worked full time during certain periods. Four of the women had worked in farm labor picking chili or lettuce, and four had worked in local canneries. Two of the women supplemented these periods of farm labor with work as domestic servants. At the time of the study, only two of the women (Carmen Ornclas and Isela Sotelo) had never worked outside their homes in the United States. Isela, however, had worked as a maid before her marriage.

As opposed to what is often believed about first-generation Mexican immigrants, then, most of the adults in the study were not involved in farm labor. For the men, working in the fields was essentially a first job. For the women, it provided seasonal employment when it was needed or wanted. Most individuals in the study, especially those who were originally from rural areas, looked upon farm labor (*los files, la labor*) as work that was always there to fall back on. It was not, however, the kind of work that they wanted for their children. As one mother (María Elena Ramírez) put it, "*Quiero que mis hijos trabajen adentro, en la sombra*" (I want my children to work inside, in the shade). She did not want them to work as hard as her husband did or to suffer the hardships that he had suffered.

In making connections in order to find work, the family collective wisdom was invaluable. Héctor Leyba, for example, was brought into the cement finishing trade by Reina's brothers, all three of whom were considered to be skilled and highly sought-after *cementeros*. Similarly, Reina Leyba was able to get her job at the factory because one of her younger sisters had worked there for some years. In each case, members of the family knew the ropes. In every case, the better jobs were obtained through relatives.

Surviving in the job, however, was not always problem free. It was often the case that the family wisdom did not cover situations that had to be confronted. For example, when there was an attempt to unionize the clothing manufacturing plant where she worked, Reina Leyba began to receive leaflets and pamphlets from different people. She also received what appeared to her to be "official" letters that she was asked to sign. The letters, leaflets, and pamphlets were all read by members of the family who could read English—especially by the sister who had worked there previously—but because the situation was beyond their experience, there was little guidance they could give her. Reina, then, devised her own strategy for getting different interpretations of the written material. She described it as follows: "*Pues voy y le pregunto a una y voy y le pregunto a otra. Así a ver si me contestan*" (Well, I go and I ask one [woman] and I go and ask another. That way maybe they'll give me an answer.) Her fear was that: "*Y de repente que me digan, pues no tiene trabajo. Y en este papel ya firmó su renuncia*" (And what if suddenly they say, well, you don't have a job. And on that paper you signed your resignation).

Surviving in the workplace, then, involved vigilance, not letting down one's guard, not assuming that just hard work would take care of it. In an unfamiliar world, nothing could be taken for granted, and strategies had to be continually developed to anticipate difficulties and problems.

During the 3 years of the study, many difficulties and problems arose for the 10 families. Ernesto Cerda lost his job in the janitorial business. Pedro Soto had a difficult time finding even seasonal work in construction because of his age. Joaquín Ramírez spent months working only a few days a week, and even the cement finishers, Chuy Castro and Héctor Leyba, were laid off several times.

For these families, not working meant not eating. Relatives could help for a week or so. Children could be sent back to relatives in Mexico, wives could clean houses, and, if the adults knew enough about the system, they could collect unemployment. For the male to be out of work, however, even temporarily, was in itself a frightening prospect. Few things provoked as high a level of anxiety in every member of the family.

Un Negocito (A Small Business)

For most of the families, the ideal of "making it" involved being able to start their own business. No matter how good the salary, no matter how regular the job, it was still not as good as being one's own boss. When asked to give examples of people they knew in Mexico who had been "successful," both men and women inevitably mentioned acquaintances who had started their own "*negocitos*" (little businesses). For most of the adults in the study, a *negocito* was a fantasy, like winning "*el gordo*" (the big prize) in the Mexican lottery.

For the Tinajero family, starting a *negocito* was not just a fantasy. Javier Tinajero had worked in the restaurant business during a 20-year period, and he was convinced that he could be successful again. As will be evident in the following description of the Tinajero restaurant, "making it" in the entrepreneurial track is not easy for laboring immigrants.

The Tinajero Restaurant. At the time the study began, the Tinajeros as a family had been in Las Fuentes only a few months. When questioned about her husband's occupation, however, Socorro Tinajero responded confidently, in spite of our surprised response, that he was making arrangements to open a small restaurant. Her surroundings (a small, crowded apartment in one of the neighborhood's worst sections) did not suggest that the family had the resources to undertake such an endeavor, nor did the fact that, according to Socorro, her husband spoke barely enough English to get by.

Within a few months, it became clear to us that we had underestimated both Socorro and her husband, Javier. They did, in fact, open up a small (8 tables) restaurant on the side of town in which there were few restaurants of all types. Javier cooked with Socorro's assistance, and at different times one of their three older children (Rolando, 8, Alejandro, 7, or Marica, 5) would be brought to the restaurant to work also. The baby (Emma Alicia, 1) and the children not "on duty" would be kept by Socorro's mother, who lived with them. In order to communicate with customers, the Tinajeros hired a bilingual waitress to whom they paid minimum wage.

During the first year the restaurant was in business, the couple spent from 8:00 A.M. to 10:00 P.M. at the restaurant every day of the week. They continued to live in the crowded apartment, and either Javier or Socorro would drive an old dilapidated blue car that rattled as it made its way down the street. Socorro spent her days helping to cook, serve, and wash dishes at the restaurant. She was also responsible for buying goods and supplies that were not available for delivery, supervising the household, running home to check up on children, washing clothes at a nearby laundromat, and shopping for the family.

The restaurant was open for breakfast, lunch, and dinner. During the early months, there were days when not a single customer came in. Later on, as the word spread, the restaurant began to develop a group of weekly and even daily regulars. By the end of the second year of the study, business was steady, and the Tinajeros were able to put down a down payment on a three-bedroom house on the north side of the barrio. They were also able to buy a used station wagon, a vehicle that the Tinajero children really liked.

Socorro was both competent and energetic and a key partner in the new business. She talked proudly of the fact that after arriving in Juárez in her late teens, she went to work as a chambermaid in a large tourist hotel. In ten years, she went from chambermaid to supervisor to *"ama de llaves"* (house-keeper) for the hotel. After working in that position for some years, she accepted a job (with a similar title and responsibilities) that offered more money at a rival hotel. For a girl from rural Zacatecas who had arrived in Juárez with a fifth-grade education, Socorro felt that she had done quite well.

It was at that point that (as Socorro's mother said somewhat sadly) *"So-corro se enredó con Javier"* (Socorro got mixed up with Javier). She bought into his dream and followed him to the United States, first to Denver, then to Washington State, and finally to Las Fuentes. *"Hemos andado rodando"* (We've been wandering around), Socorro commented with some bitterness, *"mientras que los parientes de Javier se hicieron más ricos de lo que estaban cuando él se fue"* (while Javier's relatives in the restaurant business became even richer than they were when Javier left).

Getting money to start a restaurant was not easy. Javier had been in the United States since 1963, and he knew the business well. But starting over was more difficult than he had anticipated. His own story of the struggle to do so reflects both his extraordinary determination and the fact that small businesses cannot be started without money.

For Javier, learning about the restaurant business had been, in part, a lucky break. He recalled:

Me hice amigo de un concinero. Me dijo-si gustas, yo te enseño. Comencé con un restaurant de 19 asientos. Vendía $35 de las 8 a las 2 de la tarde. Luego después $200. Pero era donde estaba feo, empecé en otra parte. Se fue levantando con el tiempo. Vendía $300 a $500 al mediodía. Las recetas eran secretas. Mi comida era la que trabajaba.

I became friends with a cook. He said, "If you like, I'll teach you." I started with a restaurant that had 19 seats. I sold $35 from 8 to 2 in the afternoon. Then it was $200. But it was located where it was ugly. I started somewhere else. It started picking up with time. I sold between $300 and $500 at noontime. The recipes were a secret. It was my food that was working.

For a number of years, he did well. He brought in two cousins from Mexico to work with him, and even let one of his cousins take over a second restaurant he started but didn't have time to take care of. After a bitter divorce from his first wife and losing about $20,000 to her, he found himself bankrupt. Because he did not fully understand what filing for bankruptcy meant, and because apparently his lawyer did not explain whatever options he had, he followed his first instinct, left Denver, and returned to Mexico. He recalled bitterly, "*Salí, cerré las puertas y me fui*" (I went out, locked the doors, and I left).

He went back to the border, tried a few different jobs, and finally met and married Socorro. In the meantime, the cousin to whom he had "given" his second small restaurant had made it big. He had become a millionaire in less than 10 years. Javier spoke of him with envy, of his trips to Spain and Rome, and of the four houses that he owned in Denver. But he also was grateful to him for a loan of $4,000 that he had used to supplement his savings in order to open the restaurant in Las Fuentes.

Raising money to start again was the biggest struggle for the Tinajero family. After going back to Denver for a short period, Javier moved his family to Washington State because he heard there was plenty of work there. And indeed there was—back-breaking work in the fields using short hoes.[2] Socorro worked in canneries and picked both chili and grapes. Her children were cared for by assorted strangers, and the proud chief housekeeper of a luxury hotel became only another picker in the fields. Mexico and the border were very far way.

For a period of time, they lived in their car with their oldest son and a baby. Then they lived in a trailer but had to sell their car and walk to work. Javier recalled that he had been very lucky and that he had gotten what was considered a very good job in a slaughterhouse. He worked every night from 11:00 to 6:00 in the morning loading heavy crates. He remembered how everything hurt, how his back and his arms ached horribly for the first months, because he had not done this kind of heavy work in years. Eventually, however, he got used to the work and stayed there seven years. Things seemed better for Javier because they started to save a little money and the dream of getting a restaurant seemed possible again.

The trick to saving money, Javier believed, was to have a little business on the side. In Washington State both Javier and Socorro had jobs, but they also started raising hogs. At first they lost money, but after a few years, they began to do well. They skimped and saved and did without, and 10 years and 2 more children later, the dream finally appeared to be on its way to becoming a reality.

Just setting up, however, had been difficult. There were many regulations governing the opening of a restaurant. Javier had to learn how the system worked in a new state where he had never done business before. Javier explained to us that he found out which offices in the county to go to by asking the owners of several different Mexican restaurants in the area. Some people helped him and some didn't, but finally he had a clear picture of what he needed to do. He just needed help. For example, in order to apply for a permit to open the restaurant, he asked help of a cordial Chicana who was a secretary at the office where the papers needed to be filed. He offered to pay for her time and she accepted his offer. Javier recalled that it had taken them three hours, but with her help they had filled out all the necessary forms.

For Javier, the key issue was not language. He appeared impatient at my questions that sought to determine how much English he spoke and how much he understood. In his opinion, "*Los que quieren entender, entienden*" (Those people that want to understand, do so). In other words, people understand other people when they *want* to understand them. Javier believed that even if he could speak perfect English, if Americans didn't like him just because he was Mexican, they would claim not to understand him. On the other hand, he had always found that Americans who *did* like Mexicans had always managed to understand him in spite of many language limitations.

Javier, then, had learned that to "make it" and to work within the regulations that govern what he wanted to do, he had to look for people of goodwill, for people who would go out of their way to help a total stranger. As both Javier and Socorro recounted the many different tasks that preceded the actual opening of the restaurant and the many tasks that still continued, Javier's resourcefulness became even more evident. In order to get started, Javier had to get around in a new city where he knew no one. He had to find space to rent, make the necessary modifications to the place, buy furniture and equipment, get a neon sign made, get menus printed, set up a bank account, get insurance, advertise locally, make arrangements to buy goods and supplies, hire a bilingual waitress, deal with health inspections, collect sales taxes, cook, clean, and wash dishes.

Socorro helped a great deal. Because she could read and write better than Javier, she was in charge of their checking account, of deducting Social Security from the waitress's check, of making payments as needed, and of handing over to their accountant all the necessary records and receipts. She was also studying English two nights a week at a local adult education center. For Socorro, working within the American system was still very strange. Recalling how things were done in the hotel industry in Mexico, she often expressed frustration with the ways things were done in the United States. But she learned fast, and she had a very good head for business.

Proud as Javier was about simply having gotten a restaurant launched in the face of so many difficulties and complications, he wanted much more. With his cousin, the Denver millionaire restaurant owner, as a model, Javier dreamed of becoming really successful. Socorro, on the other hand, compared their life in Las Fuentes to what it had been in Washington State. She was happy the days of raising hogs and picking grapes were over, but at the end of three years, she also knew that Javier was not happy. Things were not going the way he had hoped, and as the study ended, he was making plans to leave Las Fuentes to find another city where there was more potential.

Starting a business, even for a man who had spent many years in this country learning the business, was difficult. It required: (1) knowledge of the business itself, (2) knowledge of the fact that the business was embedded in a system of rules and regulations, (3) knowledge about how information about the system could be obtained, and (4) a certain amount of operating capital. Without knowledge and without capital, it is unlikely that immigrants such as the other 17 adults described here would be able to get started in setting up even very small *negocitos*. The dream remained, however, and individuals spent long hours discussing new ideas (i.e., selling tacos at noon at the factory and selling knitted baby clothes). Except for Federico Gómez, who did yard work on the side to supplement his income, none of these ideas were ever acted on. Starting a small business remained an elusive goal for 9 of the 10 families.

FINDING HOUSING

In Las Fuentes, rental housing located in the east side barrio was generally expensive and of very poor quality. Persons who owned rentals had moved out of the neighborhood and appeared not to care about crumbling walls and disintegrating stucco. For example, when we conducted our survey of the neighborhood, we spoke to a number of Chicano landlords who viewed their newly arrived *Mexicano* tenants with great contempt. They saw them as dirty, ignorant, primitive people who would stupidly clog pipes and damage bathroom plumbing. Because of this, they were reluctant to make even minor repairs or improvements. In addition to earning a living, then, finding adequate housing required an investment of a great deal of the time and energy for all of the families in the study.[3]

Overcrowding was typical of the conditions in which almost all of the families lived. For example, the Leyba family, a total of three children and two adults, lived in a one-bedroom house, and the Sotelo family, a total of eight children and two adults, lived in a two-bedroom house. Even Pedro and Velma Soto, who were building their own house, were overcrowded. The three-bedroom, one-bath house was occupied for a period by five adults and five children.

It is interesting to note that during the entire period of the study, I heard no complaints or even comments about overcrowding. My questions about how space was allocated to different children or about use of a single bathroom by so many people were generally responded to with little energy or interest. Comments such as "*Nos acomodamos todos*" (We all manage to fit) or "*Unos se esperan y otros se aguantan*" (Some wait and some hold it) were common. It was clearly a non-problem. The fact that several children slept in one bed or that each child might not have a specific spot in which she slept every night did not appear to be particularly important. In the case of visiting relatives, moreover, it was expected that they would share beds with children of the same sex.

The struggle to find adequate housing, then, did not necessarily involve finding larger quarters. For the most part, adequate housing was defined as being reasonably priced (around $200 per month), having a working bathroom (running water, working toilet), and having some source of heat for use during the winter months. For some of the families, hot running water was not seen as an absolute necessity. Since water could be heated on the stove for bathing and washing, they were happy to have cold running water.

Obtaining Housing Assistance

For the poorest families in the study (Sotelo, Ramírez, Ornelas, Cerda), the ideal solution to finding adequate housing was seen as being able to obtain housing assistance. Such assistance involved qualifying as a needy family and being able to rent a house that met program approval. In theory, when a family qualified and found adequate housing (i.e., in good repair), a large part of their rent would be paid by the housing assistance program.

Unfortunately, for most of the families in the study, it was almost impossible to get into houses or apartments that would meet program require-ments. The required deposit and first several months' rent for large housing units that were in good repair were beyond the ability of the families to pay. This created an impossible bind because in order to qualify for assistance, a family had to be living in the very house that would be approved. Since this process often took several months, family members needed to be able to pay rent on their own for a considerable period.

As a result, families ended up moving into whatever housing was avail-able that they could afford. They then spent much time and energy waiting for inspections by program personnel to see if the house they were in would qualify for assistance. When inspectors did come, often after months of wait-ing, they usually obtained not approval, but a list of repairs that needed to be made before approval could be given. The first house that the Ramírez family lived in, for example, did not meet requirements because the only heater in the house was not working. They had hoped that the inspector would not notice, but since she arrived on a very cold day and María Elena and the children had their coats on, the problem was hard to miss. As might be expected, they were not successful in getting the owner to make the needed repairs. Within a few months, then, they moved again and started the process once more.

For the Sotelo family, obtaining housing assistance was even more difficult. The size of the family required that they find at least a four-bedroom house. Moreover, since a former landlord had accused Terrence of tearing up walls and doors (on one occasion when he was drinking), Isela had been told that her chances of getting any housing assistance at all were very slim.

Of these four families, then, only Carmen Ornelas was able to obtain housing assistance. This was in part because the owner had personally helped Carmen to file the necessary paperwork to obtain approval. The other three families moved frequently during the three years of the study.

Living in Public Housing Projects

Of the 10 families in the study, only the Castro family had been success-ful in obtaining public housing. Their success was due to the family's collec-tive wisdom, that is, to the fact that two older brothers had themselves lived in the projects for several years. After what was considered a very short wait-ing period of about a year and a half, Rosario and Chuy Castro moved into a four-bedroom unit in one of the city's four projects along with their six children. Soon afterward, Chuy's mother, Doña Pepa, moved into a one-bedroom unit in the same project.

In general, the projects were reasonably maintained. Housing units were one-story duplexes built out of cement block. Kitchens included refrigerators and stoves that were old but in good repair. Floors were covered with linoleum and bathrooms had tub baths. Walls were generally freshly painted before a new family moved in.

The project where the Castros lived was located almost at the edge of the east side neighborhood. As opposed to the barrio itself, most of the residents of the projects were poor whites, poor Blacks, or poor Chicanos. Few recent immigrants lived there, and families like the newly arrived Castros had a sense that the second- and third-generation Mexican-origin children had become too rough. The Castros tried to have as little as possible to do with their neighbors.

Building a House

Both the Leyba and the Pedro Soto families were involved in building a house during the three years of the study. The two men worked in the construction business, and they both saw building a house as a process that could be accomplished a little at a time with help from relatives. In both cases, the real problem involved buying the land that the house would be built on.

In the case of the Pedro Soto family, Pedro's savings of almost 20 years went into the purchase of a small corner lot in the east side barrio. After the lot was bought, enough money was left only to pour the slab. It took another two years for the walls and the roof to go up and for the family to move in. Little by little, what was essentially an empty shell with a cement floor was made into a three-bedroom, one-bathroom house with a large living room, and adjoining kitchen. At the time the study began, fake wood paneling was up in the living room, as was a bright green commercial-grade carpet. An old porcelain sink and dish drainer unit had been installed in the kitchen, as had two white metal cabinets. A small stove and ancient refrigerator were proud possessions.

In the case of the Leyba family, their purchase of a desert lot was part of a family effort. Two of Reina's brothers had bought property out in the unimproved section of the county, as had two of her younger sisters and their husbands. Because there were no roads and no utilities in place, a fairly good-sized lot could be obtained for about $1,000. The area was far from schools and from town, but more and more houses were going up every day. The dream of owning a house was possible out in the dry and very barren hills.

For the Leybas the project took almost three years. Since Reina was working at the clothing factory and Héctor was working in cement finishing, they were able to make payments on their lot every month for about a year. As soon as the lot was paid for, Héctor began building the house himself.

His brothers-in-law helped, as did Reina on the weekends. When the house was finished, it had two bedrooms, one bath, a large living room, and an adjoining kitchen. It was made of cement block and had a cement floor. There was no electricity and no water connected to the house, but from a nearby light pole, Héctor and his relatives had rigged a 220 extension cord that ran about 100 feet and came into the house. There was a septic tank, and plans to build a well. In the meantime, water was carried in from town in two big barrels.

Of the two men, only Pedro obtained a building permit. Fortunately for both families, there was little interest by city officials in what went on in the east side barrio and almost no interest at all by county officials in what went on in Desert Acres, so there was no anxiety about construction being up to code or passing inspection of any sort. In building their houses, both the Sotos and the Leybas had done exactly what they would have done in Mexico. They considered that building a house was a private matter that did not involve adherence to external regulations. For the moment, they were lucky that neighbors did not complain, zoning restrictions (if any) were not being enforced, and they had time to labor long hours to make their dream a reality.

Buying a House in the Barrio

Two of the families, the Gómezes and the Tinajeros, were able to buy houses in the east side barrio. Federico Gómez, who was employed as a house painter in the physical plant department of the local university, had no trouble applying and qualifying for a mortgage. When the study began, he and Eulalia had just moved into a two-bedroom, one-bathroom house in the east side barrio. It was a stuccoed adobe surrounded by a chain-link fence. Every penny of the money Eulalia earned in her brother's restaurant went to buy something else for the house or to fix and paint and repair what was not quite perfect yet. The linoleum in the kitchen sparkled, the Formica counter and matching wood cabinets gleamed, and the almond-colored appliances (stove and refrigerator) were brand new. The small living room was plushly carpeted, and gold-colored knickknacks decorated the walls along with large color photographs of the two children.

During the second year of the study, Javier Tinajero was also able to buy a house. He chose carefully so that it would be close to the school the children attended and so that it would have room to house other relatives. It had three bedrooms, one bath, a living room, a kitchen, and a walled-in carport. Javier also wanted a big yard so that he could plant a garden and grow vegetables for the family and the restaurant.

In the case of Javier Tinajero, the process of buying a house was a familiar one. He had owned a house in Denver and he knew about mortgages, loans, down payments, and insurance. In Federico Gómez's case, the process required strong guidance from his brother and advice from co-workers. Even after he had bought the house, he was not very clear on exactly what the process had been. For Federico, the idea of paying off his mortgage and really owning the house someday was a strong goal.

Overall, then, for the families in the study, finding adequate housing involved much effort and much physical and emotional energy. For the poorest families, the struggle to find living space where the plumbing worked was a major challenge. For the families engaged in building their houses, the physical labor was extraordinarily intense. Moreover, when they moved in, the houses were still unfinished and lacked very basic comforts such as running water and electricity. Work did not stop. After the regular job, there was always another task to be completed.

STAYING HEALTHY

As I have pointed out above, surviving in a new world for the adults in the study involved learning how to use available services and learning how to work within established systems. In most cases, however, success or failure in uncovering how particular systems worked was not a matter of life or death. The same was not true of medical care. When members of the family became ill, when it was clear that home remedies and self-medication had not worked, access to professional medical care became essential.

Neither the adults nor the children could be described as sickly. Children caught colds and came down with normal childhood illnesses. They were cared for as children had been for generations. Stomachaches thought to be "*empachos*" (a condition resulting from eating too much or eating the wrong thing) were treated by grandmothers with massages and hot compresses. Sore throats were wrapped in flannel after a warm ointment was applied, and both Mercurochrome and iodine were applied to cuts. Together with home remedies and teas made from a variety of herbs, the families followed the tradition of sharing medication. Leftover pills were saved and then passed to others who appeared to have the same malady. Additionally, because of the proximity of the Mexican border, it was possible for individuals to drive several hours and obtain either medicine or medical care in Juárez. Since many medications (e.g., antibiotics, birth control pills) that are available only by prescription in the United States are available over the counter in Mexico, most families routinely stocked up on those items they considered to be crucial to their good health. Also, ordinarily one member of the extended family was identified as "*la que inyecta*" (the person that gives shots) and had the role of providing this service to others in the family. "*Inyecciones*" (injections or shots, available over the counter) were considered essential for treating an extremely bad cold, for building up someone's strength after an illness, and for more serious kinds of conditions. Medication used for such *inyecciones* was generally acquired at pharmacies in Juárez by asking a pharmacist, for example, *¿Qué me inyecto para los dolores de las piernas?* (What kind of a shot should I have for pains in the legs?) Pharmacists generally asked a number of questions and made suggestions.

Families, then, were not primarily dependent on American-style health care. Some individuals, especially those who had worked in the Juárez area and knew that regularly employed individuals were insured by their employers because it was required by law in Mexico, expected that a system comparable to the socialized medical system there[4] existed in the United States. Because of this fundamental assumption, it took several of the family networks a long time to disentangle their expectations from the reality of how things worked here.

Only Reina Leyba at her factory job and Federico Gómez at his physical plant job had medical coverage. Interestingly enough, however, neither was aware of what portion of the coverage was paid by the employee. Both thought that medical coverage was totally covered by their employers.

In cases of serious illness, then, obtaining adequate medical care was a major difficulty for most of the families. Even for those individuals who had good information networks and knew about available services, actually getting seen and treated by medical personnel required exceptional determination. Few members of the medical profession, even those of Mexican origin, spoke Spanish well enough to communicate well with upset and distraught patients. Family members brought in to interpret were often taxed beyond their capacity, as were volunteer interpreters in medical clinics and hospitals. Because of this, serious "errors" were often made, and lives were put in danger.

Rosario Castro, for example, vividly recalled her experience at a local general hospital when she came down with acute appendicitis. After sitting in the emergency room waiting room for several hours, the family was finally able to fill out the necessary forms that made it clear that, as indigents, they were eligible for services. They persevered because others in the family had been treated there many times. When she was finally examined, Rosario, who was in extreme pain, tried to explain her symptoms to a "Spanish-speaking" nurse. Apparently, she was either not understood or her condition was not taken seriously. She was sent home and told to rest for about four days.

Desperate at seeing his wife in such extreme pain, Chuy drove to the Mexican border. He remembered driving as fast as his car would go. He and his daughter were afraid that Rosario would die on the way to the hospital in Juárez. But they were lucky, and she made it in time. Immediately upon their arrival at a private hospital in Juárez, Rosario underwent emergency surgery and her appendix was removed. Chuy gave them what little cash he had, and the family committed itself to paying the hospital and doctor over a six-month period after the surgery was over.

For the Castros, this experience meant that the American medical profession could not be trusted, and years later, when Rosario's continuing health problems became worse, she was afraid to be treated by people who, in her mind, did not care about their patients.

For families in which there were health problems, exceptional amounts of energy were directed to exploring available options and applying to every program from which they might obtain assistance. Whatever systems were in place to help "indigent" residents of the city or county and whatever help might be available from public assistance, however, were governed by many regulations. Applying for help involved filling out long forms available exclusively in English and waiting in line for many hours. When a form was filled out incorrectly, individuals were sent to the back of the line and told to fill out a new form.

I became aware of the nature of the process of applying for help when I accompanied Rosario Castro to the welfare office, where she hoped to qualify for medical assistance. During the last two years of the study, Rosario had progressively grown thinner and had experienced almost constant gynecological problems, including frequent hemorrhaging. I had put her in touch with a Juárez doctor who, according to Rosario, told her she would probably need *"una operación."* Having heard that assistance might be available for getting treated in Las Fuentes, she wanted to explore the possibility in spite of her distrust of American doctors. Because of her family, she did not want to be in a hospital several hours away.

Our day at the welfare office was long. We stood in line for two hours simply to be given the right form. Around us were mothers with several young children and newborn babies. Some were crying, others ran around the room, and still others had come prepared to eat, nap, and spend endless hours there. The social workers and their assistants looked tired and overworked. Each person appeared to be a specialist in a single area and to have no information about related areas or questions. Any "special" situation that required departure from the ordinary routine resulted in delays, in being sent to the back of another long line, or in being told to come back on another day to see another individual.

The form we were given was in English. It asked for routine information about income, number of family members, legal residence, and the like.

Questions were printed in double columns on three legal-sized pages. Both sides of all three pages needed to be filled out completely. Rosario could make sense of many of the questions that asked for simple or routine information. There were many others, however, that were ambiguous, even for me, and required clarification. Requests for assistance with forms, however, were handled at only one window by one individual. At the time that we needed assistance, there were already 40 people standing in line ahead of us.

We decided to answer the questions as well as we could so we could hand in the completed form. Unfortunately, after several hours of working on the form, we noticed that Rosario's and her husband's signatures on the form had to be notarized. For Rosario, this was a major challenge. She had no idea what a notary public was and even less of an idea of where to find one. Had I not been present, she would have abandoned the application then. As it was, I persuaded her to consult with the family network and explained that getting things notarized in this country was a simple process.

As might be expected, Rosario did not qualify for medical assistance. Up until the end of the study, her condition grew progressively worse. She had resigned herself to getting treatment in Juárez. At least there, she argued, they would be allowed to pay a little at a time. In the meantime, she attempted to put money aside by taking on more cleaning jobs and working longer hours.

Getting medical treatment was difficult even for those individuals who were injured in accidents covered by insurance carried by others. Velma Soto, for example, was involved in an accident while working at a cannery. She struggled to get reimbursed for medical costs and medication. She was told that in order to obtain reimbursement, she would need to sign a document releasing the company from all further responsibility. Similarly, when Lola Sotelo was run over by a car and hospitalized, the driver's insurance company tried to obtain a release as soon as Lola left the hospital. Isela refused to sign the document only on instinct, not because she understood the implications of the insurance company's proposal.

Insurance company attorneys viewed first-generation immigrants as both ignorant and deceitful. Many saw them as taking advantage of the system on the advice of ambulance chasers.[5] Attorneys tried to deal with the adults in the family quickly, often through their secretaries, who acted as interpreters, before these uninformed immigrants could obtain advice from co-workers or more sophisticated relatives.

Little by little, however, experiences with personal injuries became part of the family collective wisdom. They began to realize that getting injured, especially on the job, had its advantages, and they often viewed their accidents as an opportunity to contribute to the family at a significant level. Velma, for example, based on the experience of a cousin of Pedro's who had lost the use of his hand in an industrial accident, filed suit against the cannery.

Although Velma was almost always in pain, she did not want to spend money on surgery for herself. Regaining her health was a lesser priority than bringing money into the family. Velma did not see that her injury had taken her permanently out of the labor force and that it had caused problems in her own marital relationship. What she saw was an opportunity to get a lot of money (possibly $50,000), and she did not want to "waste" the money on herself.

For Velma, learning how to file a lawsuit was no different from finding out where to buy used clothes, how to buy appliances on the installment plan, how to apply for housing assistance, or how to obtain food stamps. It was all a part of living in a new world that had "other" rules. Often the rules did not make sense, but the families in the study expected that. "*Son americanos*" (They're American), they would reason, and by implication, their rules and procedures did not need to make sense. They saw themselves as clever for figuring out how to work the system and for being able to combine its operating procedures with their own rules. Very rarely, if ever, were they aware of the costs to themselves or to their children of straddling two worlds and of compromising more and more of their values and deeply held beliefs.

But surviving meant making compromises and abandoning old ways of viewing the world. Slowly, some of the adults in the study realized that they themselves were changing because of these compromises, and they worried about what these changes meant for themselves and their children. Collecting unemployment, for example, was legal and expected. But as Rosario Castro explained to me, it was also getting paid for doing nothing. If one collected unemployment, Rosario wondered, how did one talk to one's children about the dignity of hard work?

Surviving, using what was available in the system, and learning how to work within it required energy, hard work, and information. Some families were lucky and had excellent networks of experienced relatives ready to help them. Others did not. Even with help, however, the everyday lives of the adults and children in the study were not easy. The families were poor, they lived in inadequate housing, and several of them had serious health problems. Some lived on a steady diet of beans, rice, and tortillas—all bought at the market two hours away in Ciudad Juárez. Some stood in line for hours to get free cheese, and some, like Isela Sotelo, had children who qualified for food stamps.

Figuring out what they were entitled to, finding out how to apply for special help, and living with the consequences of getting it were a constant challenge. Through all of this, the families were also raising children. They were preparing them to live life as adults in a world they did not know and would not always understand. As they would soon discover, in this country even childrearing was governed by beliefs and expectations that were quite different from their own.

CHAPTER 6

RAISING CHILDREN

Carmen Ornelas sat in one of the easy chairs in her small living room. She was out of breath and struggling to attach a metal brace on 18-month-old Anelena's legs. Anelena was severely bowlegged and had trouble walking. Carmen had just that day been successful in getting a donated brace that had been prescribed for her months before. It was obvious, however, that Anelena wanted nothing to do with it. She fussed and fretted as her mother attempted to attach it to her legs, but she did not kick or pull away. The child was obviously uncomfortable and bothered by the weight of the new appliance. I sensed that my assistant and I had probably arrived at the wrong time.

Carmen, however, did not seem bothered by our presence. When she finished installing the brace, she looked up briefly and signaled at Carmensita (then 7 years old), who quickly got up from the floor, took the child by the hand, and led her to a back bedroom. Anelena fussed a little as she walked with her new brace, but did not refuse to follow her sister. The other children, Cynthia (6), Nena (5), and José (4) sat quietly as Carmen engaged me in conversation. Cynthia, who viewed me as her special friend, sat next to me.

This same scene of the oldest child in the room taking over the care of younger siblings in order to allow their mother to engage me in conversation was repeated over and over again in the 10 homes that I visited. The rules appeared to be very clear. Children did not misbehave, clamor for attention, or take advantage of the fact that their mother had company to misbehave, try to get attention, or fight with their brothers and sisters. They responded to a raised eyebrow or to a nod that meant "Go away," or "Leave the room," or "Take your brother and change him."

Seen from a mainstream, middle-class, American perspective, these children might seem quite unusual. If one expects, for example, that conversations with mothers whose young children are present will inevitably involve constant interruptions as the mother attends to children's requests, remarks, or actions, the idea that very young children might be expected to be quiet, not to interrupt adult conversations, and not to misbehave is most noteworthy. But, in fact, in these families one rule was quite clear: *Cuando hay visita, los niños no molestan* (When there is company, children are not to bother the adults).

None of the mothers in the study considered their children's behavior particularly noteworthy. Indeed, in every case, as I asked questions about thoughts and views about childrearing, I found that there appeared to be no anxieties about rearing children. While they were considered important, children were *not* the focus of most of the family energy. I learned that because the primary goal of the family was to succeed as a unit, children were seen to contribute to these goals when they functioned well within the system as a whole, neither disrupting its balance nor causing the family to devote its energy to nonessential concerns.

In this chapter, I describe some of the childrearing practices of the 10 families. I talk about the ways in which mothers defined themselves and their roles, and the ways in which their siblings and family members were involved in raising children to become good adults.

THE ROLE OF CHILDREN IN FAMILIES

In general, a child's position in the family depended both on the order of birth with relation to other siblings and on personality characteristics as they were perceived by the family. Older siblings were expected to look after younger children and were normally given the authority to enforce family rules. This recognition of the older sibling's authority was operative on many levels. For example, if an adult attempted to engage a younger child in conversation when an older sibling was present, the younger child would defer to the older and not respond. Instead, the older child would answer for the younger.

All children, however, were not treated the same way. As babies, little ones were given much individual attention. In fact, infants seemed to belong in a special way to the entire extended family. Both siblings and cousins were expected to and did take delight in the family baby. For example, at the time that a youngster began to walk and talk, all members of the family were anxious to display "*la nueva gracia*" (the new ability). Loud approval greeted attempts to communicate. Older children eagerly shared with adults the fact that the baby had now said this or that. The baby was then requested to display his new word or expression for the adults present, for relatives who arrived later and had not heard the new expression, and even for visitors such as ourselves.

The pattern of expecting children to display abilities or knowledge did not continue into childhood. Once language had been acquired, children were no longer requested to perform. There was very little interest in "testing" children to see if they had acquired this or that piece of information. In short, children beyond the age of three were not made the center of attention of family interaction.

How a child was treated by siblings both older and younger was directly influenced by what was perceived to be his "*carácter*" (temperament). Judgments about children's personalities and temperaments were made early by both the parents and the extended family and resulted in the labeling of individual children. One child in a family might be known as "*el sentido*" (the sensitive one), "*la flojona*" (the lazy one), or "*el peleonero*" (the one who likes to fight). This labeling process reflected the family's perception of the differences among the children in the family, but more importantly, it also established clear roles and rules of interaction for the children. A child who was clobbered by *el peleonero,* for example, was told that this was deserved, because after all she knew that the child was a *peleonero* and would hit other children. This procedure, then, allowed families to deal with individual differences without devoting energy to changing what were perhaps only temporary undesirable behaviors. It also allowed the family system to function as a unit within which members complemented each other's strengths and weaknesses.

TEACHING CHILDREN

The general philosophy about how children learned to do household chores and other tasks was expressed by the comment, *Los pone uno a hacer las cosas* (one has the children do things [that one wants them to learn]). Thus, if it was considered desirable for a child to learn to wash dishes, she began by washing the dishes. It was expected that the child would either be able to do the task, or that it would be done at an unacceptable level. If it was unacceptable, the adult or older siblings could point out why this was so and suggest improvement for the next time the task was done. While carrying out the task, however, the child was free to ask questions about the process. These questions were answered and the information desired was given. No attempt was made to "get the child to think" or to test his/her underlying assumptions. Evaluation of the task was made according to the specific standards of the activity in question; the dishes were clean or they were not.

Tasks selected for learning depended on age and personality type. It was believed that there were ages at which children could not do certain things (e.g., wash dishes, dust, wring out clothes, etc.), and certain people who could not do certain things. No stigma appeared to be attached to the judgment that a child could not do a particular kind of task. Often the comment about a particular child's limitations was followed by a reference to another relative who could not do the same thing and yet could do other things well.

It is important for me to point out that in none of the 10 families did I ever observe mothers engaged in the deliberate teaching of their children. Except for *consejos* (a special genre of verbal teaching activity that I will describe at some length below), mothers did not directly teach children to do particular tasks. For most everyday things (like learning to use the toilet and learning to tie their shoes), it was simply assumed that children would learn as they observed their older brothers and sisters. *Se van enseñando* (They learn as they go along), I was told. What this meant is that it was older siblings who might actually engage in active teaching of different types. Thus, Lucila Castro at six years old was taught by her next older sister Susana (then 9) how to braid her own hair. Pamela Sotelo (then 5) showed her little sister Ada (then 3) how to tie her shoes, and Carmensita Ornelas (then 6) taught her sister Cynthia (then 5) how to use a dustpan to pick up dirt and dust after sweeping the floor. In each case, the older child taught the skill to the younger in order to save herself some work. The children were not asked by the mother to teach their siblings. It was the children themselves who initiated both the teaching and the learning.

It was also often the case that other relatives—especially visiting grandmothers—would decide to give instruction to the children in something they themselves liked to do. The instruction that I witnessed involved older children (9 years and older) in tasks such as sewing, knitting, and darning. In each case, adults carried on the task as the child imitated the adult with a smaller and simpler version of what the adult was doing. In the case of darning socks, for example, Doña Pepa Castro taught Elena (12) by giving her a sock with a very small hole to darn. She herself worked on a larger version of the same problem. Doña Pepa handed Elena a sock with an orange in it and started the needle for her. She then went back to her own sock, inserted the needle, and proceeded to darn the sock slowly while she talked Elena through the task as well. As she talked, she called attention to particular points that were important.

Fíjate bien. Hay que hacer el nudo para que no quede boludo. Lo metes asína y lo (luego) lo vas cerrando poco a poquito, asína.	Pay close attention. You have to make the knot so that it doesn't make a lump. You put it in like this and then you start closing it little by little like this.

Elena followed along and tried to darn her sock while simultaneously paying close attention to her grandmother's darning. She worked slowly and stopped often to ask her grandmother if she was, in fact, doing it right.

In this particular case, I was told that Elena had been eagerly asking to be taught how to darn. Doña Pepa decided that *como ya se fija tanto* (since she already watches so closely), it was time to give her direct instruction. In the case of darning, Doña Pepa felt that it was important to point out to learners that bulky darns can be very uncomfortable. The art of darning involved closing even very large holes in such a way that they were flat and didn't hurt the feet. She believed that most people could start darning by themselves, but she was also convinced that unless someone pointed out *lo mero importante del trabajo* (what was really important about the task), it would simply not be done correctly.

Teaching children how to carry out household tasks, then, was seen as a very natural process that would simply happen in the course of everyday life. Children learned as they became ready to do so. Sometimes an adult might deliberately choose to share particular points of wisdom about a specific task, but this was not considered to be the primary responsibility of the mother. For the most part, however, children simply taught each other. When the younger child mastered a task, the older sibling could announce it proudly. More importantly, however, he or she could also be rid of that particular responsibility.

FAMILY INTERACTION

In all of the 10 families the mother's role was well defined and well understood by everyone. In observing mothers interact with their children, including their very young children, I noted that they provided guidance, parceled out work, gave directions, organized the household, cooked meals, cleaned, and raised their children. Children were children, but they were also expected to do what they were told, to get along with their siblings, and not to see themselves as the focus of their mother's existence.

"*Respeto*" for the mother's role was very much in evidence in what the children did *not* do. As the Ornelas example made clear, even children under two years old did not interrupt conversations between their mother and other adults. They did not demand attention, act up, or otherwise disturb her. At most, they sat quietly by her side and listened to the conversation. When a directive was given, it was followed promptly. If a younger child did not do so, an older sibling soon made certain that the youngster did what he had been told.

Out of *respeto,* children were expected to wait until their mother was finished with whatever activity she was involved in before they asked for her attention. Adults were considered to be more important than children, and children did not expect to control either their mother's attention or her interaction with others. Mothers saw themselves as having certain rights and privileges. One of these rights was the expectation that their children, beginning at a very early age, would make few unnecessary demands on their energy or time.

Isela Sotelo, for example, in spite of her devotion to her family and the amount of effort that she put into making certain that they all kept afloat, had very clear expectations of even her youngest children. She expected, for instance, that they would not wake her up if she was sleeping, that they would not make more work for her, and that they would do as much as they could for themselves.

Even baby Chepe, Reina Leyba's little boy, who was 4 at the end of the study and the family pet, was expected not to be a nuisance to his mother. If he needed something and it could not be provided by older siblings or cousins, Chepe had been taught to approach his mother and whisper in her ear if she was busy or talking to others. Reina would not have impressed the members of her extended family if she had interrupted her conversation with them to engage him in interaction. She would have been considered rude to her adult female relatives, and the child would have been seen as not being taught to show respect for his mother.

Young children who constantly hung on their mothers were considered to be "*niños molestos*" (bothersome children), and mothers who gave signs of catering to such behavior were chastised by members of the family as being at fault for not teaching them better. Mothers did not expect to have to chase their children or plead with them to carry out directives. When they witnessed such scenes between Anglo mothers and their children at local supermarkets, they were quick to criticize. For them, it was important for children to learn very early "*quien manda*" (who gave the orders). There were no pretenses about running democratic households. Parents, especially mothers, considered that they knew what to do and that as the adults and the parents, they had a right to "make" their children do what they were told.

For children to talk back to their mother or to argue with her was considered to be a "*falta de respeto*" (disrespectful). When it happened, the mother was quick to point out, "*No somos iguales, tú y yo*" (We are not equals, you and I). Questioning authority head-on was not encouraged. Whatever questioning was done was permitted in older children who could be considered to be developing their own judgment. Generally such questioning was carried out in the context of listening to and responding to "*consejos*" (spontaneous homilies or moral lectures), not in the context of disagreeing with a parental decision or arguing about the suitability of a directive.

As children grew older, mothers depended on a combination of strategies to keep their children out of trouble. One strategy involved appealing to the notion of *respeto* and to the children's duties and obligations as sons or daughters. The other strategy involved an appeal for consideration of the special individual characteristics of the mother (her illness, her worries, and her other problems).

PARENTAL RESPONSIBILITIES

Parental responsibilities were similar in all the families. The normal pattern was considered to consist of the father working outside the home and the mother working primarily in the home with some occasional part-time employment when the opportunity arose.

During the period that their mothers were working, children were normally kept by relatives. When families were forced to put children in child care centers, they recalled the experience as traumatic. The very idea of leaving children with "*desconocidos*" (strangers) was most upsetting. Rosario Castro, for example, recalled how when her mother-in law, Doña Pepa, was ill, she had been forced to leave Lucila, then 3, in a child care center for migrant workers.

Se me partía el alma dejarla. Lloraba tanto. Decía—yo me quiero ir con mi abuelita Pepa. No, pos con su abuelita estaba feliz.	It broke my heart to leave her there. She cried so much. She would say, "I want to go with my grandmother Pepa." With her grandmother, she was so happy.

Leaving children with strangers, then, was an acceptable alternative only when no members of the family were available to care for them.

HOUSEHOLD CHORES

While women might joke among themselves about how "*no se dejaron*" (they didn't put up with something or other) from their husbands, in the husband's presence the wife looked after her husband's physical comfort (e.g., served his dinner and cleaned up after him) and was seldom confrontational. This was seen as part of a wife's role and not necessarily as being dependent on the personal relationship between two individuals. As Socorro Tinajero said when she talked about her obligations at home, "*Aunque yo sé que él cocina y todo, él es el hombre y yo en la casa le sirvo*" (Even though I know that he can cook and everything, he is the man, and at home I serve him).

Wives were responsible for the cooking and all household chores. Male children were rarely expected to help in these activities. Somewhat more was expected of female children, but generally great demands were not made of them either. For example, if the mother was not employed outside the home and if the work involved was not overly demanding, female children were asked to take on certain tasks only *"para que se enseñen"* (so they could learn to do them), not because the mother believed such tasks were their responsibility. It was thought that female children would have their own responsibilities later and that life would be hard enough. It was important that they be allowed to be children.

It will be recalled that Reina Leyba, for example, grew quite angry at her husband when she discovered that while she worked the 3-to-11 shift at the factory, he was making 8-year-old Maya wash all the supper dishes and take care of baby Chepe, who was then about 10 months old. She reported arguing with her husband and saying: *"Maya tiene que jugar, es una criatura todavía"* (Maya has to play, she's still a child). Since she prepared food before she left for work, Reina did not think that her husband had much of a burden. However, when it became clear to her that he resented having to wash dishes, she asked that they be stacked and left for her to do the next morning. It was a better solution than having Maya take on the task every night.

Allowing them to be children did not mean, however, that young people did not have to help when family circumstances required it. On the contrary, it was assumed that children would at a moment's notice be able to look after younger children, to keep them out of trouble, and to make certain that they were safe. They were not taught how to do this. It was assumed that by simply living in the household and observing how things were done, they would know how to do what was needed. For example, when a mother was unable to carry on normal household activities for whatever reason, it was simply expected that the oldest available female child would take on these responsibilities and carry them out well.

FAMILY STRUCTURE

For the 10 families included in the study, *family,* as a term, included relatives on both the husband's and wife's sides who either lived in the area or visited the household for extended periods of time. Indeed, as I described previously, most households had a resident "floating population," that is, cousins, grandmothers, aunts, uncles, or whole other families who visited for months at a time.

Family fun and entertainment also took place within the extended family. Picnics, visits to flea markets, birthday parties, holiday celebrations, renting of movies, and so forth were considered to be more fun when a large number of family members were present. Opportunities for the family to get together were sought after actively. Even small events were organized with great enthusiasm, and much time and thought was given to planning food and making arrangements for everyone to be there. Grandmothers, in particular, were considered to be the heart of the family, and much of the extended family's activity centered around spending time with "*la abuelita*" (the grandmother).

As a result of the time spent with extended families, children played almost exclusively with other siblings or with cousins. Men in the family interacted with their male in-laws or male relatives, and women primarily spent time with their female relatives and in-laws.

It was interesting that the distinction between blood relatives and in-laws was not particularly salient. Since only one family (the Gómezes) had relatives on both sides living in the Las Fuentes area, most of the adults in the study were not forced to make choices between two extended families. Generally, in interacting with family members at large gatherings, it was difficult for me to identify in-laws exclusively from their behavior. Among the women in particular, the tendency seemed to be for wives of sons to become very close to both their husband's sisters and their husband's mother. In the case of the Cerda family, for example, the wives of Gloria's two brothers spent most of their time at the home of Doña Cuca, Gloria's mother. They stopped by daily, spent Sundays with her, and organized most events around her household. This was even the case for Pamela, the wife of the youngest brother, who was an Anglo, spoke little Spanish, and had her own family living in the area. Having been ostracized by her own parents and siblings for marrying a *Mexicano,* she became quite close to her new family and behaved much as they did.

The extended family, as might be expected, had a great deal of influence on its members. Children's behavior, if unacceptable, was discussed, and advice was freely given about what mothers should do to encourage change. Adults were expected to be both interested and concerned not only about their own children, but also about the behavior of all the young children in the family. It was considered acceptable for adults to reprimand children when they witnessed misbehavior.

Extended families also had a strong investment in the health of the marriages of all the couples in the family. There were few secrets, and women in the family were especially sensitive to changes in behavior or mood and to other signs that might signal trouble. In the case of Rosario Castro, for example, Chuy's mother, sisters, and brothers were quite aware of his drinking and of the problems it created for Rosario and her children. They did not pry or ask Rosario questions directly. Still, they remained informed about Chuy's condition, and on several occasions one of the older brothers took Chuy aside in order to remind him of his obligations.

Advice was freely given. Young wives were cautioned to show *respeto* for their husbands, which included asking their permission to attend family gatherings. Part of the role of being a wife included being aware of the fact that a wife did not make decisions by herself. For new wives, it was felt to be particularly important that the husband approve of the interaction with the extended family. If he came to resent his wife's involvement with her family, this would in turn lead to a potentially serious conflict. By asking permission from the very beginning, a husband would be made to feel that his opinion was important. The wife would have shown her *respeto* of his role as her husband.

CONSEJOS

The majority of the teaching in the 10 families was carried out by means of "*consejos*" (spontaneous homilies designed to influence behaviors and attitudes). *Consejos* were important because mothers considered *la educación de los hijos* (the moral education of their children) to be their primary responsibility.

As might be gathered from my translation of the Spanish term *educación,* this term cannot be translated completely using the English word *education.* What English speakers call *education* is school or book learning. What Spanish speakers call "*educación*" has a much broader meaning and includes both manners and moral values. For example, when a child is scolded and told that his behavior (e.g., picking his nose) "*es mala educación,*" this means that it is bad manners. When a child or an adult is described as being "*muy mal educado,*" this means that she is very rude and has, in fact, not been reared appropriately.

Educando a los hijos, then, included teaching children how to behave, how to act around others, and also what was good and what was moral. It included teaching the expectations of the roles that they would play in life and the rules of conduct that had to be followed in order to be successful in them. This teaching, or rather, this indoctrination, began very early and generally took place whenever there was any verbal interaction between adults and children. Adults, particularly mothers, believed that their role as "educators" required that they engage constantly in the practice of "*dando consejos*" (guiding their children). They also believed that children needed to be told such things over and over again in order to internalize them thoroughly. As one mother (Amelia Soto) put it: "*Les digo y les digo, para que se les vaya grabando*" (I tell them and I tell them so that it can become engraved in their memory).

Consejos were tailored to the age of the children and generally began when a child was considered to be able to understand. For very young children, *consejos* were often embedded in moral tales. For example, when Vicky Cerda's grandmother decided that Vicky was becoming a gossip, she embedded this teaching in the following tale:

Una vez yo conocí a una niña que todo el tiempo andaba contando todo lo que oía. Si oía que su tía dicía una cosa, se lo contaba a su abuelita, y a su mamá, y a su otra tía.—Que ya me tía se pelió con su comadre.—Que ya mi tía se compró un vestido rojo. Parecía cedazo. Lo que le dicían contaba. Un día, su abuelita se econtró un dinero en la calle. Era mucho dinero y la abuelita taba muy necesitada. Cuando la niña oyó a la abuelita contándole a su mamá, ya le andaba por decirle a todo mundo. Y sí, le dijo al primo, y a la vecina, y al que iba pasando. ¿Y qué crees que pasó? Esa noche, se le metieron a la casa a la abuelita y la robaron. Fíjate. Y to por culpa de la niña. Por eso no es bueno andar chismiando y contando las cosas.

I once knew a little girl that was always telling everything she heard. If she heard her aunt say something, she would tell her grandmother, and her mother and her other aunt. "My aunt had a fight with her comadre." "My aunt bought a new red dress." She was like a sieve. Whatever she was told, she would tell somebody else. One day, her grandmother found some money on the street. It was a lot of money and the grandmother was very poor. When the little girl heard the grandmother telling her mother, she couldn't wait to tell everyone. And she did. She told her cousin and the neighbor, and people walking by on the street. And what do you think happened? That night someone broke into the grandmother's house and robbed her. And it was all the little girl's fault. That's why it's not good to be gossiping and telling things.

In other cases, *consejos* were attached to ordinary conversation. Principles and rules of behavior were worked in wherever they would fit. When Saúl Soto came home from school, for example, the following exchange took place:

VELMA: *A ver Saúl ven aquí, cómo te fue en la escuela.*

Saúl, come here. How were things at school?

SAÚL: *Bien.*

Okay.

VELMA: *¿Cómo te portaste?*

How did you behave?

SAÚL: *Bien.*

Okay.

VELMA: *¿No te peleaste?*

You didn't fight?

SAÚL: *No.*

No.

VELMA: *Acuérdate que los niños buenos*   Remember that good boys don't go
no se andan peleando. A esos niños   around fighting. Everything goes
siempre les va mejor.   better for those boys.

In this particular case, Velma worried a great deal about Saúl's aggressiveness. She constantly talked to him about not being a bully and about not hitting other children.

In discussing their children or asking about my children, the subject of *consejos* was a frequent one. I was often asked, *Y usté ¿qué les decía a sus hijos?* (What did you tell your children at that age?) about certain behaviors or certain principles. I would then recall my own small homilies to my two children, and they, in turn, would share what they had said or would say to their children. For example, Reina Leyba was worried about her then 11-year-old daughter Maya. She was fighting with her cousins and siblings, isolating herself, and making up stories. Reina reported how she was handling the situation and what she normally said to Maya:

Yo le digo que tiene que tener más cariño   I tell her that she has to give more
para poder recibir, si no al final se queda   love in order to get it, otherwise
sola. Llora, se pone a llorar porque le em-   she will end up alone. She cries, she
piezo a dar consejos. Le digo no seas   starts to cry because I start to give
tonta. Tú eres mi única niña que tengo   her *consejos*. I tell her, don't be fool-
yo. Yo no voy a tener más. Tú compre-   ish. You are my only little girl. I'm
nde que no debes de ser así. A ratitos me   not going to have any more. You
dolía estarle diciendo.   must understand that you shouldn't
    be that way. At moments, it hurt
    me to be telling her that.

Consejos covered an immense amount of ground. Older girls were lectured to about being virtuous, and young men were told about the importance of hard work. Young children were constantly reminded that it was good to be *hermanables* (to get along well with their brothers and sisters), and even married daughters were constantly reminded of what good wives and mothers should do. Generally the content of the *consejos* could be boiled down to a simple general statement or rule of behavior that was often explicitly stated by the individual doing the lecturing:

A las maestras se les respeta porque están allí para enseñarte. (You have to
    respect teachers because they are there to teach you.)
Cuando los niños cuentan mentiras, nadie les cree nada. (When children tell
    lies, no one believes anything they say.)

La esposa tiene que saber llevar su casa. (Wives have to know how to manage their households.)

The emphasis on this constant, ongoing teaching, particularly by female parents, created a type of interaction between mothers and children that generally conformed to one of the following patterns:

Pattern A
Turn 1: Mother questions child about activities.
Turn 2: Child responds.
Turn 3: Mother gives *consejos*.

Pattern B
Turn 1: Mother observes child's objectionable behavior and reprimands child.
Turn 2: Mother gives *consejos*.

Pattern C
Turn 1: Child nominates topic.
Turn 2: Mother engages in conversation about topic.
Turn 3: Mother steers conversation to broader issues and gives *consejos*.

This verbal interaction centering around *consejos* was very different from that found by Heath (1983) in certain middle-class American homes. In these 10 families, adults managed the direction of the conversations, and indeed engaged in the conversation solely or primarily for the purpose of teaching the child something. As opposed to the kind of interaction found by Heath among the families in Roadville where children were expected to display information (the ABC's, the colors) or recount in detail what happened at school, in these families, children were asked questions primarily to determine what kinds of guidance they might need.

While there was much laughter and joy in all of the families observed, when interactions focused on children's behavior and when *consejos* were being given, mothers were serious and stern and conveyed to their children the fact that they meant business. Ordinarily, if any joking took place, it was initiated by the adult. Because of the *respeto* that children were expected to have for their parents, they could not enter into teasing or joking behavior without permission, that is, without a sign of some sort that such behavior would be tolerated.

DISCIPLINE

As was seen in the discussion of *consejos* above, children's behavior problems were generally handled by anticipating those problems and by attempting to inculcate values and beliefs that would lead to the avoidance of unacceptable conduct. In all of the households, there were clear limits for all of the children.

Nevertheless, some children caused their parents more problems than others. Saúl Soto drove his mother, Velma, crazy with his fighting. Julio, Carmen Ornelas's 9-year-old, was a trial to his mother, who constantly complained about his misbehavior and his rudeness. Terry Sotelo Jr. was spoiled by his father and often ignored his mother. In those cases, more extreme measures were used. Saúl was spanked often. Julio was not allowed to watch TV. Terry was ignored by his mother and not spoken to for several days.

In the case of older children and severe problems of misbehavior that had serious consequences, physical punishment by the father was still considered to be the ultimate solution. For example, when Rebeca Castro at 14 played hooky for several days and Rosario found out about it, she wanted to make sure that Rebeca learned her lesson. Rosario recalled that Chuy had really hit Rebeca hard.

Yo fui y la encontré en la calle y me la traje de las greñas. Ya aquí se la di a su papá y él la agarró a trancazos. Pa que aprendiera y no se le fuera a olvidar.	I went and found her coming down the street and I pulled her home by her hair. Here at home I handed her to her father and he really lit into her. So that she would learn and so she wouldn't forget.

During the last year of the study, however, schools and other social agencies had begun campaigns to try to make people aware of the problems of child abuse. Posters in English and Spanish were everywhere around the city, including local convenience stores, urging people to report suspected cases of abuse. Much discussion went on within the family networks about what this meant, and I was often questioned about what I knew about the matter. Many of the kinds of corporal punishment that the mothers had been subjected to as children, such as hitting children with belts, were specifically mentioned on posters as manifestations of child abuse. There was fear that children would report parents if they were spanked and confusion about how these children were going to be kept in line if they could accuse their parents of abuse and not be punished at all. Among the families, there was not a sense that children needed to be beaten, but there was a belief very much akin to the old-fashioned American notion expressed in the saying, "Spare the rod and spoil the child." They believed very much in pointing out the right path through *consejos,* but they also felt certain that there were times when circumstances called for something more.

RESPETO

The relationship between the mothers and their children cannot be understood without an examination of one of the most important notions guiding interaction between individuals in these families. This notion is *respeto,* a concept that goes much beyond the meaning of the English term *respect.* The English notion of *respect* suggests some of the elements of the concept of *respeto,* but excludes many others.

Respeto in its broadest sense is a set of attitudes toward individuals and/ or the roles that they occupy. It is believed that certain roles demand or require particular types of behavior. *Respeto,* while important among strangers, is especially significant among members of the family. Having *respeto* for one's family involves functioning according to specific views about the nature of the roles filled by the various members of the family (e.g., husband, wife, son, brother). It also involves demonstrating personal regard for the individual who happens to occupy that role.

In the 10 families, roles and role obligations were particularly important. When speaking about the family and about ways in which it was seen to function well, reference was always made, not exclusively to individuals, but to the characteristics of particular roles that were thought to be the key to a successful family.

Comments such as *"La madre tiene que encargarse de la conducta de los hijos"* (Mothers have got to take responsibility for their children's behavior) and *"Los hijos tienen que obedecer"* (Children have to be obedient) reflect a set of rules that were accepted as governing the behavior of individuals occupying particular roles. Attitudes and expectations about roles served as a blueprint that guided the behavior of individuals as well as the response of other members of the family to their behavior.

The role of the father, for example, was seen to involve providing for his family as well as serving as an authority figure for his children. He was supposed to make sacrifices, work long hours, and ideally provide a good example for his sons. The role of the mother was seen to include managing the household in its broadest sense and raising the children to become good human beings. Household management, as I pointed out in the profiles of the 10 women in the study, involved working both inside and outside the home, negotiating the system, policing family members requiring such supervision, working in the family business when there was one, and taking care of traditionally "female" household chores. The role of children was less well defined. However, as *buenos hijos* (good sons and daughters), they had an obligation to be considerate, obedient, and appreciative of their parents' efforts. As little children, they were not expected to contribute directly to the family in any large sense. However, they were expected, even at a very young age, not to behave in a manner that would result in more work for their parents. They were expected not to be selfish, to look after their siblings, and not to draw energy away from common family goals.

The view of the roles of father, mother, wife, and husband were traditional ones. There was little flexibility in the ways in which individuals could choose to live those roles. From very early on, children were socialized to accept certain definitions for these roles and to expect that they themselves would fill them in these ways. The ideal for an individual member of the family was for him or her to fill the role as expected and, in so doing, to personally earn respect (*darse a respetar*) due to that effort. Nevertheless, when a family member failed in key obligations that were part of the role he occupied, *respeto* was still owed by family members to the role itself. For this reason, for example, even though Chuy Castro was a problem drinker and often disappointed and angered his children, Rosario's role as both a mother and a wife demanded that she act as though Chuy's role, rather than his behavior, entitled him to *respeto* from his children. In Rosario Castro's words:

Aunque su padre sea así o sea esto, él no quiere que agarren el ejemplo que les da. El quiere que de todas maneras sean buenos y ustedes tienen que respetarlo porque es su padre.	Even though your father might be this or that, he doesn't want you to follow his example. He wants you to be good anyway and you have to respect him because he's your father.

Interactions between family members, then, were guided by respect for particular persons as well as respect for the obligations, rights, and privileges of the roles occupied by each individual. Older brothers, for example, had certain responsibilities to the family and to younger siblings, as well as certain privileges. Younger siblings were expected to respect their older siblings' authority and to understand the relationship between the privileges and obligations that were part of that role.

Children were also expected to develop a sense of role boundaries and an understanding of how behaviors appropriate in one role might conflict with behaviors appropriate for another. Since, for example, the role of sister (to male siblings) required that a young woman not make her sexuality in anyway noticeable, it was considered inappropriate for her to be involved in public displays of affection with her boyfriend (or even her husband) in front of her brother. This was considered a *falta de respeto,* an offense to his sense of dignity in his role as brother.

The action of *faltar al respeto* (to offend another's sense of dignity) was considered to be a serious affront. From a very early age, children were expected to follow complex and strict rules of behavior. *"Tienen que aprender a respetar"* (They have to learn how respect works) was a guiding principle for raising children. Indeed, after a certain age (roughly 4 or 5), rules of behavior were thought to be quite clear, and it was generally assumed that such *faltas de respeto* were deliberate. It was feared that if such *faltas* took place frequently between individuals, the result would be that they would end up *"perdiéndose todo el respeto"* (losing all respect for each other as individuals and all respect for the roles in question).

Respeto, then, involved both the presentation of self before others as well as a recognition and acceptance of the needs of those persons with whom interactions took place. It also involved a knowledge of the boundaries of roles and role relationships and of the responsibilities each individual had when acting in each role. Children were cautioned often not to be *irrespetuosos* (disrespectful); and, at the same time, older young people were warned to behave in the manner prescribed for their particular roles so that they themselves might not invite disrespect.

SCHOOL SUCCESS, LEARNING, AND HUMAN TALENT

In addition to their views about how children learned at home, the parents in the study shared a number of notions and ideas about school success, learning, and human talent. I identified the following general beliefs as underlying most of these views:

1. Individuals who do well in school are not necessarily *muy listos* (very clever or intelligent). They may be only book smart, or even worse, *macheteros* (rather limited individuals who hack away at a subject like machete users until they finally understand).
2. Some people are more *cerrados de cabeza* (closed-headed) than are others. They do not learn as easily in school.
3. Some persons who do well in school are not particularly gifted. They simply rely on their memories to get by. Memory, however, is *la inteligencia de los tontos* (the intelligence of people who are not very smart).
4. All people have particular talents. There are things that they are naturally good at and others that they have difficulty with. They should

do what they are naturally good at in their lives rather than try to be what they are not.

The adults in the study expressed very positive attitudes toward education. At the same time, none of these adults equated academic success with exceptional abilities or talents. That a person had more formal schooling was not seen as evidence of anything more than the fact that he or she had had the opportunity to go to school and the desire to do so. They could give many examples, however, of people with *mucha escuela* (a lot of education) who had few real-life skills. They could also point to many of their acquaintances who had little schooling and who, in their eyes, were quite successful. They could even point to children in their own families and describe one of them as *muy listo, todo capta, todo se la pega* (very smart, catches on to everything, remembers everything), and another as simply a *machetero* (one who hacks or pounds away at his studies), just a kid who *se quema las pestañas* (burns his eyelashes) by studying. For these families, the latter child was not the smartest in the family. He was merely a diligent kid who labored away tediously. Of course he would do well in school, but this had nothing to do with real talent.

In the Castro family, for example, Elena was seen to be a *machetera*. She was also seen as *seria* (serious/shy) and not particularly interesting or bright. Lola Sotelo was also considered to be a *machetera* by her family and often ridiculed by Isela for thinking herself brighter than the rest of the children.

A subtle distinction was made between being *aplicado* (applying oneself to one's studies) and a *machetero*. A child who was considered to be *aplicado* simply applied natural talents to doing good work. The talent was there, and she applied it to the task at hand. She was not making something out of nothing or trying to.

Conversely, when a child who was considered to be bright did not make good progress at school, the problem was defined as *no se aplica* (she doesn't apply herself). In the Ramírez family, the reason that Rosana was held back was seen to be due to precisely that reason. As María Elena put it, "*Si se aplicara, si pusiera atención, haría mejor trabajo*" (If she applied herself, if she paid attention, she would do better work). In all cases in which parents pushed their children to achieve, it was done with those children who were considered to have natural ability but who had not yet learned to use that ability well.

In addition to believing that doing well in school was not necessarily evidence of ability, family members also believed that certain people were more *cerrados de cabeza* (had a harder time learning) than others. When describing, for example, a child who was doing poorly in school, they would often speak of the problem as follows: "*Es que no le entran las cosas*" (Things just don't penetrate [his head]). Carmen Ornelas described her daughter Cynthia as *más cerrada* (more closed-headed) in comparison to her daughter Nena, whom she considered to be *la más lista* (the brightest) in spite of her mediocre performance in school. For Carmen, there was a real difference between her children, a difference that she saw on an everyday basis. On the basis of their behavior at home, Carmen believed that Cynthia had limitations and that Nena was outstanding. It mattered little that Nena did not excel in school or that her teachers expressed concern about her ability. Carmen insisted that Nena's problem was simply that she did not apply herself, whereas Cynthia's problem, although she was not certain about this, might have something to do with her being *más cerrada* (see Chapter 7).

Socorro Tinajero also worried a great deal that her daughter Marica might really be *cerrada de cabeza* and not simply a child who was not *aplicada*. She spoke about working with her and worried about pushing her too hard.

El otro día hasta le pegué porque no me quería enseñar las palabras que le encargan. Decía que no se le pegaban. Pero rápido que se le pegaron. Y ya el siguiente jueves ya me las enseñó, pero ya leyéndolas. Y no que antes, no sabía ni que palabras eran, ni qué letras. Y pobrecita, me da tanta lástima. Le digo, "Si tu maestra quiere que lo hagas de vuelta es para que te enseñes más." Tal vez le estoy apretando más de lo que puede y ella está sintiendo.	The other day I even hit her because she didn't want to show me the words she had. She said that they wouldn't stick. But they stuck really fast. And then the next Thursday she showed them to me, but reading them already. And not like before when she didn't know what words they were or what letters. And poor thing. I feel so sorry for her. I tell her, "If your teacher wants you to do it again, it's so you'll learn more." Maybe I'm tightening up on her more than she can do and she is feeling it.

For both mothers, this was a dilemma. When did poor school performance mean that a child had poor work habits, and when did it mean that the child did not have the required natural ability?

Except for the memorization of the multiplication tables, rote learning was not considered to be "real" learning by the adults in the study. Children were often told such things as: "*No te lo aprendas de memoria. Tienes que entender lo que estás haciendo*" (Don't learn it by heart. You have to understand what you are doing). Often the parents had a very limited idea of what might be involved in learning particular subjects, and the advice made little sense. For example, when Rebeca Castro was learning how to type and mentioned that she had to learn the keyboard by memory, her mother cautioned her not to do so. In her opinion, Rebeca had to *entender las cosas primero* (under-stand things first).

Misguided as this advice might seem, the deeper value had to do with the belief that people who might "know" a lot of facts were not necessarily more talented than those who have not learned these same facts. *Macheteros*, in fact, were seen as the kinds of individuals who substituted memory for talent. The term *machetero/a* was often used to refer to children who exhib-ited such behavior in the hope of helping them to develop a more realistic sense of their own talents. As Isela Sotelo said about her daughter Lola:

Esta niña se está creyendo mucho y luego se va a dar un buen golpe. En la escuela luego las vuelan.	This child is really getting a big head and she is going to get hurt hard. At school, they often make them cocky.

Here, too, a familiar theme was repeated often. For all of its momentary glory, school success could ultimately be harmful.

Even though the categories of *listo, cerrado de cabeza, aplicado* and the like were used frequently by all members of the families about their children, these adults also shared a profound belief in the fact that all people were naturally good at doing certain things and not others. Some people, for ex-ample, were naturally musical and could play any tune on guitar or piano by ear. Some people could repair almost anything. Some people could sing. Some people were good with numbers, and some people could sell anything to anyone. The secret of life, then, was finding out what one was good at, and doing it as well as one could. They believed that it made little sense to fit a square peg into a round hole; thus, when young teens were seen to be pounding away at a task, spending long hours to learn something, or doing and redoing a particular project, they were advised that in life they should try something that came a bit more easily to them naturally. There was a concern that if they were not careful, they would end up in unhappy lives doing something that they would never be truly good at.

"*Confórmate con lo que eres. Y lo que puedes hacer, hazlo bien*" (Be content with what you are. And what you can do, do well). This was the advice given to Federico Gómez by his father, who did not see in him signs of his becoming a good farmer. But this was also a theme that ran through the entire study as we asked questions about education, and as we obviously expected answers that were not forthcoming. In their own subtle way, each of the families let us know that maybe *we* were a bit misguided, that maybe it was our priorities that weren't straight. After all, they had already figured things out, and they had a lot less formal education than we did. Some people were good at school things and others were not. What was important was that life provided different roads for different people.

ENGLISH LANGUAGE LEARNING AND FUTURE SUCCESS

In spite of the fact that they understood little about exactly what jobs were available and how people went about getting them, all of the families in the study were very much aware of the importance of English. When we asked how much English each member of the family spoke and which language they wanted their children to speak, all parents stated firmly that they wanted their children to speak it well. Pedro Soto emphasized that they were children who had been born here and that in order to "*abrirse paso en la vida*" (get ahead in life), they had to learn both languages. The most extreme position was voiced by Reina Leyba in one conversation with me.

GV: *Por ejemplo, si yo le dijera que sus hijos van a aprender inglés pero que poco a poquito van a ir hablando menos español, ¿usted qué diría?*

For example, if I told you that your children are going to learn English but that little by little they are going to speak less Spanish, what would you say?

REINA: *Que le hace.*

It doesn't matter.

GV: *Con tal de que hablaran en inglés, ¿aunque se les olvidara el español?*

As long as they spoke English, it would be all right if they forgot Spanish?

REINA: *No, yo me daría mañas para que no se les olvidara.*

No, I would figure out ways so that they wouldn't forget it.

For the parents, then, the value of English was unquestionable. They viewed it as basic and essential for themselves and for their children. Often, however, the fact that English quickly became a secret language for the children became a problem for the family. For example, one mother, María Elena Ramírez, commented that when she heard the children speaking English to one another and laughing after she had just reprimanded them, she was certain that they were being disrespectful. She also suspected that they were *diciendo malas razones* (using swear words) and teaching them to their younger siblings. The fact that children could speak about parents *in front of them* in ways that they could not understand gave the mothers and fathers who did not speak English the feeling that their authority was in jeopardy.

Families were also concerned about the children's use of English outside the home with strangers. Reina Leyba, for example, prohibited her children from speaking to each other in English in public and from responding to persons outside the family in this language. Her great fear was that Maya and Josué did not know English well enough to know what they were saying. She was afraid that they would say the wrong thing and, without meaning to, bring trouble to the family.

In spite of these difficulties, however, the children of relatives who had just arrived were lectured about the importance of English. For example, when María Elena Ramírez's 15-year-old niece, Marta (the daughter of the sister who had moved in with the family), was introduced to me, I was pulled into a discussion about the importance of English and schooling. María Elena was actually delivering a set of *consejos,* and she used my participation to reinforce her position.

MARÍA ELENA: *Nomás que no la hacemos que . . . mi hermana la quiere mandar a la escuela pero no quiere ir.*	It's just that we can't make her . . . my sister wants to send her to school but she doesn't want to go.
GV: *¿No quieres ir? ¿Por qué?*	You don't want to go? Why?
MARTA: *No me gusta aquí, es diferente*	I don't like it here, it's different.
MARÍA ELENA: *¿Cómo sabes si no has ido a la escuela?*	How do you know if you haven't gone to school?
MARTA: *Pero es que aquí no me gusta por las tareas.*	But I don't like it here because of the homework.
MARÍA ELENA: *Yo le digo que no pierda la oportunida ésta, pos porque la oportunida que tiene de aprender el inglés. Le digo yo que sabiendo el inglés tienen más oportunidades de cualquier trabajo.*	I tell her not to miss out on this opportunity, because of the opportunity that she has of learning English. I tell her that people who know English have more opportunities for any kind of a job.

The conversation continued in the same tone. I questioned Marta about why she didn't want to learn English and tried to persuade her that there would be many other young people at school that would also be starting out. Her aunt, María Elena, on the other hand, repeated her main message:

No quiere. Ya mi hermana . . . ya le entra por arrevés y por derecho y no quiere. Dice que no. No sabe qu'el inglés hace mucha falta. A mí me regaña mucho la tía de Joaquín. A mí me dice, "Yo no sé que tantos años que	She doesn't want to. My sister already . . . she tries to get her to go one way and another and she doesn't want to. She says no. She doesn't know that you really need English. Joaquín's aunt scolds me.

tienen aquí. ¿Por qué no han   She says, "I don't know how many
aprendido?"   years you've been here. Why
                                         haven't you learned?"

It was clear that in spite of the trouble she had experienced with her own
children when they made fun of her English or used the language in order
to exclude her, María Elena—like the other parents in the study—was convinced of its importance.

RAISING CHILDREN: A COLLECTIVE ENDEAVOR

Raising or rearing children among the 10 families was characterized by
the involvement of parents, siblings, and other family members. Indeed, the
key defining theme for this endeavor was the fact that it was a truly collective
undertaking. In a very fundamental sense, children belonged not just to their
parents or to their mothers. Indeed, they belonged to and were shared with
the entire family. Raising children to become good adults, then, involved all
the individuals who cared for them.

At the same time, children, no matter how young, were not the single
or primary focus of parents'—especially mothers'—energies. Perhaps because most women in the study had many children or perhaps because members of the family were available to share these responsibilities, the mothers
did not appear particularly anxious or concerned about the process of raising
children. They simply expected that their children would love them and
respect them as well.

In the families studied, then, children learned early that they must not
"disrupt" the family environment. They shared space and toys with siblings
and cousins, and they took responsibility for younger children. They also
learned what behaviors would be tolerated by others in the family and what
behaviors they in turn must tolerate in others. Children made few demands
for extra attention from parents and relatives. Moreover, because roles were
not shared, children were not put in the position of competing for a prized
label or position within the family.

The differences between the childrearing practices of these 10 families
and those of mainstream, middle-class American families are many. From my
perspective, these differences involve a fundamental contrast in values about
parent–child relationships and about the particular role mothers play in their
children's lives. American middle-class mothers' behavior around their
youngsters and their sense of what mothers should and should not do are
in many ways unlike the behavior and the attitudes of these working-class
Mexican women.

Be that as it might, the 10 mothers in this study, like mothers in other groups around the world, were raising their children in ways that were congruent with their deeply held views about parent–child relationships and about maternal roles in particular. They were also raising children with the help, love, and assistance of a very large network of extended family. They cared deeply about their children, and as they struggled to make it in their new country, they sought to guide their youngsters to become good human beings.[1]

CHAPTER 7

THE SCHOOL CONTEXT

LINCOLN SCHOOL

Lincoln School was located in the heart of the east side barrio. It sat on the corner of a main thoroughfare and a small street, and twice a day the comings and goings of the children would bring traffic almost to a standstill on the busy street. Most neighborhood children walked to school from their homes, which were often many blocks away. The younger children were generally accompanied by their mothers and by two or three younger siblings, who were either nudged forward or carried along.

The school itself—a redbrick, one-story building—was surrounded by an unusually large playground. It had ancient equipment, but an effort had been made to keep it freshly painted. There were young trees around the edge of the playground, grass in some areas, and a high chain-link fence on the side of the playground that faced the busy street.

At first glance, the school building looked old, but it was apparent that it was in good repair. Inside, the building showed evidence of care and attention. The wide hallways were clean and waxed, and the walls were covered with examples of children's artwork. Classroom doors displayed children's photographs, the teacher's name, and the room number. Most had large windows on one side and were bright and sunny and perhaps only a little too warm in the fall and spring. Teachers appeared to go to great pains to make the school and the classrooms attractive.

Lincoln School was one of two schools in the Las Fuentes area where bilingual classes were available for children who did not speak English. Generally known as the "Mexican" school, it was a pleasant and friendly place and reflected the principal's deep commitment to the neighborhood children. The principal, Mr. Vasquez, a Chicano native of Las Fuentes, was a fluent Spanish speaker who made every effort to make the newly arrived Mexican parents feel welcome in his school. The teachers, who included both Anglos and Hispanics, appeared to be supportive of Mr. Vasquez.

THE FOCAL CHILDREN AND THEIR SCHOOL PLACEMENT

Of the forty-seven children in the 10 families, we selected 6 4-year-olds and 6 5-year-olds as focal children. For each of the focal children, information was gathered in the school setting during the three-year period of the study. Children were observed in their regular classrooms, in pullout programs, and in the school yard. Teachers, teacher aides, and other school personnel who worked with the children were interviewed at the end of each year.

It will be noted that all but three of the focal children attended Lincoln School. Amapola and Jasmín Soto attended River School, the school located closest to the farm where they lived. Victoria Cerda was deliberately sent to a school outside the barrio by her mother, Gloria Cerda, who had always found Park School to be particularly pretty. Bilingual programs were not available at either of the schools attended by these children. Figure 7.1 summarizes the children's placement during the three-year period.

As will be seen from the above summaries of the children who attended Lincoln School, only two youngsters were enrolled in the regular monolingual English program. All the other children were enrolled in the bilingual program. Of the nine focal children at Lincoln, three were recommended for retention during the project period. One child was recommended for retention twice.

The children who attended Park School and River School were all enrolled in the regular monolingual English program. At River School, special help was available in ESL in the form of a pullout program. Of the three children attending schools other than Lincoln, one was recommended for retention.

As do most children everywhere in this country, the children of the families in the study spent much of their time in school. Some did better than others in their classes, but in general, they did not excel. In fact, in 7 of the 10 families at least one child in the family was retained in grade. Of the 33 school-aged children in the 10 families, only 2 did well in school.

Some of the children were lucky. They were able to blend in well with other children. They were seen by their teachers as making progress, and at the end of the year they were promoted to the next grade. Others were not so lucky. What they brought with them, what their mothers had so carefully taught them, did not prepare them for the world of school. Their teachers viewed them as having communication problems or social development problems or as simply coming from homes where the parents did not really care a great deal about education.

Pamela Sotelo, for example, spent her kindergarten year saying nothing at all. She did not play with other children or respond when they spoke to

Figure 7.1
Children's School Placement and Progress

Children at Lincoln School

	First Year		Second Year		Third Year	
	PROGRAM	COMMENTS	PROGRAM	COMMENTS	PROGRAM	COMMENTS
Cynthia Ornelas	4 years old Not in school		Kindergarten Regular English	Concern about progress expressed	1st grade Bilingual education program	Retention recommended
Lucila Castro	4 years old Not in school		Kindergarten Bilingual education program		1st grade Bilingual education program	
Keith Sotelo	4 years old Not in school		Kindergarten Bilingual education program		1st grade Bilingual education program	
Federico Gómez	4 years old Not in school		Kindergarten Bilingual education program		1st grade Bilingual education program	
Saúl Soto	Kindergarten Bilingual education program		1st grade Regular English	Retention recommended	2nd grade Regular English	Retention recommended
Joel Ramírez	Kindergarten Bilingual education program		1st grade Bilingual education program		2nd grade Bilingual education program	

FIGURE 7.1
continued

	First Year PROGRAM	First Year COMMENTS	Second Year PROGRAM	Second Year COMMENTS	Third Year PROGRAM	Third Year COMMENTS
Pamela Sotelo	Kindergarten Bilingual education program	Referred to communication program	1st grade Bilingual education program		2nd grade Bilingual education program	
Josué Leyba	Kindergarten Bilingual education program		1st grade Bilingual education program		2nd grade Bilingual education program	
Marica Tinajero	Kindergarten Bilingual education program		1st grade Bilingual education program		2nd grade Bilingual education program	Retention recommended

Children Not at Lincoln School

	First Year PROGRAM	First Year COMMENTS	Second Year PROGRAM	Second Year COMMENTS	Third Year PROGRAM	Third Year COMMENTS
River School						
Jasmín Soto	4 years old Not in school		Kindergarten Regular English	Concern about progress expressed	1st grade Regular Program	Retention recommended
Amapola Soto	Kindergarten Regular English		1st grade Regular English		2nd grade Regular English	
Park School						
Victoria Cerda	5 years old Not in school		1st grade Regular English		2nd grade Regular English	

her. In the play yard she would seek out her sister or her brother or sit quietly observing the other children play. The only times she spoke was to whisper in Spanish to an elderly woman who volunteered in the classroom. And yet she cut and pasted and scribbled and colored. She imitated other children's behavior and appeared to make sense of even difficult instructions given in English.

Cynthia Ornelas was also quiet. She kept mainly to herself and tried to impress the teacher by volunteering to clean up or straighten up what the other children had left in disarray. She did not usually run and play with the other children, and at times she appeared to be much older than her five years. She wore only dresses to school and sat very properly, like a little lady. On very cold days, she wore a large knit shawl that belonged to her mother and that did not look at all like the colorful jackets the other children wore.

Josué Leyba took everything in. He watched everyone and everything carefully. He took his time doing his work and produced neat pictures. He took great pride in showing us his artwork, which was generally selected for posting on the bulletin board. Because he was a quiet and cooperative child, his behavior at kindergarten graduation surprised everyone. "*Yo no me quiero poner vestido*" (I don't want to wear a dress), he screamed at his mother as she tried to help him into a white graduation gown. "*Yo no soy vieja*" (I'm not an old woman). Josué had a very clear sense of what it was to be a male in his culture. He did not want to wear what appeared to him to be women's clothes. His mother tried to explain that both boys and girls wore gowns at graduation, and in the end Josué marched out with the others sullenly, his eyes swollen from crying. He still did not understand.

Seen from a mainstream perspective, without an understanding of why children might behave differently, many of the 12 children in the study did seem strange. Some teachers were confused. Some were worried. Some simply felt that it would take the children time to become like their classmates. As Cynthia's teacher pointed out to us in an interview at the end of the kindergarten year, it was possible that these children would "snap out of it." In describing Cynthia and her conclusions about her, however, she nevertheless painted a picture of a very "odd" little girl indeed.

> Well, at the beginning she would just sit down at the table . . . wouldn't participate even if they had free play. Everybody would be playing around, she would just sit and look at everybody without even trying to participate . . .
>
> If somebody was arguing with her at the table or telling her something, she'd just look at him, and you know, and wouldn't tell him anything. Unless I'd go up to her and ask her, is he bothering you, or is she bothering you? Umhum, [Cynthia says] he kicked me, he took my paper, he scribbled, you know?

Whenever somebody was playing she thought that was like that's not what we're supposed to be doing, you know, we're supposed to be working or sitting down. Somebody else would just get up and play, and she wouldn't. She'd ask permission, or whatever, you know, she wouldn't just go up there. When something was, uh, you know, when I was cleaning a table she'd go up there and she'd ask me do you need some help . . .

I would say, ah, she doesn't look very alert. She seems tired, you know. She's not a very vibrant little girl jumping around, moving around, talking, not, laughing, not a very happy joyful little girl, you know, kind of like quiet, reserved . . .

Well, I think she was like reserved in trying not to run and jump and hop and do what the other kids did. She was trying to be too grown up, too soon, you know, so she couldn't see herself hopping and jumping, ah, skipping around like all the other kids. She'd go down the slide and walk around, and climb, and come down, but if she had a dress, which she always did, she wouldn't go up any higher, and you know, sometimes she was here and she'd be hanging upside down, and somebody would mention oh, Cynthia this and that and she wouldn't do that again. She was very self-conscious about herself and what she was supposed to do and what she wasn't supposed to— too much in the sense that she was too grown up, you know?

During this interview, the teacher went on to say that she predicted that Cynthia would be in the lowest reading group the following year and would need a tutor for reading. She perceived the child as not having enough experience in school-related activities and as being unwilling to try something if she was afraid that she would do it wrong.

To prod her into conjecturing about Cynthia's future, given her experience with teachers at that particular school and the curriculum, we asked the following question:

If you looked at her in the next year or so doing first grade work, and you've already predicted that you think she's going to be in the lowest of the reading groups, and so on, do you see her being retained in first grade? Having problems up the road?

As expected, the prognosis was not particularly encouraging, and it was unclear what exactly might help Cynthia. Comparing her to her two older siblings, the teacher responded:

She might snap out of it, she's got it in her, all she has to do is realize she can do it, and she can snap out of it, you know. It's just something that hasn't clicked yet, some of the other kids click a lot earlier and they keep going and it doesn't bother them, but I don't think it's something that will stay with her forever, if she just, you know, puts her mind to it, she's got it . . . she's, I think she has more in her than the other two kids that came in, thinking and logic and everything else.

In point of fact, this child might indeed "snap out of it" if she happened to be a youngster who could accept and function within the very different expectations of the school and the home context. On the other hand, by the time she began to "act" like the other children, she might already have been identified as "slow"; or she might have been placed in the lowest reading group and pulled out for special instruction several times during the day. She might, in fact, become just another child who didn't make it.

Cynthia and many of the other children in the study appeared very different from other, more "American" children. Indeed, they did not seem to be very "normal." Teachers' efforts to engage them in fantasy or pretend play were often met with discomfort. The children did not want to be silly. They did not want to play at being rabbits or donkeys or chickens. To teachers trained to believe that all young children like such play, the youngsters' refusal to cooperate and participate seemed odd indeed.

Seen, however, from a framework of how the 12 children in the study were being socialized to succeed within their home contexts, their behavior in school made perfect sense. For example, children whose entire world was the extended family, who were raised to distrust outsiders and to play only with siblings, would, of course, seem either extraordinarily shy or socially retarded to teachers. The children who spent the entire kindergarten year standing alone on the playground, refusing to respond when other children spoke to them, and talking only in a whisper to Spanish-speaking senior-citizen volunteers had learned their lessons well. They knew that they should distrust outsiders, and they had learned not to make friends with strange children. At home, however, these same youngsters chattered happily with their siblings and, as familiarity and trust grew, also with us. At school, they did not trust the teachers yet, and they had not yet learned how to enjoy other children. What was sad was that the teachers in our study had no way of making sense of this behavior. They simply believed that all "normal" youngsters naturally interacted with other children and that something was wrong with Pamela, and Cynthia, and other children like them.

There is other evidence that the expectations and assumptions the children made about what their behavior should be in the school environment placed them at a disadvantage. Put simply, they expected school to be like home and for adults to behave the way adults normally did in the home context. As children trained not to be disruptive, not to call attention to themselves, not to interrupt adult speech, and so forth, they behaved appropriately by following familiar rules of interaction. They did not speak out loud, ask for the teacher's attention, volunteer, or call out answers. They generally sat quietly, taking everything in, and when they had a question, they approached the person that most resembled a family member—the grandmother-like figure of the volunteer aid—just as they had been trained to do by their mothers in front of company, and they whispered a question or a remark.

The "odd" deportment continued beyond the kindergarten years. Indeed, most of the children in the study, even by second grade, seemed not to have become comfortable with "displaying information." Coming from a context where performance for the sake of performance was not expected, where "testing-type" interactions did not take place with adults, and where there were no rewards for such behavior, it took them time to "snap out of it" and to catch on to the fact that what was rewarded in the classroom was the ability to display information on request.

If they were going to do well in American schools, however, the children had to "catch on" quickly. To impress teachers favorably, they had to be ready to perform and indeed outperform their peers. In the school context, it was expected that youngsters should want to outshine the others, to be the best, to be selected for certain privileges, and to compete for attention and limited rewards. But the desire to outperform others did not develop overnight. The children in the study, accustomed to their own secure niche in the family structure—for which they did not have to compete—were unskilled at the game. They were used to having allowances made because of their special characteristics, to their parents' saying, for example, "*es muy despacioso*" (he does things slowly) or "*es muy sentido*" (he's very sensitive), and they were surprised when these same characteristics were never taken into account by the teacher.

Indeed, as I observed the children, much of the time I wondered why they were not all hopelessly confused by the school experience. Even when they worked well, started a task that was assigned, and finished it promptly, they were often admonished for not waiting for directions, or for not reciting parts of the directions before beginning the task. They soon found out that in the school context, there were ways of learning that had more to do with telling than with doing. How different this was from being asked to do something at home!

And the evaluation of the work was different, too. Comments from teachers, even when negative, were incredibly vague as compared to the evaluative remarks made about tasks at home. They were told, "You can do neater work than that" or "You have to work harder on your b's," and not the equivalent of "You left egg yolk on three plates," which would be, "Your b's have to start here and end here and look like this."

The examples of mismatch were many. It is equally clear from our data, however, that not all teachers responded to these children's behavior and characteristics in the same way. Teachers' values and beliefs about appropriate school behavior were different, and both Anglos and Hispanics varied in their response to the same children. We found sensitive teachers in both ethnic groups who believed these children could succeed. But we also found very mainstream-oriented teachers in both groups who had little patience with newly arrived Mexican children and their families.

As I pointed out in the description of the retention of Saúl Soto, the parents were of little help. For them, American schools were unfamiliar institutions. They expected them to be like the schools they had known or attended in Mexico, and they were continually surprised and taken aback by the differences. Assumptions that they made about what schools did, about what they expected of children, and about what they expected of parents were undoubtedly wrong. On many occasions, they discovered that they could not help their children even when they were treated unfairly.

All 10 mothers, however, believed that they had prepared their children well for school. They had taught them to be respectful, and they had taught them to behave. They did not know that other, more "American" mothers had also taught their children their colors, letters, and numbers. They naively believed that letters, colors, and numbers were part of what their children would learn at school.

In this chapter, it is my intention to describe and examine the mismatches and the differences that appeared to affect the interactions between children, teachers, and parents during the three years of the study. I will argue that misunderstandings between parents and school personnel took place at several levels and were due to different factors. Some of the misunderstandings between teachers and parents occurred because the parents were new immigrants who knew very little about schools in general and even less about American schools. They brought old fears, expectations, and assumptions with them; and family networks collected new information that was not always based on a full understanding of how things worked in this country.

Other misunderstandings were more profound and far more serious. These had to do with expectations that teachers had about what families should be, how they should view education, and how they should behave because of these beliefs. Their models of "good" and "supportive" families did not encompass values and beliefs about life and living that failed to place at the center individual achievement and success.

In this chapter, then, I will focus on the educational backgrounds of the parents in the study and on their lack of familiarity with American schools. I will preface this description and discussion with an overview of the attitudes toward education expressed by members of the 10 families. I will then exam-

FIGURE 7.2
Parents' Educational Background

Family Name	HUSBAND		WIFE	
	Name	Education	Name	Education
Soto	Pedro	1st grade	Velma	3rd grade
Soto	Arturo	none	Amelia	5th grade
Ornelas	n.a.		Carmen	secundaria comercio
Sotelo	Terrence	high school	Isela	2nd grade
Leyba	Héctor	6th grade	Reina	3rd grade
Castro	Chuy	3rd grade	Rosario	3rd grade
Gómez	Federico	secundaria	Eulalia	entered 7th grade (Las Fuentes Schools)
Tinajero	Javier	2nd grade	Socorro	5th grade
Ramírez	Joaquin	secundaria	María Elena	none
Cerda	Ernesto	none	Gloria	9th grade (Las Fuentes Schools)

ine and describe the many misunderstandings that arose for them because of the suppositions they made about American schools and because of their lack of knowledge about the educational system in this country.

THE EDUCATIONAL EXPERIENCES OF THE ADULTS

With two exceptions, the parents in the study had very little formal education. As I have tried to make clear in Figure 7.2, only three individuals had finished elementary school in Mexico. Of the two women who attended school in the United States, one did not complete seventh grade, and the other dropped out after ninth grade.

For many of the adults in the study, education was a sensitive topic. I do not know if it was particularly so because I, in my role of *maestra,* was raising the issue or if the sensitivity was due to a general sense that it was important to have gone to school. In Figure 7.2, then, I have entered what I believe to be the most accurate information obtainable from the adults in question or from members of their family.

Pedro and Velma Soto, for example, were typical of the adults who appeared to be embarrassed when I asked them about the number of years of schooling completed by the adults in the family. Neither had much exposure to formal education, and both were uncomfortable when discussing the subject of schooling. When I asked Pedro in the first interview how many years of schooling he had completed, he responded that he had completed third grade. During the course of the study, however, the number of years claimed to have been completed varied. At one point the number increased to six, and at another it decreased to one. According to Velma, however, Pedro finished only the first grade, a fact that she insisted did not prevent him from learning to read and write. It is difficult to say, however, how true this claim actually was.

Both Pedro and Velma were quite emphatic in insisting that Pedro could both read and write. While it is possible, of course, that Pedro did read, newspapers and magazines and other materials were never seen in the household, and Pedro was never observed either reading or writing. From this we cannot conclude that Pedro was illiterate or marginally literate. We can only say that during the three years of the study we saw no evidence of these abilities whatsoever. What we did see was an extreme sensitivity in responding to questions about reading and writing and an insecurity that was reflected in his sensitivity. What this tells us is that Pedro was quite aware of the importance of reading (at least for social if not economic reasons) and about the fact that illiteracy carries with it a strong stigma.

Velma was less sensitive about her educational background and more willing to talk about her experiences with us. For example, when asked specifically if she remembered how she had been taught to read, she responded:

No, porque era muy vaga. Yo me salía de la escuela (laughs with sister who is present) yo me salía de la escuela a jugar con el chavalo de esta . . . (speaks to her mother who is also present) como se nombra, la novia del profesor Salvador, Amá? Me salía por abajo, yo me acuerdo que me salía por abajo de todas las bancas hasta que salía hasta la puerta.	No, because I was very naughty. I used to leave school, I used to leave school to play with what's her name's kid, what's her name, the girlfriend of Salvador the teacher, Ma? I would get out underneath, I remember that I would get out under all the desks until I got out to the door.

She insisted, however, that this behavior did not keep her from making progress in school and from learning:

No, pos yo me apliqué mucho porque no pensaba, no quería que me ganaran las demás muchachas. No quería ser más burra que las demás.	Well, I applied myself because I didn't think, I didn't want the other girls to get ahead of me. I didn't want to be dumber than the rest of them.

Velma's responses to questions about how many years of schooling she completed, however, varied. On one occasion she stated that she had finished sixth grade, but on another occasion she implied that she had made it only to third grade. From her comments about other members of the family, it appears that the completion of primary school (grade six) in Mexico marked achievement of a special sort in her mind. Talking about one of her sisters, for example, she said with some pride: "*Ella sí terminó su sexto año. Ella sí lo logró*" (She did finish sixth grade. She was able to do that).

Given this perception of what constitutes academic success, it is not surprising that Velma (except when schooling was referred to spontaneously and not focused on) always sought to present herself as having completed sixth grade. She could do so with some legitimacy because she could indeed read and write in Spanish and was even able to attempt reading in English.

Regrets About Having Received Little Schooling

Some of the parents who had received very little education expressed regret at not having had the opportunity to stay in school. It is not clear whether they would have had the same feelings had they remained in Mexico, but in the United States they had come to see that going to school was normal and that most young people stayed in school for many years. In several families, it was the case that the children had already gone beyond the level of education of their parents. This made the parents sensitive about the issue and aware of their own limitations in the eyes of their children.

María Elena Ramírez, for example, recalled with some bitterness that her stepfather had not sent her to school because she was needed at home to care for her younger siblings. "*No me quiso mandar. Dijo que pa qué*" (He didn't want to send me. He said what for).

Isela Sotelo was embarrassed at having to admit that she had gone only as far as the second grade. She emphasized the fact, however, that she could still read and write. "*Pero yo sí sé leer y escribir. Bueno, no me hacen tonta*" (But I can read and write. Anyway, they can't fool me).

Overall, the sentiment expressed by those individuals who had not had much schooling was that life circumstances had prevented them from getting a formal education. They were much less precise in their answers when they were asked how their lives might have been different if they had obtained an education in Mexico. Only Velma Soto and Socorro Tinajero gave examples of the kinds of jobs they might have had in Mexico if they had more schooling. Velma stated that she would have gone to nursing school, and Socorro claimed that she would have moved up quickly in hotel management. None of the other individuals had life experiences in which formal education would have made much difference. The most they could offer in response to my questions about what would have been different was, in the words of Rosario Castro, "*No, pos 'hora les ayudara más a los hijos*" (Well, now I could help the children more).

Attitudes Toward Education

Without exception, parents expressed very positive views about education. They felt that education was important and that it was their duty as parents to send their children to school. These positive views were communicated to me in a number of forms, and because of this, I am convinced that they were genuine expressions of their feelings and beliefs. Comments about schooling and education came up frequently, and these comments went beyond the responses given to my direct questions about the importance of education.

In the case of Amelia Soto, for example, her views about formal education came into sharp focus when she became angry at her daughter Lorena for dropping out of high school. Lorena, it will be recalled, married a young man from Juárez and decided to live there with him. Amelia missed her daughter but, more than anything else, she lamented the fact that Lorena had dropped out of school. It was a topic that she returned to frequently with us. She was willing to do anything, she claimed, including putting up with a son-in-law she did not like, if only Lorena returned to school.

At the beginning, when Amelia went on at great length about Lorena, I suspected that she might be trying to impress us with her interest in education. But soon it became clear that her real worry had to do with the example that Lorena had set for the other children. Because she was the oldest, Lorena's actions deeply affected her siblings. Amelia was especially worried about her son Virgilio, who was 15 when Lorena left school. She did not want him to abandon school and end up working on a farm, like his father.

She had figured out that in the United States, people who didn't finish high school had fewer choices.

Rosario Castro also made clear what her feelings were about education not only to us, but also to her children in every way that she could. Indeed, we discovered just how important she thought education was when she recounted how she had made both Rebeca and Miguel sit through first and second grade again, rather than have them spend a year without schooling. Apparently, when Rosario first moved to Juárez, she had been unable to get her children into school. In Juárez, public schools are always very crowded and cannot accommodate all the children in the city. It is not unusual for parents to attempt to register their children at several schools only to find out that there is no more room. Rosario was lucky, however, because she located one of her former teachers from the village, who was then teaching in Juárez. She persuaded this teacher to allow her children to enter her combined first and second grade classroom even though Miguel and Rebeca were much older than the other children. It did not matter to Rosario that her children did not want to go. She was determined that they would attend school, and she had no patience with their objections. She answered her children's protests by saying, "*Que grandota ni que nada, tú vas*" (Big or not, you're going). For Rosario, what was important was that her children would attend school. It did not matter that they were repeating work that they had already had in their village school years before. She did not think about it in those terms. What she cared about was that both Miguel and Rebeca saw themselves as still enrolled in school, and that they did not begin to believe that there were reasons for dropping out.

In the United States, Rosario's children were pushed by her same determination and by her commitment to education. Rosario taught her children to respect their teachers and had little tolerance for their complaints about them. In Rosario's words: "*Las maestras están ay pa enseñarles, y ustedes están ay pa aprender*" (Teachers are there to teach you and you're there to learn). However, she was more than willing to do battle with teachers, to talk with high school counselors, and to insist that she be called whenever her children did not show up at school.

The same kind of strong feelings about education were held by María Elena Ramírez. It will be recalled that she expressed a similar kind of attitude toward schooling when she scolded her niece Marta for not attending school. For María Elena, there was a direct relationship between the kinds of jobs that could be obtained in this country and the amount of education people had.

Isela Sotelo was also a strong supporter of education. She spoke several times not only about her ambitions for her daughter Sara, but also about her own ambition to go to school and to learn English. Although it was clear that she had many insecurities about her ability to do well, she hoped classes for adults would be offered soon at the neighborhood school:

Yo estoy esperando que haiga unas clases alli en la escuela. Yo quiero ir pero con al- guien que yo tenga confianza. A veces pienso que no voy a decir algo bien. Pero yo pienso que para entrar a la escuela tiene uno que pasar, ¿verdad? por todo. Se van a reir de uno.	I'm waiting for classes to be given at the school. I want to go but with someone that I trust. Sometimes I think that I am not going to say something right. But I think that to enter school one has to go through everything. People are going to laugh at you.

For Isela, going to school involved sacrifices, and she spoke about education in those terms. Her *consejos* to her two older daughters often focused on the importance of making those sacrifices for the future.

Socorro Tinajero also had great faith in education. Her experience, however, made her far less insecure than the other mothers in the study. She seemed proud of what she had accomplished with her fifth grade education and she spoke of herself as "*aprendiendo algo más todos los días*" (learning something every day). During the third year of the study, Socorro did decide to enroll in school in order to learn English. She felt she was making good progress.

Even Eulalia Gómez, who herself had dropped out of school in the middle of the seventh grade after arriving in the United States, was deeply committed to education and deeply involved in her son Federico's schooling. When she found out, for example, that Federico (then in 2nd grade) had spelling tests every Friday and that a sheet was sent home with the words he should study, she made Federico write each word up and down an entire page, a total of about 100 times. When Federico complained *¿Pa qué me pones tantas?* (Why do you give me so many [words]), his mother replied: *Pa que no saques tantas mal* (So you won't have so many wrong). Much as Eulalia spoiled Federico in other ways, she was focused on his doing well in school. In spite of his protests, Eulalia designed a home study program of the type that was required of her during the few years that she had attended school in Mexico. It was strict and mechanistic and involved much rote learning. Federico hated it, and it is unclear how much it helped him in his work at school. Eulalia, however, was doing the best that she could. Given her knowledge and experience, this was the only way she knew how to help.

In different ways, parents in the study demonstrated that they valued schooling. They were aware of their own limited opportunities, and they wanted their children to have more. Even in the face of the many competing demands on the family system, children's schooling was still considered important.

Confusions and Misunderstandings

Commitment and interest in education, however, were not enough to make up for the parents' lack of familiarity with U.S. institutions. In spite of their good intentions, there was much that the families did not understand about American schools. There was much confusion about programs, requirements, and grading. There was much misinformation within the family collective experience about what worked and what did not.

As in the case of Saúl Soto, the parents in the study did not have a clear idea about the choice of programs offered by the school that their children attended. When they arrived at Lincoln School, the individual registering children often made a decision to place them in bilingual education programs on the basis of the fact that the only language spoken at home was Spanish. In theory, parents approved the decision, but rarely, if ever, was the nature of the difference between programs explained to them. In several cases, if the bilingual classrooms were already filled, children were placed in regular English programs. Again, parents were asked to approve the placement, but were given very little information about other options available to them. For example, when we questioned both Isela Sotelo and her daughter Sara to try to determine what kinds of programs the older children in the family had been enrolled in, we found that our question was not understood.

GV: *¿Están en salón bilingüe?*	Are they in a bilingual classroom?
ISELA: *¿Qué quiere decir bilingüe?*	What does bilingual mean?
GV: *Bueno les dan instrucción en español y en inglés, en las dos lenguas.*	Well, they teach them in Spanish and in English, in two languages.
ISELA: *Se me hace de las dos porque traen papeles en español y en inglés.*	I think in two because they bring papers in Spanish and in English.
GV: *¿No le pidió permiso la escuela a usted cuando empezó la niña? ¿No firmó usted un papel dándoles permiso para . . .*	Didn't the school ask your permission when your little girl started? Didn't you sign a paper giving them permission for . . .
ISELA: *Algo especial así, no.*	Something special like that, no.

In this case, Isela was aware of the fact that her children brought home papers from school in both English and Spanish. From this she surmised that, according to my definition, they must be receiving bilingual instruction.

When questioned further, however, it became clear that for Isela the language used in the instruction of her children had never been an issue.

At Lincoln School, the situation was made even more complex because of the fact that many of the teachers were bilingual Chicanos. Some of these individuals were assigned to bilingual classrooms. Others, however, were teachers of regular English language programs. Because they were personally bilingual, some teachers used Spanish, as needed, to communicate in the classroom with children who had just arrived from Mexico. For this reason, then, although Sara Sotelo had been at Lincoln for several years and had arrived there when she spoke no English, she did not know whether she was in a bilingual program or not. When questioned, she said that her current teacher was Mr. Alvar and that he often spoke in Spanish to the group of other sixth graders who did not speak English. To her knowledge, however, he did not make assignments in Spanish or teach in Spanish to the whole class.[1]

There were other kinds of misunderstandings as well. For example, Velma Soto expected that schools and school personnel would care about her children's well-being and about their behavior both in and out of school. Since she was concerned about Saúl's pugnacious behavior, during the second year of the study, she went to the school to talk to the principal to ask for help in dealing with him. Little help was forthcoming, however, because Saúl was not a problem at school. Not surprisingly, Velma did not understand why she could not obtain the assistance she needed to deal with Saúl. From her perspective, it was simply that the teachers did not really care about her son.

Further confirmation of the school's lack of interest and caring was the fact that Saúl's teacher did not respond to her requests asking that Saúl not be given fish at lunch. Apparently, Saúl was allergic to fish and got very sick after eating it. Velma assumed that the teacher was the person to be made aware of the problem, and she sent a message to her via her other son, then eight-year-old Juan Pedro. It appears, however, that either Juan Pedro did not deliver the message or that the teacher did not consider it to be her role to pass on the information to the appropriate school personnel. In spite of Velma's efforts, Saúl continued to be given fish along with the other children, and he continued to get sick and to miss school for at least a day or two afterward.

Had Velma sent a note instead of a message, it might have been that she would have received some response from the teacher or another individual. Velma, however, did not know that in American schools, the appropriate way of handling such matters involves either talking to the teacher personally or sending a note. Velma had no way of knowing that sending an oral message via a slightly older child might not be taken seriously.

For Velma, then, her children's schools seemed to be places where there was little interest in either the children's overall behavior or in their health or well-being. This view was reinforced when her 13-year-old daughter, Aydé, complained that she was not allowed to go to the bathroom when she needed to during school hours. Since Aydé had recurring bladder infections and did, in fact, have to use the bathroom frequently, Velma found the school's treatment of her daughter unreasonable. She became quite angry and in response decided to keep Aydé home for several weeks. In the following, somewhat disjointed conversation about the situation with one of the project's research assistants, it became clear that Velma had been misled by her daughter Aydé about the school rules for going to the bathroom.

VELMA: *Ahorita tuve que sacar a ésta también por otro problema.*

I've just now had to take this one out because of another problem.

RESEARCH ASSISTANT: *¿Aydé?*

Aydé?

VELMA: *. . . me dijo que las regañan las maestras, que son muy estrictas, que dicen que tienen que yo creo ir una vez al baño, por nueve semanas.*

. . . she told me that the teachers scold them, that they are very strict, that they say that they have to I think they can go to the bathroom one time in nine weeks.

RESEARCH ASSISTANT (TO AYDÉ): *¿Cuántas veces van al baño?*

How many times do you go to the bathroom?

AYDÉ: *Cada nueve meses.*

Every nine months.

RESEARCH ASSISTANT: *¡Las llevan al baño!*

(In surprised tone) They take you to the bathroom!

AYDÉ: *Nueve semanas, cada nueve semanas.*

Nine weeks, every nine weeks.

RESEARCH ASSISTANT: *¿Durante la clase?*

During class?

AYDÉ: *No, o sí, durante la clase nos dan un pase cada nueve semanas no-más uno.*

No, I mean yes, during class they give us one pass every nine weeks, just one.

RESEARCH ASSISTANT: *¿Es regla de la escuela o de la maestra?*

Is that a school rule or a teacher's rule?

AYDÉ: *Regla de la escuela.*

A school rule.

VELMA: *Y el otro día, vino y como pa-dece de la vejiga, venía con el estó-mago muy inflamado, o sea que ya la tuve que llevar una vez al hospital y*

And the other day, she came and since she has bladder problems, her stomach was very swollen, I had to take her to the hospital once and

la sondearon, le pusieron una sonda | they had to use a catheter, they put
para que orinara. Y el otro día volvió | in a catheter so that she could uri-
a llegar igual. | nate. And the other day, she came
 | in again the same way.

RESEARCH ASSISTANT: *¿Y por qué no* | And why don't you write a note to
le escribe una nota a la maestra, o que | the teacher, or your husband?
su esposo?

Aydé quickly rejected the suggestion that her mother send a note and vehemently stated that she wanted to move to another school. The research assistant, still convinced that she could make Velma understand the importance of handling such problems with a note, ignored Aydé's comment and tactfully suggested:

Vamos a hacerle la lucha a ver si man- | Let's try, let's see if by sending a
dando una nota que tiene problemas de | note saying that she has bladder
la vejiga y que requiere su doctor o algo | problems and that her doctor re-
. . . ir al baño cuando desea, no hacie- | quires or something for her to go to
ndo abuso, pero cuando necesite ir, tiene | the bathroom when she wants to,
que ir, a ver si les pone atención. | not abusing this, but when she
 | needs to go, let's see if they pay
 | attention.

Velma did not focus on the research assistant's suggestion in the least. Still intent at communicating her displeasure about the way in which the school treated her daughter, she responded, "*Desde que vino y me dijo eso, no lo puedo creer todavía*" (Since she came and she told me that, I still can't believe it).

As will be obvious, Aydé told her mother that she was allowed to go to the bathroom only once every nine weeks. What was really true is that Aydé could get a hall pass to go to the bathroom *during class* only once during each nine-week period. Velma had no notion of what a hall pass was or why Aydé might need one. Aydé, on the other hand, knew much more than she had told her mother. She clearly knew that there was time to go to the bathroom between classes and at lunchtime. But since Velma did not know how junior high schools worked, she imagined that Aydé sat in the same classroom all day and was not allowed to go to the bathroom. Quite naturally, this seemed unusually strict.

What this segment also reveals, however, is that Velma could very easily be manipulated by her children. Because she did not know how schools worked, she simply believed what she was told. Moreover, because of her sense that the schools were unresponsive, she did not feel that she could in any way change what was happening at school to her daughter. Her only recourse, then, was to remove her child from school.

Another kind of misunderstanding involved the interpretation of routine school communications with the family. Something as "simple" as the reading of report cards was not simple at all for the 10 families. I began looking into this issue after the difficulty of understanding report cards was made clear to me by observing the Soto family.

After Saúl was recommended for retention in first grade, Velma began to take a special interest in her children's grades. She talked to them often about doing well in school. One afternoon, I happened to be visiting when the children arrived with their report cards for the past nine-week grading period. Juan Pedro, the eight-year-old, arrived in tears. Apparently his mother had told him that she expected all A's on his report card, and he had not received a single A.

I looked at the report card and saw that it contained mainly C's, one B in math (down from a previous A), one B in reading, and two F's in social studies. It was clear that Velma had no notion about whether Juan Pedro had improved in particular subjects or had gotten worse in others. It was, in fact, the case that several C's were up from C-'s and D's, but this meant nothing to Velma. She now knew that A's were important in American schools. Juan Pedro, on the other hand, had no way of understanding what he was doing wrong. The F's in social studies included no comments from the teacher about what his problems or failings were or what he might do differently.

I sat patiently with Juan Pedro and tried to explain what the report card meant and what the different subjects were. I also tried to elicit his notions about what he did in school in social studies, or in math, or in reading. Because this discussion took place in front of Velma, I hoped to educate her in interpreting report cards without offending her in any way. I even explained to Juan Pedro that big jumps from a D to an A seldom happened and that improvement took place slowly over time. That was why, I argued, he should look at the grades that had gone up and be proud of having made progress. Improvement, I insisted, was a really good indicator of his work in the last nine weeks.

Velma listened attentively, but I was not sure that she had understood what I was saying. She made comments such as "*Ya ves, mijo*" (You see, son) and "*Hazle caso a la señora*" (Pay attention to the lady), but did not respond to any of the points that I was making. When I had finished talking to Juan Pedro, she then gave me Saúl's report card and asked me to look at it. Saúl had handed it to his mother with some indifference, and Velma commented that he already knew that he would not pass that year.

Saúl's report card was even more difficult to read than Juan Pedro's. As do many elementary school report cards, the early grades at Lincoln broke down language and reading and math into multiple components. Categories such as "recognizes words and word meanings," "uses phonics skills," and "knows number facts and operations" each had a separate grade of N (needs improvement), S (satisfactory), and E (excellent). I found it extraordinarily challenging to try to explain what each of the categories meant and why each was grouped the way it was. At the end, I had a sense that Velma was making an enormous effort, but that she really had understood little of what I said. Since I had mentioned writing, Velma replied:

Bueno nada menos ahorita estaba dicien-do—Mire, mijo, para que pueda com-poner la letra necesita hacer esto. Para que se te ablande la canilla. Digo yo, a nosotros nos ponían desde el tercer año.	Well actually, I was just saying, "Look, son, so that your handwrit-ing can get better, you need to do this. (Shakes her wrist) So that your wrist gets soft." That's what I say, that's what they had us do from third grade on.

What became evident to me was that, as all schools do, Lincoln School made the assumption that parents would be able to make sense of their children's report cards. School personnel expected that they were familiar with how schools operated, how grades were given, and what the different subjects were (e.g., language arts, social studies). There appeared to be no aware-ness of the fact that for parents who do not have such familiarity, report cards mean almost nothing. Even when they are translated into their own language—as is often the case in bilingual education programs—the con-cepts themselves may still be totally foreign and incomprehensible.

PARENTAL "INVOLVEMENT" IN SCHOOL

As might be expected, very few of the families had any concept of "involvement" in their children's education as defined by the schools. As was the case for the white working-class families studied by Lareau (1989), par-ents in the study did not impress teachers with their willingness to "help" the schools educate their children. At the very most, those parents whose family networks had established that it was important for parents to be seen at school by their children's teachers ordinarily went to open house at the beginning of the school year.

Of the eight families whose children attended Lincoln School, one par-ent in five of the families attended open houses during the first, second, and third years of the study. These families were the Castros, the Gómezes, the

Ramírezes, the Leybas, and the Tinajeros. Parents who did not feel confident in English were accompanied by an older child who could serve as translator, if needed.

For the most part, parents viewed their role at open houses as visiting their children's classroom and looking over their papers and drawings. They did not see it as an opportunity to personally meet their children's teacher. With the exception of Federico Gómez and Joaquín Ramírez, none of the parents made it a point to go up and talk to the teacher during any of the three open houses attended. When questioned about their impressions about open house and about why they believed open houses were held, no one mentioned that it was an opportunity to find out about their children's school progress or that one of its purposes was to give parents an idea about the nature of the school program. They saw it, rather, as a pleasant social event that children liked to go to. Since many teachers gave extra points to children when their parents were present at open house, the older children put pressure on their parents to attend.

Overall, then, open houses were seen as a time in which the principal, Mr. Vasquez, spoke to all the parents in the auditorium and made it a point to speak Spanish during a portion of his talk. They saw it as a time in which they got to see exactly where their children's classrooms were, where they had lunch, and how far or how near they were to the classrooms of siblings and cousins. Even the more sophisticated parents (e.g., Federico Gómez and Joaquín Ramírez) did not have a sense that they could learn a great deal about how their children spent their time at school or about teacher expectations from listening to the presentations during open house.

In addition to open house, at least one parent attended all festive events to which they were invited. In spite of busy schedules and many younger children at home, only one of the families (the Pedro Soto family) did not have parents in attendance at kindergarten graduation. During the first year, three out of the five families who had children in kindergarten at Lincoln school attended graduation (Ramírez, Sotelo, and Leyba). During the second year, all four of the families were represented (Ornelas, Castro, Sotelo, and Gómez). It is important to note, that Isela Sotelo attended the second-year graduation (Keith's graduation) a week after Vanessa had been born. She carried Vanessa with her and took Abby, 1, and Ada, 3, with her as well.

The families also attended enchilada suppers and Mother's Day celebrations. Again, usually only one of the parents was in attendance, and there was little interaction with school personnel.

Parental involvement, then, was limited to ceremonial occasions at which there was little time for teachers to talk about children's progress. Parents made an appearance to please the children, to whom those things mattered, and felt that they had done their duty. None of the families knew about PTA, about volunteering to work at the school, or about other ways in which they might become "involved" in their children's education.

PARENTAL INTERACTIONS WITH SCHOOL PERSONNEL

When parents interacted with school personnel, they did so only on those occasions in which they felt that their children needed their intervention or when they had been asked to come to the school by the teacher. Even when asked to come, however, it was often the case that parents did not respond. In some instances, the request came at a bad time (e.g., when the father, who spoke the most English, was away), and in other instances, notes (generally written in English) asking parents to call and make an appointment were interpreted as invitations that did not have to be accepted. In many families, however, neither of the two parents felt competent enough to deal with school personnel. They were embarrassed, and found almost any excuse not to go to the school and "*ponerse en evidencia*" (show how ignorant or incapable they were).

Even when some parents were as deeply committed to their children doing well in school as was Eulalia Gómez, they hesitated to speak to the teacher herself. Eulalia, for example, spoke only to the teacher's aide, who not only spoke Spanish well, but who also seemed to Eulalia more approachable than the teacher:

A ella es a la que le pregunto, porque como ella era la que siempre me saludaba cuando iba a recoger a Federico, pos se me hacía más fácil.	I always ask her since she was the one that always said hello to me when I went to get Federico, so it seemed easier.

Reina Leyba also spoke only to the aide even when she was very upset about the fact that her daughter, Maya, was being kept after school. Regardless of the fact that it was not acceptable to Reina for Maya to be kept after the regular school dismissal, she did not dare talk to the teacher.

No no sé, hasta le dije a ver si te apuras de salir de esa escuela porque yo no he ido a conocer a esa maestra. No quiero conocerla. Me platicó mi cuñada que es muy caraja, y luego le dije yo voy a hablar, porque yo estoy pagando pa que me los traiga un señor y me los lleve a la	No, I don't know, I even said, let's see if you hurry up and get out of the school because I haven't gone to meet the teacher. I don't want to meet her. My sister-in-law told me that she's a real mean one and then I said I'm going to go say some-

escuela. Y me los deja, después de la clase a Maya, y le dije voy ir a hablar con esa maestra y me dice, y no, no me animé.	thing because I'm paying so that a man takes them back and forth to school. And she keeps them, keeps Maya after class, and I said, I'm going to go talk to the teacher and she said . . . and no, I didn't have the courage to.

Reina could not describe the teacher, and did not know her name. When we asked her to describe her other interactions with her, she responded:

Déjeme y le enseño un retrato Es uno de cada uno de la clase. Ella es la maestra de Josué. Pero ésta. Es una señora que le dicen granma. Le ayuda. Con ella hablamos. Con ella, sí. Con la que hablamos, hasta nos dijo que ellas tenían tiempo, ellas tienían más tiempo más que, más que, sí podíamos hablar más que con la maestra. Ese es del programa que ellos van, uste sabe como programa bilingüe o como que, otro programa, son con las que hablamos más.	Let me show you a picture. It's one from each, from their class. She's Josué's teacher. But this one. This is a lady that they call grandma. She helps her. It was her we talked to. With her, yes, the one we talked to, she even told us that they had time, they had more time, more than, more than, yes, we could talk more than with the teacher. This one is from the program that they go to, you know, like a bilingual program or like, another program, those are the ones we talk to the most.

The truth of the matter was that Reina herself had not talked to any of the teachers. It was her husband, who was home in the evenings and who went to open house, who had seen the children's teachers. When both Reina and Héctor did go to school on one occasion, they followed the extended family's advice and chose not to risk antagonizing the teacher. In Reina's case, her apprehensiveness at talking with the teacher reflected a certain degree of *vergüenza* (embarrassment), but more than anything, it reflected caution. She had been warned by the extended family about the dangers of saying the wrong thing to teachers and that much harm could be done by teachers who took a dislike to particular children.

In comparison to Reina, Rosario Castro, her sister-in-law, paid little attention to this domain of family wisdom. She constantly visited schools and did whatever she could to keep on top of how her children were doing. She was particularly concerned about Miguel and Rebeca, who, as teenagers, were seen to be in more danger than the younger children. Things were particularly difficult for Miguel, who had arrived in Las Fuentes from two years of sitting in a first- and second-grade classroom in Juárez. Miguel was placed immediately in a junior high school and experienced a major cultural shock. As Rosario recalled:

Se escondía en un rincón. Hasta que salió Mr. Padilla y nos dijo "déjenme traerle una chavala pa que le ayude." Usté cree, como era de serio. "Yo no quiero una mujer," decía, "que me traigan un hombre." Pero la chavala le ayudó a todo.	He would hide in a corner. Until Mr. Padilla came out and told us, "Let me bring him a girl to help him." Can you imagine, as shy as he was. "I don't want a woman," he said, "I want them to bring me a man." But the girl helped him in everything.

Still, things did not go smoothly with Miguel. When he moved to the local high school, Rosario started to suspect that he was in trouble of some sort. She wanted to go to school and look into what was happening, but was told by Miguel that teachers did not want mothers to come to the school at all. Rosario asked everyone she could whether what Miguel said was true or not, and when she determined that it wasn't, she went to the school and was referred to a counselor. She found out that Miguel was hanging out with a crowd of very rough kids and that they all had been accused by a bus driver of smoking pot. Armed with that information, she confronted Miguel and told him that she had made arrangements at the school to contact her whenever he was absent or his homework was missing. She then made it a point of dropping by the school periodically so that Miguel would know that she was watching after him. In her words *"Arbol que crece torcido, nunca de endereza"* (So the twig is bent . . .).

Unlike Reina, Rosario was not afraid of antagonizing teachers. She often talked to the principal at Alamo Junior High School, through an interpreter, to straighten things out for Rebeca. On one occasion when Rebeca was thrown out of class for fighting with another girl, Rosario complained to the principal because the other girl had not been thrown out also. In her view, it was clear that the teacher personally disliked Rebeca. Rosario felt that it had been necessary for her to confront the teacher about the situation. She recalled that she talked to him in front of the principal and said:

Que le hace que no se puedan ver. Usted está aquí para enseñar. Usted tiene mucho estudio y yo no, pero yo sé que usted está aquí para darles estudio a los alumnos, no para que le caigan bien.	It doesn't matter if you can't stand each other. You are here to teach. You have a lot of schooling and I don't, but I know that you are here to teach students, not to like them.

Rosario's interventions, however, were not always effective. On several occasions, for example, teacher–parent conferences initiated by Rosario did not really accomplish very much for the child in question. Once, when her daughter Susana was upset because she had been placed in a lower reading group, she complained to her mother. Rosario, who spoke of herself as a *"mujer de pelo en pecho"* (a woman with hair on her chest), went immediately to find out what the problem was. She later recounted the experience as follows:

Sacaron a Susana del grupo en el que estaba. Llegó y me dijo y yo fui a preguntar por qué. Me dijo la maestra que estaba en el grupo más alto y que no es que no pueda con el trabajo, pero que la bajó del grupo para darle más tiempo de que se aprendiera las palabras.

They took Susana out of the group she was in. She came in (from school) and told me and I went to ask why. The teacher told me that she used to be in the highest group and that it isn't that she can't do the work, but she put her in a lower group to give her more time to learn the words.

When questioned further, it became clear that Rosario had no idea that the group in question was a reading group or that the child was having problems with sounding out words. She did not question the teacher's action further and simply urged her daughter to "learn her words." In her own mind, she had intervened on behalf of her daughter and determined that Susana needed to put more work into her studies. It was now Susana's job to work harder.

It is important to note that all interactions with school personnel that were initiated by parents (rather than their children) had to do not with academics, but with behavior. Parents considered it to be their proper role to ask: "*¿Cómo se porta?*" (How does he behave?). Since this was the parents' realm of responsibility, they thought it to be their duty to be informed of the children's *conducta* (conduct). Moreover, they believed that it was the school's duty to help them raise well-behaved and -disciplined children. For this reason, Velma Soto sought the school's assistance in dealing with Saúl, and Rosario Castro asked the school counselor to keep her informed about Miguel's attendance. They believed that keeping children from straying off the straight and narrow was their most important obligation as parents.

Indeed, when school practices were seen to make that task and obligation harder, it created much concern and serious conflict for the families. This occurred, for example, in the case of the time-honored American tradition of keeping children after school. Mothers who had strict rules about when their children were to come home and who viewed hanging out with neighborhood children as potentially dangerous considered teachers who interfered with these procedures to be inconsiderate, capricious, and overstepping their boundaries. They were, in fact, providing built-in excuses for lateness that children might use in inappropriate ways. As might be imagined, however, the mothers would have had a very hard time explaining to their children's teachers the implications and ramifications of a seemingly harmless school practice. It is most unlikely that the profound nature of their concern would have been understood or responded to positively by school personnel.

PARENTAL INVOLVEMENT IN CHILDREN'S SCHOOLWORK

As Chapter 6 made clear, the 10 mothers in the study saw themselves as participating actively in their children's *educación,* that is, in raising their children to be good and well-behaved human beings. They did not, however, see themselves as adjunct schoolteachers. They did not see their role as involving the teaching of school subjects. In their own experience in school, this had been the province of the teacher. Mothers, on the other hand, had been responsible for the moral upbringing of their children. Parental teaching involved guiding youngsters, molding them with *consejos,* and supervising them carefully.

When American teachers expected that Mexican working-class mothers would "help" their children with their schoolwork, they were making assumptions about abilities that the mothers did not have. Moreover, they were also making assumptions about the universality of what, in American schools, counts as knowledge. For example, when Mrs. Lockley complained that Velma Soto had not taught Saúl his ABC's, she did not consider that the teaching and the learning of the alphabet might not be equally valued in all school contexts. She could not possibly imagine that there might be very valid reasons why parents might not have prepared their children for school by teaching them the alphabet, and it was difficult for her to consider that parents might not understand, even when told, why learning the ABC's was so important.

Indeed, the learning of the alphabet by children is an example of how parents' experiences did not help them make sense of their new world. In Mexico, the ability to recite the alphabet *per se* is not considered particularly important. Instead, recognition of syllables containing a consonant and a vowel is considered fundamental to reading. A child who can recognize and call out combinations such as *ba, be, bi, bo, bu* and *da, de, di, do, du* containing the five Spanish vowels is considered to be making progress toward reading. And indeed, most reading instruction begins by having children work with such combinations. What is important is the *sound* of the letter combinations and not their names.

Given this experience, the parents in the study could not anticipate that in this country, teachers expected the children to know their ABC's, that is, to be able to recite the alphabet by the time they began first grade. More importantly, the parents were not aware that for many teachers, knowing the alphabet was an indicator of children's abilities and of parents' "involvement" in their education. By not making certain that their children arrived in school with the "right" knowledge, they were, in fact, condemning their children to placement in the lowest reading groups. Unfortunately, as was the case for Saúl, as well as for many of the other children, this placement was the beginning of an endless cycle of academic failure.

THE SCHOOL CONTEXT: A SUMMARY

For the children, the teachers, and the parents, the school context presented many challenges. Teachers tried their best and appeared to fail. Children brought with them skills they had learned at home and found them inappropriate. Parents felt helpless, confused, and angry.

Both the schools and the families made assumptions about each other. Schools expected a "standard" family, a family whose members were educated, who were familiar with how schools worked, and who saw their role as complementing the teacher's in developing children's academic abilities. It did not occur to school personnel that parents might not know the appropriate ways to communicate with the teachers, that they might feel embarrassed about writing notes filled with errors, and that they might not even understand how to interpret their children's report cards. When children came to school without certain skills that their families, in good faith, believed the teachers should teach (e.g., the alphabet, the colors, the numbers), school personnel assumed parental indifference, troubled homes, and little interest in education.

The parents, on the other hand, were living lives that required large amounts of energy just to survive. They had little formal schooling and few notions about what schools expected of them and their children. And yet, they valued education. The collective family wisdom had already instilled in them a sense of the importance of high school graduation. They wanted their children to have good jobs, and they wanted them to have whatever education they would need in order to get such jobs.

As the next chapter will make clear, however, the parents' notions about "good" jobs were not "standard" notions. Education occupied a particular place within their life plans that was not entirely congruent with the place it occupies in the middle-class American world. As I will argue, the misunderstandings, such as those presented in this chapter, that are caused by lack of information can be adjusted. Teachers can be informed about what parents do not know, and parents can be taught how American schools work. What is not as easily fixed are values and beliefs that run counter to views held in Western industrialized countries about individual success and school achievement.

CHAPTER 8

EDUCATION AND LIFE CHANCES

As I attempted to make clear in the preceding chapter, interactions between newly arrived Mexican-origin families and school personnel were characterized by much confusion and misunderstanding. Much of the confusion had to do with the fact that the families were recent immigrants who lacked familiarity with schools and made incorrect assumptions about the nature of the educational system. Problematic as these confusions and misunderstandings were, however, it is easy to argue that schools and school personnel can ordinarily make an effort to resolve such differences and difficulties. Parents can be taught about the American educational system, and individual teachers can be made more sensitive to the many things new immigrants do not know about what teachers and schools expect of their children.

I will argue here that in addition to these superficial misunderstandings, there were other profound differences between the 10 newly arrived immigrant families and the families that schools assume and expect. These differences had to do with values and beliefs about the nature of life itself and what is important. In particular, they had to do views about the relationship between parents and children that involve notions about success, ideas about good jobs, and opinions about what is attainable at what cost.

In terms of many of these differences, the 10 Mexican immigrant families were neither exceptional nor unique. Indeed, many of the values held deeply by the 19 adults in the study have been found to be characteristic of several other groups of immigrants who arrived in this country early in this century. As a number of scholars have made clear (e.g., Berrol, 1982; Bodnar, 1982; Fass, 1988; Handlin, 1982; LaGumina, 1982; Mathews, 1966; Perlmann, 1988; Portes & Bach, 1985; Weiss, 1982; Williams, 1938/ 1969), various immigrant groups did not consider their values to be compatible with those held by American public schools. More importantly, these values were also found to be problematic by the native-born white population.

In this chapter, I will attempt to describe some of the values and beliefs held by members of the 10 families by talking about the life plans and blueprints for living that undergirded their lives as they struggled to survive in their new world. I will provide a context for understanding these values and beliefs by describing something about the world from which the 10 families came. Very specifically, I will talk about education in Mexico and about its role in the lives of what Selby and associates (1990) have termed "ordinary" Mexicans.[1] I will argue that for large numbers of people in Mexico, neither education nor schooling have the same meaning that they have in the United States. For a number of complex reasons that I will attempt to describe here, definitions of success and accomplishment are different in the Mexican context. Indeed, for many ordinary Mexican families, individual success and accomplishment are generally held in lesser esteem than are people's abilities to maintain ties across generations and to make an honest living somewhere close to home.

In sum, what I hope to suggest is that many Mexican immigrants— such as those who were part of this study—come from a world in which conceptions about personal development are grounded in economic, spiritual, and moral considerations that seem quite foreign to most Americans. Indeed, as I have suggested in Chapter 2, Mexican-origin immigrants bring to the United States an understanding of *life chances*—of how and how far people can unfold, what they can achieve, and what is meaningful—that is derived from the social conditions in which they lived in Mexico.[2]

The term *life chances* is an important one. Dahrendorf (1978) defines it as the "sum total of opportunities offered to the individual by his society or by a more specific position occupied in society." According to Dahrendorf (pp. 29–31), life chances are a function of both *options* and *ligatures*, the exact combinations of which can vary. *Options* are "possibilities of choice, or alternatives of action given in the social structure." *Ligatures* are bonds, linkages and allegiances that "give meaning to the place the individual occupies." Dahrendorf argues that until recently, the extension of life chances in modern industrialized societies inevitably meant the reduction of human linkages and bonds. Ligatures or bonds had to be severed so that individuals could take advantage of the options offered to them by modern society.

What this study of recent Mexican immigrants suggests is that individuals, who come from a nonindustrialized nation understand bonds and linkages well. What they cannot immediately envision is the sum total of choices that are available to them in highly industrialized nations. When they arrive in the United States, for example, they begin to discover the differences in life chances available to them here over a period of time. They must also discover, however, how to bring into balance the new opportunities or options encountered in their new world with their strongly held values and perspectives. They must seek this balance in the face of the strongly held American notion that in order to access such options, they must abandon old beliefs.

The families in this study came from a world in which relationships and human ties were far more important than options or choices. These values, beliefs, and ideas about life and living were the product of their generation, their class, their regional origins, and certainly of the life chances that were available to them in Mexico. In their views about the world, they reflected these life chances. What they believed was possible had been shaped by the lives they and their parents had lived elsewhere.

TRADITIONAL VALUES AMONG THE TEN FAMILIES

The Sotos, the Castros, the Leybas, the Ramírezes, the Gómezes, and indeed all of the 10 families in the study and their relatives brought with them to this country traditional cultural values of the rural areas of the state of Chihuahua. These values survived the move both to the large border city of Ciudad Juárez as well as to the semirural U.S. community of Las Fuentes. The fact is that in Mexico, as in other "Third World" countries, even when Western education and the academic-occupational hierarchy have been established to some degree, complete success in transforming these original agrarian societies to "modern" ones has not been attained. Life in these countries has many of the characteristics of life in complex agrarian societies, in which everyday living is still governed by traditional views and values.

According to LeVine and White (1986), in many of these countries urbanization has greatly outdistanced industrialization. Limited employment, child labor, few government welfare programs, and problematic state bureaucracies are a fact of life. It is also the case that in spite of educational mobilization, these "Third World" economies cannot employ the large number of able-bodied adults that have both the credentials and the desire to obtain full-time work. In addition to unemployment, there is widespread underemployment, marginal employment, and "self-employment."

Therefore, in many "Third World" countries, the fact that many individuals have migrated to large urban areas does not necessarily mean that they have discarded their agrarian values or social identities. In LeVine and White's (1986) words:

> More surprisingly, perhaps—at least from an economic point of view—many of those who do have permanent employment in the city, with the security and esteem offered by the modern sector, also retain their agrarian social identities, and their attachments to the ends and means of life as defined by the rural communities in which they grew up. Thus a large part of the population remains agrarian in its outlook and values, even when living in the city, and even when aware that their outlook and values do not accord with those of the modern world. (p. 174)

If LeVine and White's (1986) interpretation of the ethnographic record is correct, agrarian values are not confined to primitive rural villages. They are alive and well in the large urban metropolitan areas of "Third World" countries such as Mexico, and they are increasingly present in the United States among newly arrived immigrants from many different parts of the world. These values include filial loyalty, reciprocity, conformity to social conventions, and maintaining social linkages.

In traditional societies, its members derive benefits that include not individual glory, but rather security, trust, and continuity. They feel secure in their interdependencies with other human beings. Agrarian cultures offer to their members a sense of permanence and continuity, an awareness of being part of a larger entity—of a human group whose history they share. What is worth doing in agrarian societies are those actions and activities that result in the establishment of reciprocal relationships with members of the community or that contribute to the welfare of the family unit. Satisfaction is to be derived from living life very much the way it was lived by others in the same community in previous generations.

The Adults and Their Values

All 19 adults came to this country with fully formed internalized models of what life should be. They had hopes and ambitions that were compatible with their values, and they did not examine their assumptions and expectations. Each day they struggled to survive in a new context that was very different from the world they had known, but it did not occur to them that values involving, for example, the way in which children were raised would need to be questioned. They fully expected that their children would grow up with the same notions of reciprocity, respect, and responsibility that had been part of their families for generations. It is true that their notions about what was important for survival began to change quickly. For example, very soon after their arrival they discovered that high school graduation was considered essential to living life in this country. But none of the families ever imagined that choices would need to be made between, for example, young people's responsibilities to their family and their own ambitions. It was simply assumed that a son's or daughter's ambitions and aspirations would primarily involve contributing to the welfare of the family and that they would spend a large part of their lives reciprocating the many sacrifices that their parents had already made for them.

For the families, then, being in favor of education, caring about education, and wanting their children to go to school in this country did not mean that they wanted their children's values to be different from what their own had been when they were the same age. Of course they were in favor of education. They knew credentials were needed in order to obtain certain kinds of employment. But they also wanted their children to put family first. They wanted them to live nearby, to visit often, and to continue to be part of a network of close relationships and linkages.

It is important to emphasize, however, that very few individuals in the study would have been able to articulate their position about the possible conflict between education and their traditional values even if I had asked the question directly. The problem was that none of them were familiar with notions and views of success and achievement in American terms. They had no way of knowing that their own ideas and beliefs about what children should want and what families should help them achieve were very different from those held by mainstream persons in this country. Given their own world views, they naively assumed that all parents had ideas about both schooling and parenting that were similar to their own. They had not yet understood that in this country, "believing in education for one's children" involved much more than just getting them to school. Indeed, the parents in the study spoke positively about education, but, as I will discuss at greater length, their everyday microlevel practices and activities could well be called *unsupportive* by mainstream standards.

In order to establish a framework for understanding the beliefs and ideas about education brought by the 10 families as they entered the United States, in this section I will present an overview of the Mexican educational system and of the ways in which individuals, such as the adults in this study, come to understand the role of education in their own and their children's lives. By presenting this overview, I hope to illustrate why it is that newly arrived Mexican-origin people—in comparison to other newly arrived immigrants—may not look to education as a dependable means through which they can ascend the social ladder.

ORDINARY MEXICANS AND EDUCATION IN MEXICO

In spite of focused interest by the Mexican government and certain sectors of the Mexican population in the development of human capital leading to both economic growth and progress, Mexico has been generally unsuccessful in educating most of its citizens. In spite of this failure, there is much evidence that the modernization of education has been considered vital to the country's interest for a long period of time. Indeed, as other presidents had done in the past, Mexico's recent former president, Carlos Salinas de Gortari, for example, made education a national priority. Upon taking office, Salinas quickly appointed a blue-ribbon commission (the *Comisión Nacional para la Consulta sobre la Modernización de la Educación*), which was charged with examining the long-term crisis in Mexican education. As was expected, the commission presented a discouraging picture in its report, *Texto íntegro del Programa para la Modernización Educativa 1989–94* (included in full in Oria Razo, 1989). Statistics illustrative of the present crisis included the following:

There were 4.2 million illiterates over the age of 15

Approximately 20.2 million adults had not completed *primaria* (elementary school)

Every year 300,000 children (2% of the total number of children) do not have access to education

Nearly 880,000 students drop out of primary school every year

Approximately 500,000 children drop out of primary school within the first 3 years of schooling

700,000 children between the ages of 10 and 14 are not enrolled in school

Only 54% of 14.6 million students enrolled in primary school complete this level of study in the normal 6 years

More than 15,000 primary schools (20% of total schools) do not offer the full six years of primary schooling

22% of all schools have only one teacher for all grades

The average level of schooling among the Mexican population is 6 years

In 1983, there were only 331 public libraries in the entire country

It is important to note that the Mexican educational system does not exactly parallel the educational system in the United States. The former is divided into the following levels: preschool education (*educación inicial,* for children up to age 4, and *educación preescolar,* for ages 4–6), primary education (*educación primaria,* grades 1–6), lower secondary education (*educación media básica,* three years), upper secondary education (*educación media superior* or *preparatoria,* 2–3 years), and higher education (*educación superior y de posgrado*).[3] Primary and lower secondary education are controlled by the federal government through the *Secretaria de Educación Pública* (SEP), the establishment of which in 1921 marks the true beginning of public education in Mexico (Oria Razo, 1989; Valdés-Villalva & Montenegro, 1989).

While it is true that in the last decade credentialing has become increasingly important in many occupations and that there has been an expansion of the higher education system with the establishment of institutions of higher education around the country, most "ordinary" Mexicans, even at their most successful, do not go beyond the lower secondary level (the ninth year of schooling). Postsecondary education, which includes all studies beyond the ninth grade (*preparatoria* and *educación superior*), is often inaccessible in rural areas. Indeed, it is quite usual for *preparatorias* to be located in institutions of higher education and for these programs to be designed to prepare students for admission for undergraduate study. Most ordinary Mexican young people (for reasons that will be discussed below) are not prepared to leave their families and households to live in distant areas in order to complete the upper secondary level of education.

As compared to the United States, where going to school is taken for granted and where there is concern about *high school* dropouts, in Mexico, many children of ordinary families do not go to school. Children who do go often drop out within the first three years of school.[4] The dropout problem (*deserción escolar*) begins much earlier than in the United States, and the implemented solutions involve such approaches as bilingual education programs in those areas of the country in which the population does not speak Spanish; a highly developed adult education system (for persons older than 15); specialized programs throughout the country designed for children 10 to 14 who have dropped out of school; and a system of "open" education that allows students to pursue studies without attending school, by means of both television (*telesecundaria*) and radio (*radioprimaria*). Unfortunately, as critics of education have argued, approaches and solutions tend to change with every *sexenio,* that is, with every six-year term of office for the nation's president. The fact of the matter is that public education in Mexico has been faced with many difficulties and problems (Muñoz Izquierdo & Schmelkes, 1992).

EDUCATION AND SOCIAL MOBILITY

A look at the distances between "fortunate" and "less fortunate" groups within Mexico can help underscore the reasons why education and schooling play a different role in Mexico. While a complete discussion of this topic is beyond the scope of this book, the problem is well illustrated in the work of Nolasco and Acevedo (1985) on Mexico's two largest border cities, Ciudad Juárez and Tijuana. According to Nolasco and Acevedo (1985), the following five different social strata can be identified in the two cities:

1. The *marginados* (the underemployed or occasionally employed who have an income of under 1.5 minimum salaries)—40% of the population of Tijuana and 25% of the population of Ciudad Juárez.[5]
2. *Trabajadores pobres* (poor workers who have stable jobs in commerce, industry, or service and whose household income varies between 1.5 and 3 minimum salaries)—34% of the population of Tijuana and 46% of the population of Ciudad Juárez.

3. The *empleados* (persons employed in commerce, teaching, or in bureaucracies who have an income of 3 to 7 minimum salaries)—16%
of the population of Tijuana and 19% of the population of Ciudad
Juárez.[6]
4. *Ejecutivos medios, profesionistas y comerciantes* (middle-level executives,
professionals, and business people who have an income of 7 to 12
minimum salaries)—8% of the population of both cities.
5. The *alta burocracia y la burguesía* (the high bureaucracy and the bourgeoisie)—2% of the population of both cities.

Of these five strata, only the *empleados,* the *ejecutivos medios,* and the
profesionistas (26% of the population in Tijuana, 29% in Juárez) would view
schooling as directly contributing to additional opportunities. The *marginados*
and the *trabajadores pobres* would be unrealistic if they expected schooling to
move them or their children out of what are euphemistically called *las clases
populares.* For them, completing *primaria* might mean fulfilling the minimal
credential requirements for becoming assembly-line workers in the *maquila*
industry, but little more. On the other hand, the *comerciantes,* the *burguesía,*
and in particular the *alta burocracia* would in no way depend primarily on
education for ensuring their children's futures. For these individuals, connections, good marriages, and the like would be more important. Sending children to the "right" elementary and secondary schools would cement friend-
ships with the right peers and ensure connections. Education in and of itself
would be far less central. The reasons for this reside in the fact that Mexico
is a closed society. In such societies, as Musgrove (1966, p. 13) has argued in
his book *The Family, Education, and Society,* parents do not view education as
a solution.

> In a closed or caste society, with a fixed and rigid hierarchy, no amount of
> parental encouragement and pressure can secure for the child any improvement
> on the status to which he was born. By the same token, parents of higher social
> rank can rest assured that their children cannot fall below their own social level,
> however inadequate their upbringing and disastrous their education.

THE FAMILIES AND THEIR BACKGROUNDS

In attempting to make sense of the deeper beliefs about education that
were guiding the lives of the 10 families in this study, it is important to place
these individuals in the study in the 5 strata described above. It is especially
important to note that of the 10 adults who were part of the Ciudad Juárez
population for a number of years, only Carmen Ornelas in her job as a bank

teller could be considered to be a member of stratum #3, the *empleados*. She had completed *comercio,* that is, business training that is designed to prepare workers for clerical positions, and she was able to obtain what is considered to be a "good" job. All the other individuals who were employed in Juárez were part of stratum #2, *trabajadores pobres.* Several (e.g., Isela Sotelo, Gloria Cerda) had been part of the group of *marginados* for a period in their lives, and others had relatives who were still among the *marginados.*

As a result of these experiences, not to mention the experiences they had in their rural villages, most of the adults in the study had not focused on education as a key solution upon which they could depend in order to open doors for themselves in Mexico. None of the adults were acquainted with people who had "made it" by going to school. They developed different strategies for surviving, one of which was, in fact, crossing the border into the United States in order to increase the family's standard of living.[7]

Before they left Mexico, however, they had used other strategies for "making it" on a day-to-day level that had become very much a part of their lives. Both their move to the border away from their *ranchos* and their survival in the large urban area of Ciudad Juárez involved using the resources and strengths of the entire family in special ways. Insights into the kinds of strategies and tactics that Mexican families living in cities use in order to make it can be found in Selby et al.'s (1990) study of urban households in a number of Mexican cities. Focusing on what they call the urban household, these researchers conclude that in order to survive in a society in which there are vast inequalities and few opportunities, ordinary Mexicans have derived a number of "defensive" strategies. An overview of these strategies as well as the views about life and its possibilities that undergird the use of these strategies can help highlight the differences between middle-class, mainstream, or standard families in the United States and those of newly arrived Mexican-origin immigrants.

In their study, Selby and his colleagues, whose research was carried out in 10 cities and involved over 9,458 households, describe aspects of the domestic and working lives of urban Mexicans. They offer a view of a resilient household made up of family members of all ages who contribute to the household and who sacrifice what are considered "selfish" needs for the good of the family unit. In order to survive, such ordinary families must make certain that the children contribute to the household welfare by the time they are five or six and that they continue to remain closely tied to the household throughout most of their adult lives. Selby and his colleagues point out that in order to meet their everyday needs, ordinary Mexican families, large numbers of whom live in abject poverty, must use the earnings of all their members. Indeed, they argue (p. 109) that the only sure way of decisively raising a family's level of living is through the household. House-

holds that are better off "have more children, more family members participating in the workforce, lower dependency ratios, and a higher percentage
participating in migration." By working at a combination of full-time lowly
paid jobs and odd jobs of various sorts, members of the households must
make at least 1.8 *salarios mínimos* (minimum salaries) in order to get by.

The picture presented is one of "working" children, children who run
errands, sell goods in the street, perform services, and otherwise earn their
keep. According to Selby and his colleagues, for ordinary Mexicans household survival—as opposed to individual success or achievement—is a key
theme in the ideology of the family.

The possibility that education in Mexico really offers social mobility is
seriously questioned by Selby and his colleagues. They argue, moreover, that
because individuals with modest and typical educational attainments work
in lowly paid monotonous jobs, they are often viewed with disdain. Self-
employment is, therefore, held up as the ideal goal. True social mobility is
seen to reside in independent employment, and wage labor is considered to
be simply a temporary expedient.

It is important to emphasize that Selby et al. point out that, according
to World Bank figures, Mexico is one of four countries in Latin America in
which the distribution of income is most unequal. They quote Riding
(1985), who pointed out that:

> . . . the middle classes, the professionals, well-placed bureaucrats, middle level
> company executives, owners of small business . . . belong to the wealthiest 30%
> that earn 73% of the country's total income. Thus, while Mexico's very rich live
> in a style that would put all but a few American millionaires to shame, and the
> middle classes enjoy standards of suburban Americans, its majority lives in de-
> grees of poverty ranging from mere survival to outright misery.

The perspective, then, of persons who were raised in Mexico, who were
part of the majority of "ordinary" Mexicans, will be unlike the perspective
of most middle-class, mainstream Americans. Indeed, their perspective will
also be unlike that of the urban poor in this country who have access to
social services of several types. Their strategies, their conclusions about survival, and their sense of what they must do in order to make it from one day
to another will be based on entirely different ground rules.

The 10 families in the study brought with them to the United States an
internalized set of strategies that had proved to be successful either for themselves or for friends and family. Their children were seen as assets in helping
the family survive, and the families' view of the future included a sense that as
they grew older, children would contribute to the family income. Education
played a role in these strategies, certainly; but education was not focused on

as the principal means of advancement or mobility. As will be recalled in the discussion of the survival strategies of the 10 families, the view that having "*un negocito,*" a business of one's own, was the key to real success was very much present in the thinking of all of the adults. None of the parents had known people in Mexico who had become successful by going to school or pursuing advanced studies. The people who had done well had either had a *patrón* who ended up in high places, or they had been able to start a business that did well. Not surprisingly, the real dream for all of them was becoming *comerciantes,* becoming part of the group that did not work for anyone else. Being one's own boss was, in fact, the real essence of the dream.

MEXICAN-ORIGIN FAMILIES AND MICROLEVEL PRACTICES

As I pointed out in Chapter 2 by citing Lareau's work (1989), the distance that must be traveled by white, working-class parents before they can take on the behaviors and intense focus of the middle-class is great indeed. This is so in spite of the fact that the working-class persons referred to are American, white, and products of the "same" educational system as their middle-class counterparts. Not surprisingly, in comparison to white working-class households, the distances that must be traveled by newly arrived Mexican families (who bring with them traditional or agrarian values and life plans) are much, much greater. As LeVine and White (1986) have pointed out, the move from notions of childrearing in traditional societies to notions of childrearing in industrialized societies involves a "revolution" in the ways that parenting is both conceptualized and carried out.

Persons who move from largely peasant-agrarian societies to Western industrialized nations suddenly find themselves in contact with a completely different set of cultural practices and assumptions. It is as if they suddenly undergo the totality of changes experienced over time in the Western world in a very short segment of their lifetimes. As Kalantzis et al. (1989) argue in their study of Macedonian immigrants in Australia, this shift to what they term the "single culture of western industrialism" (p. 24) is not easy. While some immigrant cultural practices (e.g., food types) are easy to maintain, others are immediately discarded (e.g., arranged marriages). Still others slowly erode away as the influence of the industrialized world creeps into the lives of the new immigrants.

For the members of the 10 families in this study, the move from their rural villages to the border and then to the United States involved many changes. As I have described above, many of these changes had to do with learning how to survive in a new world and discovering how things that they had taken for granted in Mexico were different here. Nevertheless, the contact with American life did not immediately erode the deep values with which these 19 adults and their families had been raised. However, it is in the realm of school-related microlevel practices that families' adherence to their original life plans were more clearly obvious.

As I pointed out in Chapters 6 and 7, in all 10 families in the study, children were not the central focus of the family. Rather, the energy of all family members was directed at the welfare of the household as a functioning unit. This was the case partially because the move to a new environment made many demands of the adults, but it was also true that the families were household-centered rather than child-centered because their beliefs about the parent–child relationship required these behaviors. As I pointed out previously, *respeto* was a central value in the 10 Mexican families and one that demanded that children "honor" their parents in a very old-fashioned sense of that word. The children were taught to be grateful for what their parents had done for them, and they were encouraged to think about the father and mother and about their siblings before thinking about themselves. Selfishness was discouraged, and children who began contributing to the household were seen as virtuous and responsible.

The 10 families brought with them, then, views about parenting and about the role of children that were at odds with the kinds of microlevel practices engaged in by middle-class mothers and ultimately encouraged by the school. It is true that the mothers in the 10 families, like the working-class mothers studied by Lareau, did not have either the preparation or the resources to become adjunct schoolteachers for their children. They—again like the working-class mothers—tended to see school learning as the province of teachers. Moreover, they were busy with struggling to survive in a new world and with caring for very large families. Nevertheless, it is also true that the mothers in the study saw themselves as indeed responsible for the *educación* of their children, that is, for raising them to become responsible members of society as they understood it. To this "teaching" function, they devoted much of their time. Indeed, most direct interactions with their children involved mothers' giving *consejos* and directly inculcating values and expectations. What they did not encourage were demands or even requests by children for what were considered selfish needs. Thus, children in these families could not expect that their mothers would abandon plans made for the entire family or postpone their work (laundry, cleaning) on behalf of the entire family in order to cater to some "selfish" whim. Mothers, for example, could not be expected to launch an expedition to find ice cream tubs to be used as cubbies just because they were requested by a child's teacher. Neither could they be expected to take over children's chores because children had not completed a special project urgently due the next day. Mothers were busy. They were not at the service of their children. More importantly, teachers' requests did not cause the family to stop in its tracks in order to fulfill them. Directives about where to be or what to bring that American middle-class parents might find quite reasonable were considered intrusive by the adults in the study—especially by those who had children in the upper elementary years. Indeed, when children became upset and insisted that they needed something by the next day or that they needed to be at school for a particular function *because the teacher had said so,* a parent would often reply: "*La maestra no manda aquí*" (The teacher doesn't give orders here).

For all of the 10 families, the principal organizing theme around which family activities were centered had to do with the ties and close bonds that linked them to other members of the family network. An illness in the family, for example, often required taking care of a relative's children or cooking more food or even driving to Ciudad Juárez to buy medicine or to see a doctor. Children needed to be flexible. A sick family member could not be left to fend for herself just because the children had homework. If the family needed to help out, children simply went along. For children to refuse to do whatever a family emergency might require would have been unacceptable. They were being taught in clear and consistent ways that members of the family were interdependent.

Everyone was expected to be present for both joyful and somber occasions. A death in the family, for example, had special significance. Not going to the funeral was not an option. Although attending funerals meant hours or days of travel, it was the duty of all family members to be present. The men took days off from work; they stayed at home only when going might put their jobs at risk. Women packed quickly and were often ready to go at a moment's notice. As might be expected, children were pulled out of school in spite of the fact that they might miss something "important." The fact was that in comparison to the death of a loved one, schooling was hardly important. When I mentioned to Velma Soto, for example, that her going to her father's funeral at her village and her taking the children out of school was frowned on by her children's teachers, she was confused and did not understand the teachers' objections. "*Tenían que ir*" (They had to go), she said simply. "*Era su abuelo*" (He was their grandfather). For Velma, it was quite clear that teaching her children to pay their last respects to a loved one was at the very core of raising good children.

HOPES AND DREAMS

As might be expected, the ten women in the study had both hopes and dreams for their children. As might also be expected, these hopes and dreams were colored by the experiences of each of the women, by the collective wisdom of the family, and especially by their own values and beliefs. To mainstream Americans, the hopes and dreams of these women might not seem much at all. Their dreams had little to do with success or achievement as it is generally defined in this country, and their hopes had a great deal to do with simply raising good, responsible human beings.

For example, when I asked the question: *¿Qué quisiera usted para sus hijos en la vida?* (What would you like for your children in life?), answers clustered around several main themes: *Que tengan todo lo necesario* (That they have all the basic necessities), *Que mis hijas salgan bien de la casa* (That my daughters won't get pregnant before they get married), *Que mis hijos sean trabajadores y no tengan vicios* (That my sons are hard working and have no addictions), and *Que no se vayan lejos.* (That they won't go far away).

These were modest and yet very profound goals. For these 10 women, being good mothers and being considered good mothers by others had to do not with material success, not with high status achievement, but with very simple things such as having hard-working sons and and virtuous daughters. Mothers were considered to have done well if they could say that their children *"no se habían descompuesto"* (had not gone in the wrong direction). Mothers did not achieve particular status among their friends and acquaintances because their children had important jobs in faraway cities, or because they had gotten numerous awards for their athletic ability or their academic distinction. The 10 women in the study did not trade in such currency. Children were not raised to be status symbols for the family.

What mothers did boast about, as the five grandmothers in the study made evident, was that their grown children looked after them, that these children had chosen to live close by, and that they, as mothers, were provided for and sought after. A grandmother who could say, *"Mis hijos vienen todos los domingos y me sacan"* (My children come every Sunday and take me out) had something to be proud of. It meant that she had done her job of mothering well, that her children were stable, and that they valued what she had tried to do for them.

Reorienting Goals

In addition to broad and overarching goals, the mothers in the study had "smaller" aspirations for their children. Some of these goals were very imprecise and ill-defined, and in talking about them, it was clear that the families were struggling to find ways of bringing together their two worlds. They wanted what was possible for their children in this country, but they were not yet sure what that was. They had become aware that opportunities existed in the United States that had not existed for them in Mexico. Some of the women (for example, Velma Soto and Isela Sotelo) even knew that these opportunities were connected to education. Their husbands, who had each already raised a set of children here, spoke about wanting their young children to go to college (*que vayan al colegio*[8]). What wasn't clear was if the men really knew what college was and how their children would get there.

A good example of how Isela was struggling to make sense of what she knew about the world of work and about education emerged as we discussed the kind of job that she wanted for her oldest daughter, Sara.

GV: *¿Cómo qué clase de trabajo le gustaría usted que consiguiera Sara?*

Like what kind of job would you like for Sara to get?

ISELA: *¿Para ella? Pos yo digo que secretaria, un trabajo donde no se maten tanto. Weno no tampoco que gane mucho, verda,—regular. Una cierta cantidad que pueda ella (sentence left unfinished). Por ejemplo, yo digo que cuando ellas van a ir al colegio, verdad, tienen que pagar ellas, y va trabajar en un trabajo donde no va sacar ni pa eso. Le digo que un trabajo más o menos regular. Yo no digo, no sé yo en una tienda cuánto . . .*

For her? Well, I say secretary, a job where they don't kill themselves so much. Well, not that she would make a lot, right? just regular. A certain amount that she can (sentence left unfinished). For example, I say that when they go to college, okay, they have to pay and to work in a job where they are not going to get (money) even for that. I tell her a more or less regular job. I don't say, I don't know how much you could make in a store . . .

GV (addressing Sara): *Y a ti ¿qué te gusta, Sara?*

And what do you like, Sara?

SARA: *No sé, yo digo que policía pero ni pa cuando.*

I don't know. I say policeman, but that's not ever going to happen.

ISELA: *Yo le digo qu'es peligroso porque también les agarran coraje, ¿verdá? Es mejor un trabajo como secretaria, que no sea peligroso, periodista también.*

I tell her that it's dangerous because people also have a lot of anger toward them, isn't that right? A job as a secretary is better, a job that isn't dangerous, a journalist also.

Isela's world, when she lived in Juárez, had been a very small one. The women she knew worked only as domestic servants and worked very hard. She talked about her brothers, however, and tried to find parallels there:

Había uno de mis hermanos que decía mi mamá que era muy buscón, porque él estaba en la escuela y se iba a trabajar

I had a brother who my mother said was always looking to do better, because he was in school and he

cuando iba a la escuela también, pero le gustaba parte del tiempo trabajar y acarrear.	went to work when he went to school too, but he liked to work and haul things part of the time.
Y mis otros hermanos, me acuerdo en esos tiempos se dedicaban a buscar dinero de algún modo, trabajando. En la escuela no estudiaron mucho, digo yo ¿por qué será? No fueron mucho a la escuela, como aquí, si no van a jai scul (high school) no los admiten para trabajar.	And my other brothers, I remember that at that time they tried to earn money somehow, working. At school they didn't study much, I wonder why. They didn't go to school much, like here, if they don't go to high school they don't let them work.

The two brothers that Isela talked about had what she considered to be good jobs. One worked at a large dairy and delivered milk around the city, and the other worked at a water-bottling plant. In her mind, they had done well. What concerned her, as it did other mothers in the study, was that life not be as hard for sons as it had been for husbands and fathers. "*Que no se ensucien mucho*" (I would like for them not to get too dirty), Isela said softly when talking about her sons, "*Que no se ensucien mucho.*"

The difference in orientation and perspective between these mothers and the existing mainstream American position can best be appreciated in the conversation I had with Rosario Castro. In this conversation, my own middle-class Mexican views, coupled with many years of living and raising children in this country, contrasted dramatically with those held by Rosario.

During one visit to the Castro household, I had mentioned that my son, who was away at school, had been visiting recently. Since she had not met him, Rosario expressed curiosity about him and about where he lived and why. I was quite proud of him because he was a graduate student at a good university, and I went into some detail about his life. I talked about how dedicated he was, about the awards he had won at the local high school, and about how well he was doing. The conversation then continued as follows:

ROSARIO: *Oiga Lupe, y ¿cuántos años tiene su hijo?*	Say, Lupe, and how old is your son?
GV: *Tiene 24.*	He's 24.
ROSARIO: *¿Y no trabaja?*	And he doesn't work?
GV: *Bueno, no, este . . . sí. Bueno, es que está estudiando y su trabajo es estudiar. Cuando termine va a conseguir muy buen trabajo y ahorita lo que tiene que hacer es dedicarse al estudio.*	Well, no, that is, yes. Well, the thing is that he's studying and his job is to study. When he finishes he's going to get a very good job and what he's got to do now is to dedicate himself to his studies.

ROSARIO: *¿Y no le manda dinero?*	And he doesn't send you money?
GV: *No, pero yo tampoco le mando dinero a él porque consiguió una beca muy buena y le pagan todo.*	No, but I don't send him money either because he has a very good scholarship and they pay for everything.
ROSARIO: *Ajá.*	Oh, I see.
GV: *Es muy buen hijo. Siempre nos hace mucha falta.*	He's a very good son. We miss him a lot.
ROSARIO: *Sabe que Miguel también es muy buen muchachito. Siempre nos pide permiso para todo, no como otros muchachos de su edad. Y ay donde lo ve, ya trabaja, y ya me ayuda. Todos los veranos se va a Dallas, allá a trabajar con su tío en la obra. Y cuando viene me trae su cheque. "Tenga mamá," dice, "esto es para usté."*	You know Miguel (then 17) is a very good boy, too. He always asks us for permission to go places, not like other boys his age. And as a matter of fact, he works already and helps me out already. Every summer he goes to Dallas to work with his uncle in construction. And when he comes back, he gives me his check. "Here, mother," he says, "this is for you."

She said nothing more, and neither did I. However, from both Rosario's tone and her expression I knew that she felt a little sorry for me. Not only was my son far away—when he did not really have to be—but he had also not taken responsibility for me and for his sister. For Rosario, success as a mother involved teaching a young male how to be responsible. She could not conceive of the fact that a 24-year-old man was still in school and not working. In her book, I was either not a great success or I had been unlucky in having a son who only cared about himself.

A good job for Rosario was one in which one did not work too hard and in which one made a decent living. Achievement was being a good son, husband, and father. Rosario wanted her son to be honest, hardworking, and responsible. She wanted him to work and to support his family. She wanted him to find a good wife to love him and to find joy in simple ordinary things. She did not believe that he had to be outstanding or exceptional in order to be happy.

FAMILISM AS A CENTRAL VALUE

Seen from one perspective, the fact that the 10 families focused largely on their relationships to members of their extended families is evidence of their deeply familistic values. This is, in fact, the case. All 10 families in the study viewed their life chances as primarily being a function of ligatures, that is, of family bonds.

For many researchers, especially for those concerned about success and achievement in the American context, familism is problematic. It smacks of failure and low attainment. Stodtbeck's work (1958), for example, argues that in mobile industrialized societies such as the United States, ethnic groups (such as Italians) who have traditional family orientations are not as successful as those groups (e.g., the Jews) whose family orientation encourages individual credit and geographical mobility. For some scholars (e.g., Engels, 1972; Goode, 1963; Parsons, 1953), a strong family orientation is characteristic of an earlier and less sophisticated stage of family development.

I want to argue here, however, that familism can also be part of success. Indeed, among the Mexican elite, success depends not on individualism, not on independence, but on family ties and family networks. As Lomnitz and Pérez-Lizaur (1987) reveal in their study of a 60-year period in one elite Mexican family, in Mexico the merchants who became industrialists in this century did and continue to do so within a specific kinship pattern. In the authors' words:

> The new Mexican entrepreneur was not a driving individualist (as he might have been in the United States), but the leader of a large extended family, a kinship group that he brought with him up the social ladder. (p. 24)

The Gómez family studied by Lomnitz and Pérez-Lizaur, like many other successful Mexican families, used their large kin network for social mobility. In the Gómez family, sons, nephews, and daughters' husbands were brought into the family business. These men in turn brought their sons and nephews into the branch of the business that they themselves developed. Over the years, the same close ties were maintained. Members of the same family sat on each others' boards, went into partnerships with cousins, shared financial information, and received professional services from doctors and lawyers who were also part of the same family. According to Lomnitz and Pérez-Lizaur, as in the Gómez family, Mexican conglomerates are, in fact, "family enterprises that draw their management from a group of relatives" (p. 47).

Lomnitz and Pérez-Lizaur (p. 103) maintain that three factors contributed to the "continuing solidarity of the Gómez family": (1) family enterprise as a source of patron–client relations and generalized economic exchange; (2) the presence of dominant males in the family who took their roles seriously, both as prominent public figures and as employers and protectors of their relatives; and (3) the influence of centralizing women who gathered and disseminated information about their branches both within the branch and by centralizing women of other branches.

It is also important to note that in addition to the close relationships that men had within the work and business domain, members of the family were also close in many other ways. Family life was organized around the homes of the "centralizing women," and it was at family gatherings at their homes that the family ideology was transmitted. Grown and married children tended to live close to their parents and to their other siblings, and indeed whole branches of the same family moved to another part of town *together* as they were able to afford newer and larger houses. The ideal was to have everyone in the family close by.

Indeed, in the extended family described by Lomnitz and Pérez-Lizaur, the most prized value was family unity. Fulfilling family duties and remaining loyal to the family were seen as central. Both men and women, in their separate spheres, contributed to maintaining this family unity. Rather than a weakness, all members of the family, and indeed members of the society in which they lived, considered such strong family orientation to be at the heart of the family's success.

It is important to note that even among these ambitious and mobile individuals, education did not play a key role. A university education was important only to the degree that it made family members more able to contribute to the family enterprise. Many male members of the Gómez family, therefore, did not go to college. Young men who went into the family business at a young age and who did not pursue advanced study were not looked down upon. Formal education was not considered essential to either success or achievement.

In sum, what this rare study of the Mexican bourgeoisie makes clear is that Mexican society, as compared to Anglo-American society, has a very different view of family ties and relationships. In the authors' words:

> The three-generation grandfamily pattern that the Gómez have in common with the rest of Mexican society largely accounts for the cultural distinctiveness of their family life as compared with that of Anglo-Saxon societies like Britain and the United States. (pp. 5–6)

Even though I have pointed out here that the 10 families in this study brought with them traditional models of family bonds and linkages because of their largely agrarian background, it is also the case that that they brought with them such values because in Mexican society family "was and remains a privileged symbol of exchange . . . a pivot of the culture and the core of social networks" (Lomnitz & Pérez-Lizaur, 1987, p. 232). It is not just the *"marginados"* who need and use family networks. Indeed, at all levels of Mexican society, it can be conjectured that these networks are social capital and the main vehicles for economic mobility.

Lomnitz and Pérez-Lizaur point out that the Gómez family is an example of economic behavior that is at odds with classical forms of capitalism. They maintain, however, that

> When introduced into a different sociocultural setting from the one in which it originated, it [capitalism] tends to adapt to the new local conditions, including the historical context, socioeconomic conditions, and local culture. . . . Individuals turned actors of capitalism behave according to their values and their traditional system of social relations.

Arguing that the same process took place in the case of British capitalism, the authors suggest that what were heralded as "laws" of production may have been peculiar to the British sociocultural system. They contend that these laws may not be universal and that Parsons (1953) may have been wrong in arguing that there is a basic disharmony between modern democratic industrial society and the extended family.

Familism, then, may be problematic only in certain sociocultural contexts. Or, as Litwak (1960) argues, it may be problematic only in periods of emerging industrialization. Be that as it may, for practitioners, policymakers, and school administrators, what Lomnitz and Pérez-Lizaur's view of both familistic and achievement-oriented behavior should do is to raise serious questions about single views of success and achievement. The 10 Mexican families in this study—in spite of the fact that they did not understand the centrality of education in the lives of Americans—brought with them values, beliefs, and social capital that may indeed convert into economic capital. The problem—if it is a problem—is that the adults in this study had not yet figured out how to utilize family strengths—as the Mexican elite has learned—to help their children achieve economic mobility.

FAMILIES AND THEIR VALUES: A SUMMARY

To those individuals who believe that "good" parents should be actively involved in their children's academic success, the 10 mothers in the study will seem either perplexing or pitifully backward. While these parents believed that education was important, they did not put education first. Family activities did not center around children's school lives, and parents' views about their success or failure as parents were not closely tied to their children's academic performance.

The families had very simple goals: (1) They were concerned about the physical survival and health of their children; (2) they were concerned with developing their children's capacity to make a living; and (3) they were concerned with developing children's behavioral capacities for maximizing the cultural values central to them. For these families, prestige, intellectual achievement, and even wealth were less important than morality and family loyalty. Education still played a small role in their understanding of life chances in this country. They had not yet subscribed to the "new" model of parenthood that LeVine and White (1986, p. 67) have described as resulting from mass schooling. They expected reciprocity from their children, and they did not see their role as having as its principal goal optimizing life chances "for each of a few children through extended education and a measure of adult attention that had formerly been reserved for heirs to the throne."

To be fair, LeVine and White (1986) may exaggerate a bit. The fact is, however, that the views that were held by the adults in the study about themselves as parents did not support the kinds of micropractices that researchers (e.g., Clark, 1983) have described as supportive of high academic achievement. The parents valued education, but they had not yet understood that in order for their children to succeed in school in this country, they had to reexamine their most profound beliefs about the parent–child relationship.

In sum, the 19 Mexican-origin men and women in the study, like members of other immigrant groups who came before them, brought values and beliefs and strategies for surviving that they had acquired in their native towns and villages. Their distance from American schools was a product not only of confusion and lack of information about educational institutions, but also of a vague sense of unease. This same sense of unease was experienced by Irish immigrants (Handlin, 1979) when they endeavored to build their own parochial school system, by Polish immigrants (Thomas & Znaniecki, 1927) when they struggled to do the same, and by Italians (Mathews, 1966; Williams, 1938/1969) when they removed their children from school and placed them in mills and factories. Indeed, like the groups that came before them, the new Mexican immigrants in this study had much that they wanted to hold on to. Their "cultural problems" were especially similar to those encountered by newcomers in the early part of this century. Given these similarities, it is important, perhaps, to recall the cautionary statement included by Williams (1938/1969) in her preface to her book *South Italian Folkways in Europe and America:*

> Americans are apt to assume that if an immigrant is given the opportunity to enjoy the advantages this country offers, sometimes almost for the asking, he will seize them with eager hands. But this is not always true. The eager hands are not stretched out, and there is no gratitude for the offer. We conclude that he does not understand, because he is a foreigner, but it is more often we who do not understand what lies behind his refusal. Frequently the explanation lies in his folkways and mores. (p. xv)

CHAPTER 9

CHANGING FAMILIES

Many years have passed since I spent time in Las Fuentes and looked at the faces of my young focal subjects. Today, I am half a continent away, and they—I imagine—have grown tall and strong. I remember them well, however, and can see them still as they started school, their faces shining and their eyes wide and bright. Like five- and six-year-olds everywhere, they entered their new world full of expectations. They were prepared to like school and to like their teachers. For many of them, however, expectations turned into harsh realities. Excitement became resentment and distrust. The light in their eyes went out, and they sat sullen and silent among their more successful peers. I remember the change in them well, and I remember feeling both angry and powerless. I did not like what schools did to little children.

Today I do not blame the schools. I understand that the problem is larger than particular teachers or particular schools. I spend a lot of time in classrooms, and I still work closely with Mexican-origin populations. For me, the setting has changed from the desert and the borderlands to the West Coast, the ocean, and the crowded freeways. What has not changed are the newly arrived Mexican families and their children. What has also not changed is the transformation of the eagerness and the hope to the sullen silence.

Now I work in middle schools. The children I study are 11 to 14. All of them have been here only a year or two—and like the little children in my first study, most have already experienced failure.

In the course of my work, I see and talk to many teachers. These are teachers who are baffled by the large new population of immigrant students entering their schools. They feel unprepared to deal with students who do not speak English and about whose academic background they know little. Like the teachers in Las Fuentes, teachers here see these newly arrived children as different.

In most cases and with most teachers I can almost predict our conversation. When they learn that I am studying newly arrived children and their academic progress, when I ask to sit in their classrooms to listen and observe,

I sense their uneasiness. "These children are not learning," I am told. But before I am tempted to reach my own conclusions, I am given a reason for their poor performance. "The problem is the parents," teachers explain. "They don't care about education. They just won't do for their children what they need to do to help them succeed. They have little education and many are even illiterate."

I want to respond, to say something useful. But most of the time I don't know where to begin. I understand that teachers are frustrated. They are also concerned about what I will think about their teaching. They want to prepare me for what I will see. They want to make certain that I understand that it is not their fault that the children are learning little. The blame, they claim, belongs to families. If only they could be reached, I am told, the children might possibly have a chance.

In this chapter, it is my intention to once again focus on attempts currently being made by both practitioners and policymakers to reach non-mainstream families and to close the distances between homes and schools. In focusing on this issue, I hope to raise questions about the well-intentioned efforts of school personnel to educate and/or to "involve" Mexican-origin parents in their children's education. Basing my comments on the lives of the 10 families who took part in my study, I will suggest that efforts to educate parents must be examined closely and that the assumptions under-girding practices that are ultimately designed to change families must be subjected to careful scrutiny.

PARENT EDUCATION PROGRAMS

The concern about the many limitations that Mexican-origin parents place on their children that was expressed by teachers both in Las Fuentes and on the West Coast is sincere. What teachers see is the children's failure and the confusions and misunderstandings experienced by the parents. The children seem different, and the parents appear to be unsupportive. They do not respond appropriately to notes and other school communications. They do not help with homework. They seem unprepared to guide their children in the American academic world.

The teachers respond as they do because, for the most part, they have little understanding about the everyday lives of children who are poor, non-English-speaking, and part of families struggling to survive. Their vision of home life includes a view of the standard or typical middle-class family—reflected in Lareau (1989)—in which parents spend the evening gathered around their children's homework. In these families, mothers, in particular, are dedicated to teaching their children what teachers expect them to know already. Not surprisingly, teachers who have been raised with such a model of the family in mind cannot begin to imagine why Mexican mothers are not busy teaching their children the alphabet.

For many school administrators, for many policymakers and teachers, the problem is simple, and the solutions are simple, too: Mexican parents must be helped to become "involved" in their children's education; they must be taught how to help their youngsters to succeed in American schools. In short, Mexican parents, like other "disadvantaged" and minority people, must be taught how to become "good" parents.

The response of the teachers and their desire to intervene and to help is very much within the mainstream of educational thinking. As I indicated in Chapter 1, numerous efforts are currently being made to "involve" and "empower" families. As I have pointed out also, many of these efforts are based on an ideology about education, opportunity, and merit that discounts structural inequalities and attributes success or failure to individual effort.

In truth, the evidence in favor of intervening in family lives appears to be almost overwhelming. Research carried out for over three decades has persuaded many practitioners and policymakers that school success is directly connected to particular parental behaviors and values. Families such as those I described here are seen as urgently in need of remediation.

The fact is that if we examine families such as those I have described here and if we evaluate their childrearing practices against the "standards" of "good" practices identified by the research literature, the picture appears to be dismal indeed. It is evident that the 10 families in the study did not utilize the kinds of "child-training" practices that researchers (e.g., Evans & Anderson, 1973; Rosen, 1956, 1959; Rosen & D'Andrade, 1959) have described as resulting directly in high achievement motivation by children. They did not, for example, provide independence training or encourage a greater reliance on self. They did not particularly advocate autonomy. Moreover, they encouraged a collectivistic rather than an individualistic orientation. In fact, on all the dimensions that researchers following Rosen's (1956, 1959) work have identified as supporting high achievement in children, the 10 families would rank very low. Like the Mexican-American families studied by Evans and Anderson (1973), the families in the study tended to be fatalistic and present-time oriented. Worst of all, they used what the literature has characterized as "nondemocratic" family socialization practices.

Measured by the standards established by researchers who have sought to find, within families, the causes of children's low achievement, the Mexican-origin families in this study provide almost stereotypical examples of well-meaning people who did not have the ability to support their children's academic learning. For example, in many ways, they were unlike the Black families studied by Clark (1983) whose children were successful in school. These Black families used a desirable "sponsored independence" parenting style characterized by large amounts of parental involvement and interest in children's home activities: almost ritualistic parent-and-child activities involving studying, reading, writing, conversing, and creating; and regular praiseworthy sentiments expressed for the child's talents, abilities, and achievements.

At the same time, however, the parents in the 10 families were also not like the parents of unsuccessful Black students. These latter parents were either permissive or authoritarian, had limited involvement in children's home activities, and had inconsistent knowledge of their children's whereabouts and activities.

In many ways the 10 families in the study were more like the "good" model presented above in their attention to their children's behavior, in their close supervision of children's activities inside and outside the home, and in their modeling of consistent role behavior. They did not, however, engage in ritualistic activities involving reading and writing, and they did not teach their children school concepts and ideas. The 10 mothers did not see themselves as their children's adjunct schoolteachers or as particularly responsible for their children's cognitive development.

From the perspective of educators who subscribe to the notions presented in *What Works* (U.S. Department of Education, 1987), the parents in the study were not "involved" in their children's schooling. They seldom interacted with teachers, and they did not create a "curriculum of the home." In short, from the mainstream perspective, they were very much a part of what is currently perceived as a growing problem among "new" immigrants.

FIXING THE PROBLEM

The desire to fix the problem—to help families become their children's "first teachers," as described in numerous other booklets aimed at practitioners (e.g., Rich, 1987a, b)—has led to a large number of efforts directed at "educating," "involving," or "empowering" non-mainstream parents. It is important to point out, however, that these three approaches to family intervention are quite different. In theory, they have different goals, and they are designed to address related but quite distinct issues.

Parent education has generally focused on imparting instruction to parents on childrearing practices in general. Parent education programs may focus on nutrition, discipline, health, or activities that promote early learning. Parent education has had a long history in this country, and both the foci and the populations targeted by such programs have changed considerably over time.

As Berger (1987) has pointed out, "The history of parent education . . . can be pictured as the constant ebb and flow of the ocean's tide" (p. 23).

Parent involvement, on the other hand, is a movement or trend that is much more recent. It views parents' interaction with schools, teachers, and their children's schoolwork as essential to school success. In order to encourage parental involvement, schools have been urged to make a positive effort to attract parents to school functions, to encourage them to volunteer in their children's classes, and to teach them how to tutor their children at home. It is important to note that this latter thrust is very similar in orientation to the more general parent education programs described above, except that the exclusive focus of instruction is school material. Parents are given instruction in mathematics, for example, and taught how to make everyday interactions into teaching activities involving counting, sorting, and the like. Similarly, programs focusing on family literacy teach parents to read and write and encourage home interaction that centers around reading and writing. These types of programs are designed to teach families how to establish the types of ritualistic activities around school tasks that Clark (1983) and others have found to be successful.

Parent or family empowerment programs are more difficult to characterize. Many different kinds of programs have been referred to in these terms. It is not always clear, however, how *empowerment* is being defined. In theory, empowerment, as a notion borrowed from Freire (1970), involves "*conscientizçåo,*" a bringing to participants' awareness the realities of the structural inequalities in the society in which they live. Using a truly transforming definition of empowerment, family intervention programs designed to "liberate" new immigrants and their children from the positions they now occupy would involve them in a dialogue that would result in their becoming conscious of themselves as members of an oppressed class. Such a dialogue would center around the discussion of social inequality, racism, and exploitation.

In an empowerment approach to "fixing the problem," programs would be designed to help parents understand that, as opposed to what many school personnel often claim, their children's futures and school success are dependent on a complex set of factors for which they, as parents, are not responsible. If such empowerment programs were successful, parents would no longer accept blame for being "uninvolved," "uninformed," or "uneducated" parents.

It is important to emphasize, however, that such transformative work is seldom approached in so-called parental empowerment programs. At best, such endeavors offer parents information about how schools work in this country, how parents can influence the power structure on behalf of their children, whom they can enlist as allies, what legal recourse they have, and how they can help their children to succeed in school. At worst, such empowerment programs are warmed-over parent education programs in which families are persuaded that if they change their behavior at home, all will be well, in school and in the world, with their children.

Those individuals who advocate on behalf of parent involvement or parent education or parent empowerment are sincere in looking for ways in which they can break the cycle. The problem is that they are seeking to break the cycle by focusing exclusively on one explanation for the poor school performance of non-mainstream youngsters. They are subscribing to existing mythologies about the power of school to right all social wrongs, and they are failing to take into account how social inequalities, educational ideologies, educational structures, and interpersonal interactions work together to affect educational outcomes.

Indeed, what we see being played out before us is the "trilemma" that Fishkin (1983) described in his work *Justice, Equal Opportunity, and the Family.* As Fishkin points out, many profound contradictions must be resolved if members of a society believe that achievement should be rewarded and that "there should be fair competition among individuals for unequal positions in society" (p. 5). Such societies must grapple with difficult and complex choices.

Because of the importance of Fishkin's delineation of the problem, I will briefly review several of his major points. First, in order to illustrate the complexity of the choices facing societies that hope to achieve justice and equal opportunity, Fishkin begins by recalling two central liberal assumptions about equal opportunity: (1) the principle of merit, which assumes that there should be procedural fairness in evaluating individuals for different positions, and (2) the assumption of equality of life chances. Fishkin argues that in order for a competition for equal positions to be fair, equal developmental conditions for talent development must be present. If it is the case that one can predict where people "will end up in a competition merely by knowing their race or sex or family background, then the conditions under which their talents and motivations have developed must be grossly unequal" (Fishkin, 1983, p. 5).

Fishkin argues further that if the assumptions about merit and equality of life chances are combined with a third assumption about the autonomy of the family, a very difficult "trilemma" arises. Engaging in a thought experiment, Fishkin asks his readers to imagine a mythical society in which a warrior class has historically had exclusive access to positions of power and wealth. He considers what might happen in such a society if, at a particular point in time, its members decided to allow all individuals to compete for those positions of power and prestige that were formerly available only to those persons who were members of the warrior class by birth. He points out that in whatever competition might be established, the children of the warrior class, because of their background, would most likely still have an important advantage. They might be better fed and stronger physically than other children, or they might learn special skills from their parents. They might, then, in spite of open competition, still continue to occupy most of the positions available.

The solutions for the society determined to allocate opportunity justly might, then, include creating a system that would give every child, warrior class or not, the opportunity to achieve warrior status. One possibility might involve, for example, neutralizing background factors by assigning children randomly at birth to different families. In this way, children of non-warrior background could be raised by warrior families and thus receive advantages not available to them from their own parents.

Fishkin points out, however, that if one subscribes to a principle that holds that families have a right to raise their own offspring and that these rights should not be interfered with except when "essential prerequisites for adult participation in the society" are not being provided, random assignment of children to other families will violate that important principle. In Fishkin's society, then, one is left with alternatives that are problematic in different ways. If parents have the right to influence the development of their biological children, and if positions must be competed for fairly, and if different backgrounds advantage some individuals and penalize others, a society might have to accept unequal conditions and inequality of life chances. On the other hand, a society might elect to compromise somewhat around the principle of merit and to advocate using procedures for selection of individuals for unequal positions that place crucial weight on factors other than strict qualifications.

Another approach to evening out the playing field in Fishkin's society is embodied in the philosophy of family intervention programs. Fishkin points out that if one attempts to equalize life chances while leaving the principle of merit in place, coercive interferences with the family would be required in order to "level down" the advantages provided by the upper strata or to "level up" the opportunities of the lower strata. Arguing that leveling down violates the principle of family autonomy for advantaged families, Fishkin is equally as pessimistic about leveling-up strategies for disadvantaged families.

Leveling-up programs, if implemented, would have as their purpose helping non-warrior parents to "train" their children for success by using strategies and practices found to be effective for warrior families. In such programs, non-warrior parents would be taught how to manage their time, how to talk to their children, how to initiate them in warrior-like activities, and how to reward or punish different behaviors. Inevitably, if these programs were effective, non-warrior families, whatever their strengths might have been, would change in nontrivial ways. In order to raise warrior children, parents would have to take on unfamiliar parenting styles and engage in interactions with their children that might not allow them to be themselves. The costs, measured against the possible rewards available to their children, however, might seem small indeed. In the absence of a principle that would protect parents' rights to rear children as their culture and conscience dictated, however, the implementation of wide-scale parent education programs might be seen as an excellent and effective means of leveling the playing field. Parents would be taught how to be "better" parents and how to produce "better" children.

However, Fishkin contends that "leveling up strategies, whatever the precise form, must be insufficient to close the gap unless they involve a complete manipulation of all the significant causal factors affecting the disadvantaged child" (p. 82).

Fishkin's example is an enlightening one. Like the society he describes, Americans have been concerned for some time about justice and equality. We have struggled with contradictions and complexities. We believe in merit, and yet we have understood that expecting equality of outcomes without providing equality of opportunity is unjust. We have engaged, therefore, in the implementation of policies and practices that might help us resolve the contradictions in which we find ourselves. Affirmative action admissions policies, for example, reflect one response to the dilemma of unequal outcomes due to unequal opportunities. Head Start and Even Start programs reflect a desire to even out the playing field by providing early help or more help to disadvantaged children.

Some of us question whether all of our children should be warriors. Others of us struggle to compensate for differences that are a product of historical inequalities. Every day in school, however, many teachers try to help non-warrior children to become successful. They become discouraged when they fail to make a difference, and they either blame families for not providing the right background or they initiate and implement leveling-up strategies that they hope will make up for existing inequalities.

THE PROBLEM WITH FAMILY INTERVENTION

Programs that are directed at families, whether they involve parent education, bringing about parent involvement, or fomenting parent empowerment, are, in essence, interventionist. They are designed to change families.

What emerges from the scholarship on programs and policies that promote such intervention is the intense criticism leveled at such programs by a number of distinguished individuals. Irving Sigel (1983), for example, argues that questions of ethics and morality come into play whenever one intervenes in the lives of others. Examining what he terms the intervention paradigm, he maintains that "All intervention involves a power play between the strong and the weak, the knowledgeable and the uninformed" (p. 6). He further points out that "Intervention can be defined more precisely as the process whereby individuals or institutions deliberately set out to change the course of ongoing or anticipated behaviors, feelings, and attitudes of others" (pp. 7–8).

According to Sigel, the concept of the expert is basic to the intervention process. The expert's authority rests on the presumption that he already has the right and the best solutions to identified problems. Reality, Sigel reminds us, is quite different. Answers are seldom totally clear-cut. Indeed, when an expert presents himself to his own professional community, he is careful to point out the limitations of his approach given existing knowledge in the field. When facing clients, however, the expert will present himself as quite certain of the wisdom of his position. He will not communicate the limits of his knowledge or the possible side effects of the intervention. Families, Sigel contends, have a right to information such as the following:

> For example, what happens to a low-income black family's social network when it shifts its child-rearing strategies as a consequence of a parent education program? Do these changes create new adjustment problems for the family? What are the side-effects for children involved in intervention programs? Since intervention refers to alterations in developmental trends, if it is successful there should be changes which may well create disequilibrium in the child. The question is, do the intervention agents discuss such issues with the clients? Is the failure of intervention programmers to do this a failure to act in a ethical manner? What is the intervention agent's responsibility? (1983, pp. 9–10)

Focusing on the education of Black families, Sigel further argues that parent education programs directly intrude into the organization of families and attack their values, their language, and their practices of childrearing and household management. Like Schlossman (1978), he points out that the sociohistorical context in which the families find themselves is totally ignored.

> There is a serious omission of the fact that poverty is a racial or caste issue. . . . Yet there is a belief that if these black parents were to follow through on those child-rearing practices which have been identified through research with middle-income white families as benefiting children, the black children would be adequately prepared for education and would consequently get out of the poverty cycle. . . . Essentially, the low-income black families are judged to be

inadequate, incapable of coping, and incapable of instilling the appropriate (middle class) social norms, and it is the ineptness of these parents that contributes significantly to the failure of their children to cope with the existing school situation. In effect, it is the old story of blaming the victim for his or her inadequacy. The intervention programs make minimal efforts to deal with some fundamental racial and economic issues; they focus instead on parental care, most often that of the mother. We overlook the fact that mere survival at a poverty level is in itself an achievement. (Sigel, 1983, p. 10)

Parent education programs have for the most part, according to Sigel, followed the medical model. Thus, parents are never engaged or invited to participate in diagnosing the problem. They are not engaged in a cooperative and noncoercive endeavor. In fact, Sigel points out, the parent does not come to the expert for help. Instead, it is the experts who decide that certain kinds of families need certain kinds of treatment, and it is the experts who are engaged in coercive behavior. Seen from this perspective, Sigel concludes, it is evident that within parent education programs ethics pose a persistent problem.

A number of other researchers agree with the questions raised by Sigel. Schlossman (1978) argues that a new domesticity underlies federal parent education programs. This perspective tends to view families in total isolation from the rest of society and to hold mothers wholly responsible for the intellectual development of their children. He states his objection to parent education by saying, "Parent education not only tends to blame the victim; it places an inordinate share of the blame on women alone" (p. 796).

Laosa (1983) further argues that social science professionals who designed such programs reinforced popular misconceptions and stereotypes about ethnic minorities in particular on the basis of very limited research. More recently, Auerbach (1989) critically analyzes family literacy programs aimed at immigrant families and concludes that these programs are a new version of the deficit hypothesis. Auerbach argues for a social-contextual approach to family literacy that takes into account cultural practices and community concerns.

It is important to note that among individuals who work primarily in the fields of parent education, much appears to have changed since the early 1960s and 1970s. As Powell (1988, p. 5) comments, a recent trend is to attempt to match parents and programs. Another tendency is to attempt to realign the traditional balance of power between program staff and participants by asking parents to contribute to decisions about the scope and content of services received. In Powell's words, however:

Certainly the ideology and/or practices of many parent programs continue to represent the deficit model in their assumptions about parent functioning. In some instances the terms collaboration and empowerment may be nothing more than a public relations veneer for program operations where staff assert superiority by prescribing child-rearing practices. Nevertheless, criticism of the deficit perspective has led to a rhetorical if not substantive change in the ways practitioners approach relations with program participants. (Powell, 1988, pp. 10–11)

In spite of these criticisms and concerns, parent education programs under many different guises and identities appear to be firmly taking hold among educators as a whole and in particular among those concerned about Mexican-origin children. Moreover, many state and federally sponsored programs specifically require family involvement or family education components as a condition of funding. Well-meaning individuals are focusing on a single factor (maternal or parental involvement in schooling) and completely disregarding the broader context, the fact that the mother–child relationship is embedded in the family, which is itself embedded in the immigrant community, which is, in turn, a part of the wider American reality.

PARENT INTERVENTION PROGRAMS AND MEXICAN-ORIGIN PARENTS

As I have mentioned above, there are many reasons to question the efficacy of family intervention programs in general, and there are perhaps even more questions about the utility of such programs for Mexican-origin families. Indeed, when I think about the children that I followed for three years and when I remember how they and their parents lived their lives, it is difficult for me to imagine a family intervention program that would not seriously damage the delicate balance they maintained. It is true that the families were not producing successful schoolchildren. It is true that there were many things they did not know about American schools and American teachers. It is also true that they were poor and they were struggling to survive.

What is not true is that the parents in the study were bad parents, or that they did not know how to parent well, or that they did it poorly. The 10 mothers loved and cared for their children and were intensely concerned about their rearing and their future. The nine fathers worked hard to earn a living, sometimes under difficult and painful circumstances. Both fathers and mothers wanted their children to have more and to suffer less than they themselves had suffered both as adults and children. In part, they had left Mexico so that here they would have a better chance.

For all of their virtues, however, for all of their dedication to raising good human beings and responsible adults, in the eyes of their teachers, the parents were failing their children. They did not respond to school communications in a timely fashion. They did not help their children at home. And they seemed not to have understood that without education their children would never be able to "make something of themselves."

As I have endeavored to point out, members of these 10 families had different views and ideas about what "making something of oneself" might mean. In fact, they worried little about individual achievement in mainstream terms. They were guided by beliefs about childrearing that emphasized respect and obedience. They did not understand the mother's role to include teaching school lessons to her children.

As Saragoza (1983, p. 118) has maintained in his article "The Conceptualization of the History of the Chicano Family":

> . . . child-rearing, adolescence (if it occurred), marriage, and identity in Mexico were bound by the economic necessities of life. Most Mexican women were valued for their household qualities, men by the ability to work and to provide for a family. Children were taught to get up early to contribute to the family's labor, to prepare themselves for adult life—childhood was short, adolescence still shorter, and adulthood too often a gradual wearing down under the weight of harsh labor. Such a life demanded discipline, authority, deference—values that cemented the working of a family surrounded and shaped by the requirements of Mexico's distinctive historical pattern of agricultural development, especially its pervasive debt peonage.

Saragoza is speaking of the past. But as I have pointed out here, newly arrived Mexican families also reflect the same agrarian and traditional perspective on the world. I believe, moreover, that as in the past, their values and beliefs will endure for a time. Eventually, however, in spite of or perhaps because of racism, transiency, isolation, and the like, these beliefs and ideas will change. The children of these families may come to believe, as Saragoza (p. 122) has argued, that material worth is equivalent to self-worth. At that time, they may look at their parents—who are poor and have not managed to acquire material symbols of success—with embarrassment. They may view them from the perspective of the majority society, and consider them failures.

If Saragoza's historical account (1983, p. 127) is any guide to the future, what will happen to these young people is easy to predict. Once again, urban families will feel the greatest alienation. Families' confidence in their ability to socialize their children will be eroded, and they will begin to reflect "the consequences of being neither 'Mexican' nor 'American.'"

The issue for those of us concerned about Mexican-origin families is whether their children will survive as human beings. Today, these families are no longer isolated in rural areas. They are part of the urban poor. Their children are both alienated and angry, and their parents—who in Mexico would have whipped them for hanging out with gangs—are afraid of being prosecuted for "abusing" their children.

Meanwhile, in the very same cities, many teachers and school personnel are faced with the choice of giving up on what is actually a multifaceted and very complex problem or of attempting to change what little they can. In organizing parent education programs, they sincerely hope to make a difference.

I understand that these efforts are well-intentioned, but I am convinced that if there is any hope at all of protecting young people from the dangers of life in urban ghettos, it is in the hands of the families themselves. It is with their resources, with their networks, and with their traditions—even with those traditions of currently unacceptable corporal punishment—that they will be able to produce "good" children.

I worry, then, about these well-intentioned teachers—many of them of Mexican origin themselves—who might decide, for example, to help the children learn to read by involving them and their parents in the now-fashionable family literacy programs. I worry about family math programs and family nutrition programs, and toy-making projects, and health programs really designed to change the cultural practices of these very able and very strong families. Maybe the short-term effect of more family–school involvement will be achieved, but the long-term goals of the family and its own internal processes will have been tampered with. Moreover, the implementers of such programs will have thought little about the side effects of their activities. They will have had no knowledge about the effects of changing routines and activities for the entire family.

It is very clear to me, and I hope it will be somewhat evident to the reader, that in all of the families with which I spent the larger part of three years, the rhythm of the family would change entirely if the adults were to become involved in family intervention programs that resulted in changing the way they lived their lives. Indeed, if mothers were persuaded, for example, to "enrich" their children's language in the manner of American middle-class mothers, if they were to structure "talk" with their children by teaching them to display information or by expanding their children's utterances, these practices would entirely change the internal verbal interaction of the family. When and how and for what reasons mothers talk to their children would be transformed. *Consejos* might well give way to recitations by the children, to telling stories, and to playing games.

The point is that if Rosario Castro, for example, were made to believe that she should read to her children every evening, or listen to them read, or write stories, or practice multiplication tables, she would do just that. She is indeed committed to her children's schooling, and she would hope to do her best for them in spite of her many other obligations. On the other hand, she would be replacing *educación* in the Mexican sense with an American middle-class focus on schooling and school learning. Given the demands on her life, she perhaps would not have time to do the real teaching that Mexican mothers do. Her *consejos* would be hard to work into the games, make-believe stories, and school recitations. In essence, Rosario would be helping the teachers to do their jobs, but she herself would fail to do her own.

As Fishkin (1983) argues in considering the alternatives for promoting leveling-up strategies:

> Suppose, however, that all potential parents were subjected to systematic indoc-trination, or thought control, so that by the time they reached procreation they would universally be expected to comply "voluntarily" with systematic govern-ment intervention into their child-rearing practices. . . . If universal and appar-ently voluntary compliance were to come about through a campaign of indoc-trination that suppressed certain alternatives and promoted others, it would count as coercive interference and would violate the autonomy principle. Ac-cording to the earlier definition, if knowledge of the alternatives to action A has been suppressed, a person has been coerced into doing A just as effectively as if he had been threatened with dire consequences for performing any of these alternatives. Suppression and thought control may be as effective as punishment. The autonomy principle could be trivialized unless it also provided protection against such efforts at manipulating a person's awareness and understanding of alternatives. (pp. 80–81)

I am suggesting, then, that if family intervention programs are imple-mented with Mexican-origin families, they must be based on an understand-ing and an appreciation and respect for the internal dynamics of these families and for the legitimacy of their values and beliefs. Parents must not be coerced into believing that in order to rear "successful" children, they must give up the childrearing practices that they consider appropriate. They must be helped to understand the alternatives in all of their complexity. They must be made aware of the fact that a change in childrearing practices may result in unexpected consequences for their children. In this age, when there is talk about the value of diversity, both practitioners and policymakers must be willing to accept the fact that new immigrants bring with them models of living life successfully that can not only enrich our society but can also provide protection for these new Americans in what is now a very dangerous new world.

My instinct, then, is to warn both practitioners and policymakers that there are serious costs to tampering with families. In an ideal world, new immigrants could be made into middle-class Americans in a series of parent education classes. They would nevertheless still be able to parent in a way that allowed their children to keep the best of both worlds. In a real world, however, this may not be possible.

MEXICAN-ORIGIN FAMILIES:
CAN WE AND SHOULD WE INTERVENE?

The question of what to do that might "truly help" Mexican-origin children to succeed in school is a particularly difficult one. The answer to this question depends, in fact, on one's views about education in general. For example, if one views schools as sorting instruments charged with producing or reproducing a class of individuals willing to work at what Spener (1988) has termed the "bad" jobs in this country, one can easily become cynical and discouraged. It is easy to believe that little can be done in schools without changing the larger structure of society. On the other hand, if one believes in the possibility of change, it is difficult to stand idly by on the sidelines while large numbers of children suffer discouragement and failure.

For me, attempting to answer the question of how to bridge the distances between families and schools is buying into the position that school outcomes can be changed significantly for poor children by efforts made at the institutional and interpersonal levels. It presupposes a belief that changes in Mexican-origin parents can compensate for the inequality they experienced both here and in Mexico.

The truth is that I do not believe that tampering with what happens inside the "black box" of the school or the classroom can, *by itself,* change the impact of the other factors contributing to school failure. I doubt that well-meaning practitioners, researchers, and policymakers can really level the playing field even if they could change teachers, change schools, and teach Mexican-origin families to become as focused on and as dedicated to their children's school success as middle-class parents already are. I disagree with *What Works* (U.S. Dept. of Education, 1987). Affluence does indeed make a great deal of difference in schools.

On the other hand, I am not ready to abandon hope. I am not ready to see more of the hurt and disappointment in children's eyes. For all of my doubts, I want to see Mexican-origin children laugh and brag about their brilliance. I want to applaud them as they become scientists, and businesspeople, and lawyers. In fact, I want it all. Like their parents, I want them to be good human beings, responsible and caring. And like a mainstream American, I want them to succeed!

The dilemma is whether to try to "help," and whether to encourage others to help Mexican-origin children succeed. For me, the single or primary focus on academic success and achievement for the Mexican-origin population has become more and more troubling. As I have suggested, advocating the acceptance by this population of the mainstream culture of achievement with its focus on individual upward mobility will have profound human costs.

For those of us who are of Mexican origin ourselves, the double bind is particularly painful. We can either advocate that Mexican communities and individuals be helped to make whatever changes are necessary to achieve success, or we can argue that there are already successes among the population in question and that it is the majority society that must change its perspective about human values and achievement.

The contradictions and difficulties in taking either position exclusively are distressingly obvious. I want to make clear, however, that I am not advocating that Mexican-origin families should be left alone. What I am trying to suggest is that ideals about success are perhaps not incompatible with other values. I believe that it should be possible to move into a new world without completely giving up the old.

What I found among the 10 families can offer important insights about how the domains of the school and the family might be bridged by those who wish to do so. As I finish the final chapter of this book, it is my hope that those who read it will focus on the strengths of this new wave of immigrants and respect them for their courage. I am convinced that, like the immigrants that came before them, Mexican-origin people will travel the distances between where they have been, where they are, and where they must go. I am also convinced that they will do so most effectively if they are allowed to become American at their own pace and in their own way. As Oscar Handlin (1951/1973, p. 6) so eloquently expressed it when he wrote about turn-of-the-century immigrants in his book *The Uprooted:*

> The immigrants lived in crisis because they were uprooted. In transplantation, while the old roots were sundered, before the new were established, the immigrants existed in an extreme situation. The shock, and the effects of the shock, persisted for many years; and their influence reached down to generations which themselves never paid the cost of crossing.

Notes

INTRODUCTION: BETWEEN TWO WORLDS

1. Bilingual education programs are designed to provide mother-tongue support for children who do not speak English. For a complete discussion of the theory, practice, and history of bilingual education in this country, the reader is referred to Crawford (1989).

2. This particular classroom, although classified as "bilingual," did not actually provide instruction in Spanish. The teacher in this classroom was hired on a temporary basis and was not a credentialed bilingual teacher. She was, however, very much in favor of teaching in two languages and was actively working on her Spanish language skills in order to bring them up to par.

3. Blueprints for living, according to LeVine and White (1986, pp. 12–13), are models for living or "life plans" or "cognitive maps of the life course" that are "embedded in codes of conduct and local survival strategies that endow the life span with culture-specific potentials for personal development."

4. Some individuals concerned about the education of linguistic-minority children might argue that the problem was indeed linguistic. They would base this argument on Cummins's early work (1979, 1981). According to this work, the proficiencies that we observed were simply characteristic of BICS (Basic Interpersonal Communication Skills) in English. According to Cummins's early writings on this topic, children from non–English language backgrounds often experience academic difficulties because they have not yet developed English CALP (Cognitive Academic Language Proficiency), or the kind of academic language proficiency that is needed to make sense of reading and writing. Saúl, then, would have experienced problems because he had not developed this more academic English language proficiency.

While a discussion of this theory is beyond the scope of this book, in the particular setting in which the study was carried out, other children who had also *only* developed English BICS (and who had not developed CALP in their first language) did, in fact, succeed in school. Since these children shared Saúl's background, this suggests, as Cummins argues in his more recent work (1989, p. 34), that, "under achievement is not caused by lack of fluency in English. Under achievement is the result of particular kinds of interactions in school that lead minority students to mentally withdraw from academic effort." It is my intention in this book to examine the factors that contribute to these interactions.

5. Because we did not want to suggest to the families that we were actually their

children's teachers, we described ourselves as *profesoras* rather than *maestras*. *Maestra* is the word commonly used for school teacher. *Profesor/a* suggests a teaching occupation also, but one which is much broader. We explained that we were *profesoras* at a university located in the general area.

6. Patterns of getting acquainted in Mexican society require that both individuals contribute information they consider relevant or interesting to the other person. Desire to become acquainted is manifested not by asking questions but by contributing the kind of information one wants the other individual to share also.

7. A *madrina* or godmother can be acquired by a child in several ways. She can be the child's baptismal, confirmation, or first communion "sponsor." By accepting such a role, an individual becomes a *comadre* to the child's parents and is treated somewhat like extended family.

CHAPTER 1

1. For a discussion of these arguments as they relate to bilingual education policy, the reader is referred to Crawford (1989, 1992a, 1992b).

2. Steinberg (1981) directly refutes the myth of Jewish intellectualism and Catholic anti-intellectualism and argues that many poor Jews in this country did not rapidly ascend the social ladder. He coincides with Berrol (1982) in his claim that poor Jews (like poor Italians, poor Irishmen, and poor Slavs) dropped out of school quite early. He contends that cultural values were not the major or primary cause of school success and social mobility among Jews, but that the economic success of the first and even second generation led to the educational success of succeeding generations.

3. The literature on the research carried out on the effectiveness of bilingual education is voluminous. For excellent reviews of this research, the reader should refer to Cazden and Snow (1990) and Casanova and Arias (1993). Both Hakuta (1986) and August and Garcia (1988) include comprehensive overviews of language research as it relates to the education of linguistic minority students.

4. Two recent volumes contain excellent bibliographies on testing and Mexican-origin students: Keller et al. (1991) and Valdés and Figueroa (1994).

5. For a discussion of the bilingual education debate in this country, the reader is referred to Crawford (1989), Cazden and Snow (1990), Porter (1990), and Hakuta (1986).

6. Because it is not my intention to criticize particular programs, I am deliberately not referring to these various efforts by name. I will point out, however, that many "parent education" programs focus on such areas as family literacy, family involvement in education, early learning, care and feeding of newborn children, etc. A general search of the ERIC system, for example, using the descriptors *Mexican* and *family education* yields an impressive number of articles describing such efforts.

CHAPTER 2

1. Ciudad Juárez is often referred to simply as Juárez. I will use these two terms interchangeably.

2. For a complete view of these border industries, the reader is referred to Fernandez-Kelly (1983).

3. In the southwest, the term *Anglo* is used to describe all anglophone white persons of non-Hispanic background. It will be used in this sense here.

4. I am using the term *Hispanic* to include persons of Mexican ancestry. It is a cover term that includes the two groups with which this study is concerned: *Chicanos* (Mexican-Americans who have been in this country for one or more generations) and *Mexicanos* (Mexican nationals who are recent immigrants). The terms *Chicano* and *Mexican/Mexicano* will be used with this meaning here.

5. *Fotonovelas* are exactly what their name suggests: novels that are illustrated by photographs. Generally, these materials are set up "comic-book style" so that the characters in the photographs carry the action forward by means of dialogue and easily photographed actions and expressions. This genre is very popular among the working classes in Mexico.

6. During the first six months of the study, we also carried out observations in the community on a weekly schedule. Observations involved noting the ethnicity of all persons encountered, the language of interaction used among all persons, the amount of print to be seen in the environment, the language of this print, special characteristics of home and property, etc.

7. The survey of the fifty households made clear that the majority of the Hispanic residents were Chicano and not newly arrived *Mexicanos*. Moreover, of the households visited, only seven individuals could be identified as non-Hispanic.

8. One of the fathers was an exception. This particular man, Terrence Sotelo, was born on the U.S. side of the border to an Anglo mother and a *Mexicano* father. Apparently he spent some of his childhood living in both the United States and Mexico.

9. In Mexican Spanish, older women are addressed as *Doña* plus first name. The term is one of respect and is used to address or refer to persons whom it would be inappropriate (unfriendly or distant) to address as *Señora* plus last name. The term is often used, for example, to address one's mother-in-law, an older female friend of the family, or a respected acquaintance of a certain age. I personally addressed and will refer here to all of the grandmothers in the study using this form.

10. *Secundaria* can be translated into English as secondary school. However, since the school systems are different, the term requires further explanation. In Mexico, *primaria* (elementary school) consists of grades 1 through 6. This level is followed by *secundaria* (2 years) and *preparatoria* (3 years). An individual is considered qualified to begin university work after she has completed *preparatoria*.

11. In Carmen Ornelas's case, she had completed two years of schooling beyond elementary school and then elected a vocational track (private secretarial training) instead of continuing in *preparatoria*.

CHAPTER 3

1. Border crossing cards are issued to residents of border areas and allow Mexican nationals to cross into the United States to carry out business. Border crossing cards are essentially picture identification cards that contain the local border resident's

address as well as other key information. Individuals using such cards can remain in the United States for a period of no longer than 72 hours. They cannot obtain employment using such cards, and they must remain within the border area.

2. Individuals who work in the United States legally must be resident aliens and be in possession of a "green card." A green card is issued to those individuals who have legal alien status in the United States. This status allows Mexican nationals to live and to work in the country. Along the border, however, many individuals apply for and receive alien resident status but decide not to live in the United States. In the Juárez area and in other border towns, it is very common for persons who have obtained a green card to reside on the Mexican side of the border and work on the American side. These persons normally cross the border every day and show their green cards to immigration officials at points of entry.

3. Border patrol checkpoints are set up on roads and highways throughout the Southwest. All persons on the highway must stop and upon request present proper identification and proof of citizenship or legal entry. These checkpoints are not permanent and are moved frequently in order to intercept illegal aliens traveling from one part of the country to another.

4. In all Spanish language segments included in this volume, traditional orthography has been used to capture rapid speech characteristic of speakers of rural Mexican Spanish.

5. The term *mica* is used to refer to a green card (or legal resident card). It is generally laminated in plastic, formerly in mica.

6. It will be recalled that this study took place between 1983 and 1986, that is, before the passage and implementation of the Immigration Reform and Control Act of 1986. At that time, as opposed to the years immediately following the passage of the act, there were no attempts made to inform the immigrant community about procedures to be followed in obtaining legal residence in this country.

7. Family, for the 19 adults in the study, included not only the immediate family, but also grandparents, parents, aunts, and uncles, as well as adult brothers and sisters.

CHAPTER 4

1. What most residents of rural Mexico refer to as a *rancho* is not a ranch, but a small farm.

2. I find it difficult to attempt a general characterization of these women because I am aware that from a majority perspective, they may be seen as stereotypically submissive and far from the ideal "modern" American woman. I am also quite aware of the objections that some scholars have raised to the presentation of Mexican-origin women as submissive individuals who are living out traditional sex-stereotypical roles. (For an overview of research on Chicano families and the role of women within them, the reader is referred to Ibarra, 1983, and Zavella, 1987.)

It is important for me to emphasize that I am not attempting to describe *the* Chicana or Mexican-American woman in a broad sense. I am speaking of 10 newly arrived *Mexicano* women from a particular part of Mexico, of a particular social class and of a particular age.

CHAPTER 5

1. This same type of information network was found by Velez-Ibañez (1988) among the marginalized in Mexico and among the Mexican-origin population in Tucson, Arizona. Similar networks have been described by Lomnitz (1989) and Stack (1974).

2. Farm laborers are often required to work with hoes with cut-off or shortened handles. In order to work with such hoes, the laborers must bend over. This allows the foreman to look out over the field from a distance and determine who is working and who is not.

3. The Arturo Soto family was an exception. It will be recalled that Arturo Soto was allowed by his employers to live rent-free in an old farmhouse on the property where he worked.

4. Mexico has a national health insurance system made up of three separate programs. One program insures private workers, another insures public employees, and still another insures indigent individuals.

5. This information was obtained during a separate research study on the use of English and Spanish in the courtroom in the same geographical area. This study involved activity as a court interpreter in many personal injury and worker's compensation cases and included long interviews with attorneys. Results of this research relating specifically to the linguistic aspects of the project have appeared in Valdés (1986, 1990).

CHAPTER 6

1. It is important for me to point out that in describing the childrearing practices of the 10 families, it has not been my intention to suggest that these practices are unique. Cross-cultural work on child socialization practices (e.g., Whiting & Edwards, 1988; Whiting & Whiting, 1975) has made evident the fact that as Whiting and Edwards (1988, p. 17) point out, "There are a finite number of general programs governing the lives of children growing up throughout the world, as well as a finite and transculturally universal grammar of behaviors that children can use in interpersonal interaction."

CHAPTER 7

1. As was made evident in my description of Saúl Soto's kindergarten classroom, it was often difficult to understand why the term *bilingual* had been applied to a particular classroom. Indeed, at Lincoln School, many of the problems identified by Wong Fillmore (1992) as taking place in the implementation of bilingual education in schools around the country were in evidence.

At Lincoln, there was much goodwill in the school toward newly arrived children, and the principal in particular was very much in favor of bilingual education. However, there was little consensus in the school about what bilingual programs should do, and no agreement about what first language support for children actually meant. Additionally, there were not enough teachers in the school with bilingual certificates. Many experienced teachers had decided not to apply for the bilingual endorsement because of the additional work required. Some of the younger teachers who did want to be bilingual teachers and who were working on their bilingual endorsement were (like Saúl's kindergarten teacher) unfortunately very limited in their Spanish language skills.

CHAPTER 8

1. I am using the term "ordinary" following Selby et al. (1990, p. 207) to describe the majority of persons in Mexico. The term avoids the use of "working class" or "middle class" and the connotations these terms have for American and European readers. The term "ordinary" Mexicans excludes the "middle" and "upper" sectors, who represent only 10 percent of the Mexican population.

2. As was pointed out in Chapter 2, this has also been the case for other groups of immigrants who have come to the United States. As Portes et al. (1978) point out in their article "Immigrant Aspirations" (p. 242), immigrants are "decisively influenced not only by events in the United States but by experiences of whole life in a different country."

3. For an excellent English-language presentation on the Mexican educational system, the reader is directed to Villa (1982).

4. For an overview of this problem, the reader is referred to Valdés-Villalva and Montenegro (1989).

5. The *salario mínimo* is a figure roughly analogous to the minimum wage in this country. Different *salario mínimo* amounts, however, are established for different regions of the country. As opposed to an hourly wage, the *salario mínimo* is most frequently given as the amount earned by a worker on a single day, week, month, or year. Thus, a certain region may have a *salario mínimo* of 56 pesos ($8.75, U.S. currency) per day or 1680 pesos ($262, U.S. currency) per month.

The *salario mínimo* serves as an index of income level. Household income levels are often computed using *salario mínimo* equivalents. As did Nolasco and Acevedo (1985), household income levels are reported as being 1.5 times the minimum salary, 3 times the minimum salary, etc. Very low daily incomes of 1.5 minimum salaries would be equivalent to 84 pesos. At the current rate of exchange of 6.4 pesos to $1.00 U.S. currency, a person having a daily income of 1.5 minimum salaries (56 × 1.5) would make $13 per day. A person earning 7 minimum salaries (56 × 7), would earn $61 per day.

6. According to Nolasco and Acevedo (1985), it is members of this group who seek social mobility, who inform themselves about national politics, and who become teachers and university students.

7. Massey et al. (1987, pp. 174–180) provide an excellent discussion on strategies of migration used by Mexican-origin people who come to the United States.

8. In Mexican Spanish the term *colegio* generally refers to a private school. It is often used more broadly as a synonym for school. To say, for example, that one's daughter attends *un colegio de monjas* means that she attends a school run by nuns. The term is not associated with postsecondary institutions.

When the term *colegio* was used by Pedro Soto in stating his ambitions for his children, I believe that he meant it as a translation of the English word *college,* and that he was familiar, at least to some degree, with this concept. When Isela Sotelo used the term in quoting her husband and saying that his older children were *en el colegio* in Austin, Texas, it was clear that she had only the vaguest notion of what this meant.

REFERENCES

Althusser, L. (1969). *For Marx*. New York: Vintage Books.

Althusser, L., & Brewster, B. T. (Eds.). (1971). *Lenin and philosophy, and other essays*. London: New Left Books.

Arias, B. (1986). The context of education for Hispanic students: An overview. *American Journal of Education, 95*(1), 26–57.

Au, K. H., & Mason, J. J. (1981). Social organization factors in learning to read: The balance of rights hypothesis. *Reading Research Quarterly, 11*, 91–115.

Auerbach, E. (1989). Toward a social-contextual approach to family literacy. *Harvard Educational Review, 59*(2), 165–181.

August, D., & Garcia, E. (1988). *Language minority education in the United States: Research, policy and practice*. Chicago: Charles C. Thomas.

Baratz, J., & Baratz, S. (1970). Early childhood intervention: The social scientific basis of institutionalized racism. *Harvard Educational Review, 39*, 29–50.

Barbara Bush Foundation for Family Literacy. (1989). *First teachers: A family literacy handbook for parents, policy-makers, and literacy providers*. Washington, DC: Author.

Bean, F. D., & Tienda, M. (1987). *The Hispanic population of the United States*. New York: Russell Sage Foundation.

Becker, H. J., & Epstein, J. L. (1982). Parent involvement: A study of teacher practices. *Elementary School Journal, 83*, 85–102.

Bennett, W. J. (1986). *First lessons: A report on elementary education in America*. Washington, DC: U.S. Department of Education.

Bereiter, C., & Englemann, S. (1966). *Teaching disadvantaged children in preschool*. Englewood Cliffs, NJ: Prentice-Hall.

Berger, E. H. (1987). *Parents as partners in education: School and home working together* (2nd ed.). New York: Merrill.

Bernstein, B. (1977). Social class, language and socialization. In J. Karabel & A. H. Halsey (Eds.), *Power and ideology in education* (pp. 473–487). New York: Oxford University Press.

Berrol, S. (1982). Public schools and immigrants: The New York City experience. In B. J. Weiss (Ed.), *American education and the European immigrant: 1840–1940* (pp. 31–42). Chicago: University of Illinois Press.

Bloom, B. S., Davis, A., & Hess, R. (1965). *Compensatory education for cultural deprivation*. New York: Holt, Rinehart and Winston.

Bodnar, J. (1982). Schooling and the Slavic-American family, 1900–1940. In B. J. Weiss (Ed.), *American education and the European immigrant: 1840–1940*. Chicago: University of Illinois Press.

215

Boger, R. P., Richter, R. A., & Paoulucci, B. (1986). Parent as teacher: What do we know? In R. J. Giffore & R. P. Boger (Eds.), *Child rearing in the home and school* (pp. 3–29). New York: Plenum.

Bond, G. C. (1981). Social economic status and educational achievement: A review article. *Anthropology and Education Quarterly, 12*(4), 227–257.

Bourdieu, P. (1977). *Outline of a theory of practice.* Cambridge: Cambridge University Press.

Bourdieu, P., & Passeron, J. C. (1977). *Reproduction in education, society and culture.* Beverly Hills, CA: Sage.

Bourdieu, P., & Passeron, J. C. (1979). *The inheritors: French students and their relation to culture.* Chicago: University of Chicago Press.

Bowles, S., & Gintis, H. (1976). *Schooling in capitalist America.* New York: Basic Books.

Bronfenbrenner, U. (1974). *Is early intervention effective? A report on longitudinal evaluation of preschool programs.* Washington, DC: Office of Child Development, Department of Health, Education, and Welfare.

Bronfenbrenner, U. (1979). Who needs parent education? In H. J. Leichter (Ed.), *Families and communities as educators* (pp. 203–223). New York: Teachers College Press.

Buriel, R. (1983, December). Teacher student interactions and their relationship to student achievement: A comparison of Mexican-American and Anglo-American children. *Journal of Educational Psychology, 75,* 889–897.

Carnoy, M., & Levin, H. (1985). *Schooling and work in the democratic state.* Stanford, CA: Stanford University Press.

Carter, T. P. (1970). *Mexican Americans in school: A history of educational neglect.* New York: College Entrance Examination Board.

Carter, T. P., & Segura, R. D. (1979). *Mexican-Americans in school: A decade of change.* New York: College Entrance Examination Board.

Casanova, U., & Arias, M. B. (1993). Contextualizing bilingual education. In M. B. Arias & U. Casanova (Eds.), *Bilingual education: Politics, practice and research* (pp. 1–35). Chicago: University of Chicago Press.

Cazden, C., & Snow, C. (Eds.). (1990). *English plus: Issues in bilingual education.* Newbury Park, CA: Sage.

Clark, R. (1983). *Family life and school achievement: Why poor black children succeed or fail.* Chicago: University of Chicago Press.

Clark, R. M. (1988). Parents as providers of linguistic and social capital. *Educational Horizons, 66*(2), 93–95.

Coleman, J. S. (1987). Families and school. *Educational Researcher, 16,* 32–38.

Cornelius, W. A. (1976a). Mexican migration to the United States: The view from rural sending communities. In *Migration and development monograph C/76–12.* Cambridge, MA: MIT Center for International Studies.

Cornelius, W. A. (1976b). Outmigration from rural Mexican communities. *Interdisciplinary Communications Program Occasional Monograph Series, 5*(2), 1–39.

Cornelius, W. A. (1978). Mexican migration to the United States: Causes, consequences, and U.S. responses. In *Migration and development monograph C/78–9.* Cambridge, MA: MIT Center for International Studies.

Cortes, C. E. (1986). The education of language minority students: A contextual interaction model. In Bilingual Education Office (Ed.), *Social and cultural factors in schooling language minority students* (pp. 3–33). Los Angeles: Evaluation, Dissemination and Assessment Center, California State University.

Crawford, J. (1989). *Bilingual education: History, politics, theory and practice.* Trenton, NJ: Crane.

Crawford, J. (1992a). *Hold your tongue.* Reading, MA: Addison Wesley.

Crawford, J. (Ed.). (1992b). *Language loyalties.* Chicago: University of Chicago Press.

Cummins, J. (1979). Linguistic interdependence and the educational development of bilingual children. *Review of Educational Research, 49,* 222–251.

Cummins, J. (1981). The role of primary language development in promoting educational success for language minority students. In California State Department of Education, Office of Bilingual Bicultural Education, *Schooling and language minority students: A theoretical framework* (pp. 3–29). Los Angeles: California State University, Evaluation Dissemination and Assessment Center.

Cummins, J. (1989). *Empowering minority students.* Sacramento: California Association for Bilingual Education.

Dahrendorf, R. (1978). *Life chances.* Chicago: University of Chicago Press.

Dale, G. E., & Macdonald, M. (Eds.). (1980). *Education and the state, I and II.* New York: Falmer.

David, M. E. (1980). *The state, the family, and education.* London: Routledge & Kegan Paul.

Deutsch, M., Bloom, R. D., Brown, B. R., Deutsch, C. P., Goldstein, L. S., John, V. P., Katz, P. A., Levinson, A., Peisach, E. C., & Whiteman, M. (1967). *The disadvantaged child.* New York: Basic Books.

Deutsch, M., Katz, I., & Jensen, A. (1968). *Social class, race, and psychological development.* New York: Holt, Rinehart and Winston.

Diaz-Soto, L. (1988). *Families as a learning environment: Reflections on critical factors affecting differential achievements.* University Park: The Pennsylvania State University Press.

Dinerman, I. R. (1982). *Migrants and stay-at-homes: A comparative study of rural migration from Michocan, Mexico.* (Monographs on U.S.-Mexican Studies No. 5). La Jolla: Program in United States–Mexican Studies, University of California at San Diego.

Dinnerstein, L. (1982). Education and the advancement of American Jews. In B. J. Weiss (Ed.), *American education and the European immigrant: 1840–1940* (pp. 44–60). Chicago: University of Illinois Press.

Dokecki, P. R., & Moroney, R. M. (1983). To strengthen all families: A human development and community value framework. In R. Haskins & D. Adams (Eds.), *Parent education and public policy* (pp. 40–64). Norwood, NJ: Ablex.

Dominguez, J. R. (1977, Spring). School finance: The issue of equity and racial-ethnic representativeness in public education. *Social Science Quarterly, 69,* 175–199.

Drucker, E. (1971). Cognitive styles and class stereotypes. In E. Leacock (Ed.), *The culture of poverty: A critique* (pp. 41–62). New York: Simon and Schuster.

Duran, R. (1983). *Hispanic education and background: Predictors of college achievement.* New York: College Entrance Examination Board.

Durand, J., & Massey, D. S. (1992). Mexican migration to the United States: A critical review. *Latin American Research Review, 27*(2), 3–42.

Engels, F. (1972). *The origin of the family, private property and the state in the light of the researches of Lewis H. Morgan.* With an introduction and notes by E. B. Leacock. New York: International Publishers.

Epstein, J. L. (1982). *Student reactions to teacher practices of parent involvement.* Paper presented at the annual meeting of the American Education Research Association, Baltimore; The Johns Hopkins University Center for Research on Elementary and Middle Schools, Parent Involvement Report Series P–21.

Epstein, J. L. (1985). *Effects of teacher practices of parent involvement on change in students' achievement in reading and math.* Baltimore, MD: Center for Social Organization of Schools, Johns Hopkins University.

Epstein, J. L. (1986a). Parent involvement: Implications of limited English-proficient students. In C. Simich-Dudgeon (Ed.), *Issues of parent involvement and literacy* (pp. 6–16). Washington, DC: Office of Bilingual Education and Minority Language Affairs.

Epstein, J. L. (1986b). Parents' reactions to teacher practices of parent involvement. *The Elementary School Journal, 86,* 277–294.

Epstein, J. L. (1991). Effects of teacher practices of parent involvement on student achievement in reading and math. In S. Silvern (Ed.), *Advances in reading/language research, Vol. 5: Literacy through family, community, and school interaction.* Greenwich, CT: JAI Press.

Epstein, J. L., & Dauber, S. L. (1991). School programs and teacher practices of parent involvement in inner-city elementary and middle schools. *Elementary School Journal, 91*(3), 289–305.

Erickson, F., & Mohatt, J. (1982). Cultural organization of participant structure in two classrooms of Indian students. In G. D. Spindler (Ed.), *Doing the ethnography of schooling: Educational anthropology in action* (pp. 132–175). New York: Holt, Rinehart and Winston.

Espinosa, R., & Ochoa, A. (1986). Concentration of California Hispanic students in schools with low achievement: A research note. *American Journal of Education, 95,* 77–95.

Evans, F. B., & Anderson, J. G. (1973, Fall). The psychocultural origins of achievement and achievement motivation: The Mexican-American family. *Sociology of Education, 46,* 396–416.

Eysenck, H. J. (1971). *Race, intelligence and education.* London: Temple Smith.

Fairchild, H. H. (1984). School size, per-pupil expenditures, and academic achievement. *Review of Public Data Use, 12,* 221–229.

Fass, P. S. (1988). *Outside in: Minorities and the transformation of American education.* Oxford: Oxford University Press.

Fernández, R. R., & Guskin, J. T. (1981). Hispanic students and school desegregation. In W. D. Wawley (Ed.), *Effective school desegregation* (pp. 107–140). Beverly Hills, CA: Sage.

Fernandez-Kelly, M. P. (1983). *For we are sold, I and my people: Women and industry in Mexico's frontier.* Albany: State University of New York Press.

Figueroa, R. A. (1983). Test bias and Hispanic children. *Journal of Special Education, 17,* 431–440.

Figueroa, R. A. (1989). Psychological testing of linguistic-minority students: Knowledge gaps and regulations. *Exceptional Children, 56*(2), 145–152.

Fishkin, J. S. (1983). *Justice, equal opportunity, and the family.* New Haven, CT: Yale University Press.

Fligstein, N., & Fernandez, R. M. (1988). Hispanics and education. In P. S. J. Cafferty & W. C. McCready (Eds.), *Hispanics in the United States* (pp. 113–146). New Brunswick, NJ: Transaction Books.

Florin, P. R., & Dokecki, P. R. (1983). Changing families through parent and family education: Review and analysis. In I. Sigel & L. M. Laosa (Eds.), *Changing families* (pp. 23–63). New York: Plenum Press.

Foley, D. E. (1990). *Learning capitalist culture: Deep in the heart of Tejas.* Philadelphia: University of Pennsylvania Press.

Freire, P. (1970). *Pedagogy of the oppressed.* New York: Seabury Press.

Giroux, H. A. (1983). Theories of reproduction and resistance in the new sociology of education: A critical analysis. *Harvard Educational Review, 53*(3), 257–293.

Goldberg, A. S. (1974a). *Mysteries of the meritocracy.* Madison: Institute for Research on Poverty, University of Wisconsin.

Goldberg, A. S. (1974b). *Professor Jensen, meet Miss Burks.* Madison: Institute for Research on Poverty, University of Wisconsin.

Goode, W. J. (1963). *World revolution and family patterns.* New York: John Wiley.

Goodson, B. D., & Hess, R. D. (1975). *Parents as teachers of young children: An evaluative review of some contemporary concepts and programs.* Washington, DC: Bureau of Educational Personnel Development (DHEW/OE).

Gould, S. J. (1981). *The mismeasure of man.* New York: Norton.

Gramsci, A. (1971). *Selections from prison notebooks.* New York: International Publishers.

Hakuta, K. (1986). *Mirror of language: The debate on bilingualism.* New York: Basic Books.

Handlin, O. (1951/1973). *The uprooted.* Boston: Little, Brown.

Handlin, O. (1979). *Boston's immigrants.* Cambridge, MA: The Belknap Press of Harvard University Press.

Handlin, O. (1982). Education and the European immigrant. In B. J. Weiss (Ed.), *American education and the European immigrant: 1840–1940* (pp. 3–16). Chicago: University of Illinois Press.

Haro, C. (1977). Truant and low-achieving Chicano student perceptions in the high school social system. *Aztlan-International Journal of Chicano Studies Research, 8,* 99–131.

Heath, S. B. (1983). *Ways with words: Language, life and communication in communities and classrooms.* Cambridge: Cambridge University Press.

Henderson, A. (1987). *The evidence continues to grow: Parent involvement improves student achievement.* Columbia, MD: National Committee for Citizens in Education.

Henderson, R. W., & Merritt, C. B. (1968). Environmental background of Mexican-American children with different potentials for school success. *Journal of Social Psychology, 75,* 101–106.

Herrnstein, R. (1973). *I.Q. in the meritocracy.* Boston: Little, Brown.

Herrnstein, R. J., & Murray, C. (1994). *The bell curve: Intelligence and class structure in American life.* New York: Free Press.

Hess, R., & Shipman, V. (1965). Early experience and the socialization of cognitive modes in children. *Child Development, 36,* 869–886.

Hess, R., Shipman, V., Brophy, J., & Bear, R. (1968). *The cognitive environments of urban preschool children.* Chicago: The Graduate School of Education, University of Chicago.

Hunt, J. M. (1961). *Intelligence and experience.* New York: Ronald.

Hunt, J. M. (1969). *The challenge of incompetence and poverty: Papers on the role of early education.* Urbana: University of Illinois Press.

Ibarra, L. (1983). Empirical and theoretical developments in the study of Chicano families. In A. Valdez, A. Camarillo, & T. Almaguer (Eds.), *The state of Chicano research on family, labor and migration* (pp. 91–110). Stanford, CA: Stanford Center for Chicano Research.

Jasso, G., & Rosenzweig, M. R. (1990). *The new chosen people: Immigrants in the United States.* New York: Russell Sage Foundation.

Jensen, A. (1969). How much can we boost IQ and scholastic achievement. *Harvard Educational Review,* Reprint Series (2), 1–123.

Kalantzis, M., Cope, B., & Slade, D. (1989). *Minority languages and dominant culture: Issues of education, assessment and social equity.* London: Falmer Press.

Kamin, L. J. (1974). *The science and politics of I.Q.* Potomac, MD: Erlbaum.

Kamin, L. J. (1977). The politics of IQ. In P. L. Houts (Ed.), *The myth of measurability* (pp. 45–65). New York: Hart.

Keller, G. D., Deneen, J. R., & Magallan, R. J. (Eds.). (1991). *Assessment and access: Hispanics in higher education.* Albany: State University of New York Press.

Labov, W. (1973). The logic of nonstandard English. In N. Keddie (Ed.), *The myth of cultural deprivation* (pp. 21–66). Harmondsworth, England: Penguin.

LaGumina, S. J. (1982). American education and the Italian immigrant response. In B. Weiss (Ed.), *American education and the European immigrant: 1840–1940* (pp. 61–77). Chicago: University of Illinois Press.

Laosa, L. M. (1978). Maternal teaching strategies in Chicano families of varied educational and sociocultural levels. *Young Children, 49,* 1129–1135.

Laosa, L. M. (1983). Parent education, cultural pluralism, and public policy: The uncertain connection. In R. Haskins & D. Adams (Eds.), *Parent education and public policy* (pp. 331–345). Norwood, NJ: Ablex.

Laosa, L. M. (1984a). Ethnic, socioeconomic, and home language influences upon early performance on measures of abilities. *Journal of Educational Psychology, 76,* 1178–1198.

Laosa, L. M. (1984b). Social policies toward children of diverse ethnic, racial and language groups in the United States. In H. W. Stevenson & A. E. Siegel (Eds.), *Child development research and social policy (Vol. 1)* (pp. 1–109). Chicago: University of Chicago Press.

Lareau, A. (1989). *Home advantage.* London: Falmer Press.

Lareau, A., & Benson, C. (1984). The economics of home/school relationships: A cautionary note. *Phi Delta Kappan, 65*(6), 401–404.

Lazar, I. (1988). Measuring the effects of early childhood programs. *Community Education Journal, 15*(2), 8–11.

Lazar, I., Hubbell, V. R., Murray, H., Rosche, M., & Royce, J. (1977). *Summary:*

The persistence of school effects [Publication No. (OHDS) 78–30129]. Washington, DC: U.S. Government Printing Office.

LeCorgne, L. L., & Laosa, L. M. (1976). Father absence in low income Mexican-American families: Children's social adjustment and conceptual differentiations of sex role attributes. *Developmental Psychology, 12,* 470–471.

LeVine, R. A., & White, M. I. (1986). *Human conditions: The cultural basis of educational developments.* New York: Routledge.

Lewis, O. (1966). The culture of poverty. *Scientific American, 215,* 19–25.

Lewontin, R. C., Rose, S., & Kamin, L. J. (1984). *Not in our genes: Biology, ideology, and human nature.* New York: Pantheon.

Litwak, E. (1960, February). Occupational mobility and extended family cohesion. *American Sociological Review,* 9–21.

Lomnitz, L. A. (1989). *Como sobreviven los marginados* (10th ed.). Mexico City: Siglo Veintiuno Editores.

Lomnitz, L. A., & Pérez-Lizaur, M. (1987). *A Mexican elite family, 1820–1980: Kinship, class, and culture.* Princeton, NJ: Princeton University Press.

Macías, R. F. (1988). *Latino illiteracy in the United States.* Claremont, CA: Tomas Rivera Center.

Massey, D. S., Alarcon, R., Durand, J., & Gonzalez, H. (1987). *Return to Aztlan: The social process of international migration from western Mexico.* Berkeley: University of California Press.

Mathews, S. M. F. (1966). *The role of the public schools in the assimilation of the Italian immigrant in New York City, 1900–1914.* Dissertation, Fordham University.

Matute-Bianchi, M. E. (1986). Ethnic identities and patterns of school success and failure among Mexican-descent and Japanese-American students in a California high school: An ethnographic analysis. *American Journal of Education, 95*(1), 233–255.

Matute-Bianchi, M. E. (1991). Situational ethnicity and patterns of school performance among immigrant and nonimmigrant Mexican-descent students. In M. A. Gibson & J. U. Ogbu (Eds.), *Minority status and schooling: A comparative study of immigrant and involuntary minorities* (pp. 205–247). New York: Garland.

McCandless, B. R. (1952). Environment and intelligence. *American Journal of Mental Deficiency, 56,* 674–691.

McClelland, D. C. (1974). Testing for competence rather than for "intelligence." In A. Gartner, C. Greer, & F. Riessman (Eds.), *The new assault on equality* (pp. 163–197). New York: Harper & Row.

McClymer, J. F. (1982). The Americanization movement and the education of the foreign-born adult, 1914–25. In B. J. Weiss (Ed.), *American education and the European immigrant: 1840–1940* (pp. 96–116). Chicago: University of Illinois Press.

McGowan, R. J. M., & Johnson, D. L. (1984). The mother-child relationship and other antecedents of academic performance: A causal analysis. *Hispanic Journal of Behavioral Sciences, 6*(3), 205–224.

McLaughlin, M. W., & Shields, P. M. (1987). Involving low-income parents in the school: A role for policy? *Phi Delta Kappan, 69*(2), 156–160.

McRobbie, A., & McCabe, T. (1981). *Feminism for girls.* London: Routledge & Kegan Paul.

Meier, K. J., & Stewart, J. Jr. (1991). *The politics of Hispanic education: Un paso pa'lante y dos pa'tras.* Albany: State University of New York Press.

Michaels, S., & Collins, J. (1984). Oral discourse styles: Classroom interaction and the acquisition of literacy. In D. Tannen (Ed.), *Coherence in spoken and written discourse* (pp. 219–244). Norwood, NJ: Ablex.

Mines, R. (1981). *Developing a community tradition of migration: A field study in rural Zacatecas, Mexico and California settlement areas. Monographs in U.S.-Mexican Studies No. 3.* La Jolla, CA: Program in United States–Mexican Studies, University of California at San Diego.

Mines, R. (1984). Network migration and Mexican rural development. In R. C. Jones (Ed.), *Patterns of undocumented migration: Mexico and the United States* (pp. 136–155). Totowa, NJ: Rowman and Allanheld.

Mines, R., & Massey, D. S. (1985). Patterns of migration to the United States from two Mexican communities. *Latin American Research Review, 20,* 104–124.

Morrison, P. (1977). The bell shaped pitfall. In P. L. Houts (Ed.), *The myth of measurability* (pp. 82–89). New York: Hart.

Muñoz Izquierdo, C., & Schmelkes, S. (1992). Mexico: Modernization of education and the problems and challenges of basic education. In D. A. Morales-Gomez & C. A. Torres (Eds.), *Education, policy, and social change: Experiences from Latin America* (pp. 57–68). Westport, CT: Praeger.

Musgrove, F. (1966). *The family, education and society.* London: Routledge & Kegan Paul.

Nielsen, F., & Fernandez, R. M. (1981). *Hispanic students in American high schools: Background characteristics and achievement.* Washington, DC: U.S. Government Printing Office.

Nolasco, M., & Acevedo, M. L. (1985). *Los niños de la frontera.* Mexico City: Centro de Ecodesarrollo, Ediciones Oceano, S.A.

Oakes, J. (1985). *Keeping track: How schools structure inequality.* New Haven, CT: Yale University Press.

Ogbu, J. (1978). *Minority education and caste.* New York: Academic Press.

Ogbu, J. (1981). Origins of human competence: A cultural-ecological perspective. *Child Development, 52,* 413–489.

Ogbu, J. U. (1982). Socialization: A cultural ecological perspective. In K. M. Borman (Ed.), *The social life of children in a changing society* (pp. 253–267). Norwood, NJ: Ablex.

Ogbu, J. (1983). Minority status and schooling in plural societies. *Comparative Education Review, 27*(2), 168–190.

Ogbu, J. U. (1985). A cultural ecology of competence among inner-city Blacks. In M. B. Spencer, G. K. Brookins, & W. R. Allen (Eds.), *Beginnings: The social and affective development of Black children* (pp. 45–66). Hillsdale, NJ: Lawrence Erlbaum.

Ogbu, J. (1987a). Variability in minority responses to schooling: Nonimmigrants vs. immigrants. In G. Spindler & L. Spindler (Eds.), *Interpretive ethnography in education* (pp. 255–280). Hillsdale, NJ: Lawrence Erlbaum.

Ogbu, J. (1987b). Variability in minority school performance: A problem in search of an explanation. *Anthropology and Education Quarterly, 18*(4), 312–334.

Ogbu, J., & Matute-Bianchi, M. E. (1986). Understanding sociocultural factors: Knowledge, identity and school adjustment. In Bilingual Education Office (Ed.), *Beyond languages: Social and cultural factors in schooling language minority students* (pp. 73–142). Sacramento, CA: State Department of Education, Bilingual Education Office.

Olivas, M. A. (Ed.). (1986). *Latino college students*. New York: Teachers College Press.

Olneck, M. R., & Lazerson, M. (1988). The school achievement of immigrant children: 1900–1930. In B. McClellan & W. J. Reese (Eds.), *The social history of education* (pp. 257–286). Urbana: University of Illinois Press.

Olsen, L., Chang, H., Salazar, D. D. I. R., Leong, C., Perez, C. M., McClain, G., & Raffel, L. (1994). *The unfinished journey: Restructuring schools in a diverse society.* San Francisco: California Tomorrow.

Orfield, G. (1986). Hispanic education: Challenges, research, and policies. *American Journal of Education, 95*(1), 1–25.

Oria Razo, V. (1989). *Política educativa nacional: Camino a la modernidad.* Mexico City: Imagen Editores.

Orum, L. S. (1985). *The education of Hispanics: Selected statistics.* Washington, DC: National Council de La Raza.

Orum, L. S. (1986). *The education of Hispanics: Status and implications.* Washington, DC: National Council de La Raza.

Parsons, T. (1953). Revised analytical approach to the theory of social stratification. In R. Bendix & S. M. Lipset (Eds.), *Class, status and power: A reader in social stratification* (pp. 92–128). New York: Free Press.

Perlmann, J. (1988). *Ethnic differences: Schooling and social structure among the Irish, Italians, Jews and Blacks in an American city, 1880–1935.* Cambridge: Cambridge University Press.

Persell, C. H. (1977). *Education and inequality: The roots and results of stratification in America's schools.* New York: Free Press.

Philips, S. U. (1982). *The invisible culture: Communication in classroom and community on the Warm Spring Indian Reservation.* New York: Longman.

Porter, R. P. (1990). *Forked tongue: The politics of bilingual education.* New York: Basic Books.

Portes, A., & Bach, R. L. (1985). *Latin journey: Cuban and Mexican immigrants in the United States.* Berkeley: University of California Press.

Portes, A., McLeod, S. A., & Parker, R. N. (1978). Immigrant aspirations. *Sociology of Education, 51*(4), 241–260.

Powell, D. R. (1988). Emerging directions in parent-child early intervention. In D. R. Powell (Ed.), *Parent education as early childhood intervention: Emerging directions in theory, research, and practice* (pp. 1–22). Norwood, NJ: Ablex.

Reichert, J. S., & Massey, D. S. (1979). Patterns of U.S. migration from a Mexican sending community: A comparison of legal and illegal migrants. *International Migration Review, 14,* 475–491.

Reichert, J. S., & Massey, D. S. (1980). History and trends in U.S.-bound migration from a Mexican town. *International Migration Review,* 476–491.

Rich, D. (1987a). *Schools and families: Issues and actions.* Washington, DC: National Education Association.

Rich, D. (1987b). *Teachers and parents: An adult-to-adult approach*. Washington, DC: National Education Association.

Riding, A. (1985). *Distant neighbors: Portrait of the Mexicans*. New York: Knopf.

Robins, D., & Cohen, P. (1978). *Knuckle sandwich: Growing up in a working class city*. London: Pelican Books.

Rosen, B. C. (1956). The achievement syndrome: A psychocultural dimension of social stratification. *American Sociological Review, 21*(2), 203–211.

Rosen, B. C. (1959). Race, ethnicity, and the achievement syndrome. *American Sociological Review, 24*, 47–60.

Rosen, B. C., & D'Andrade, R. (1959). The psycho-social origins of achievement motivation. *Sociometry, 22*(3), 185–218.

Roth, D. R. (1974). Intelligence testing as a social activity. In A. V. Cicourel, K. H. Jennings, S. H. M. Mennings, K. C. W. Leiter, R. MacKay, H. Mehan, & D. R. Roth (Eds.), *Language use and school performance* (pp. 143–217). New York: Academic Press.

Rumberger, R. (1991). Chicano dropouts: A review of research and policy issues. In R. R. Valencia (Ed.), *Chicano school failure and success: Research and policy agendas for the 1990's* (pp. 64–89). London: Falmer Press.

Samuda, R. J. (1975). *Psychological testing of American minorities*. New York: Dodd Mead.

San Miguel, G. (1987). *"Let all of them take heed": Mexican Americans and the campaign for educational equality in Texas, 1910–1981*. Austin: University of Texas Press.

Saragoza, A. (1983). The conceptualization of the history of the Chicano family. In A. Valdes, A. Camarillo, & T. Almaguer (Eds.), *The state of Chicano research on family, labor and migration* (pp. 111–138). Stanford, CA: Stanford Center for Chicano Research.

Sarup, M. (1982). *Education, state and crisis*. London: Routledge & Kegan Paul.

Schlossman, S. L. (1976). Before home start: Notes toward a history of parent education in American, 1897–1929. *Harvard Educational Review, 46*(3), 436–467.

Schlossman, S. L. (1978). The parent education game: The politics of child psychology in the 1970s. *Teachers College Record, 79*, 788–808.

Schlossman, S. L. (1983). The formative era in American parent education: Overview and interpretation. In R. Haskins & D. Adams (Eds.), *Parent education and public policy* (pp. 7–39). Norwood, NJ: Ablex.

Schlossman, S. L. (1986). Family as educator, parent education, and the perennial family crisis. In R. J. Griffore & R. P. Boger (Eds.), *Child reading in the home and school* (pp. 31–45). New York: Plenum.

Schwartz, J. L. (1977). A is to B is to anything at all: The illogic of IQ tests. In P. L. Houts (Ed.), *The myth of measurability* (pp. 90–99). New York: Hart Publishing Company.

Selby, H. A., Murphy, A. D., & Lorenzen, S. A. (1990). *The Mexican urban household*. Austin: University of Texas Press.

Sigel, I. E. (1983). The ethics of intervention. In I. E. Sigel & L. M. Laosa (Eds.), *Changing families* (pp. 1–21). New York: Plenum.

Simich-Dudgeon, C. (1986). *Trinity-Arlington parent involvement project: Final report*. Washington, DC: U.S. Department of Education.

So, A. (1987, October/November). Hispanic teachers and the labeling of Hispanic students. *The High School Journal, 71,* 5–8.

Sowell, T. (1981). *Ethnic America: A history.* New York: Basic Books.

Spener, D. (1988). Transitional bilingual education and the socialization of immigrants. *Harvard Educational Review, 58*(2), 133–153.

Stack, C. B. (1974). *All our kin: Strategies for survival in a black community.* New York: Harper & Row.

Steinberg, S. (1981). *The ethnic myth: Race, ethnicity and class in America.* Boston: Beacon Press.

Sternberg, R. J. (Ed.). (1982). *Handbook of human intelligence.* Cambridge: Cambridge University Press.

Sternberg, R. J. (1985). *Beyond IQ: A triarchic theory of human intelligence.* Cambridge: Cambridge University Press.

Sternberg, R. J., & Detterman, D. K. (Eds.). (1986). *What is intelligence? Contemporary viewpoints on its nature and definition.* Norwood, NJ: Ablex.

Stodtbeck, F. L. (1958). Family interaction, values and achievement. In D. C. McClelland, A. L. Baldwin, U. Bronfenbrenner, & F. L. Strodtbeck (Eds.), *Talent and society* (pp. 13–191). Princeton, NJ: D. Van Nostrand Company.

Suro, R. (1990, April 11). Cavazos criticizes Hispanic parents on schooling. *New York Times,* p. B8.

Thomas, W. I., & Znaniecki, F. (1927). *The Polish peasant in Europe and America.* New York: Alfred A. Knopf.

Tobias, S., Cole, C., Zinbrin, M., & Bodlakova, V. (1982, October). Special education referrals: Failure to replicate student–teacher ethnicity interaction. *Journal of Educational Psychology, 74,* 705–707.

U.S. Commission on Civil Rights. (1972a). *Mexican American education study, Report 2: The unfinished education: Outcomes for minorities in five southwestern states.* Washington, DC: U.S. Government Printing Office.

U.S. Commission on Civil Rights. (1972b). *Mexican American education study, Report 3: The excluded student: Educational practices affecting Mexican Americans in the Southwest.* Washington, DC: U.S. Government Printing Office.

U.S. Commission on Civil Rights. (1972c). *Mexican American education study, Report 4: Mexican American education in Texas: A function of wealth.* Washington, DC: U.S. Government Printing Office.

U.S. Commission on Civil Rights. (1973). *Mexican American education study, Report 5: Teachers and students: Differences in teacher interaction with Mexican American and Anglo students.* Washington, DC: U.S. Government Printing Office.

U.S. Commission on Civil Rights. (1974). *Mexican American education study, Report 6: Toward quality education for Mexican Americans.* Washington, DC: U.S. Government Printing Office.

U.S. Department of Education. (1987). *What works: Research about teaching and learning* (2nd ed.). Washington, DC: Author.

Valdés, G. (1986). Analyzing the demands that courtroom interaction makes upon speakers of ordinary English: Toward the development of a coherent descriptive framework. *Discourse Processes, 9*(3), 269–303.

Valdés, G. (1990, Spring). When does a witness need an interpreter? Preliminary guidelines for establishing language competence and incompetence. *La Raza Law Journal, 3,* 1–27.

Valdés, G., & Figueroa, R. (1994). *Bilingualism and testing: A special case of bias.* Norwood, NJ: Ablex.

Valdés-Villalva, G., & Montenegro, J. (1989). *Causales de la deserción escolar en las escuelas primarias urbanas de Ciudad Juárez, Chihuahua, Ciclo 1985–86.* Cd. Juárez, Chih.: El Colegio de la Frontera Norte.

Valencia, R. R. (1984). *Understanding school closures: Discriminatory impact on Chicano and Black students.* Stanford, CA: Stanford Center for Chicano Research.

Valencia, R. R. (Ed.). (1991a). *Chicano school failure and success: Research and policy agendas for the 1990's.* London: Falmer Press.

Valencia, R. R. (1991b). The plight of Chicano students: An overview of schooling conditions and outcomes. In R. R. Valencia (Ed.), *Chicano school failure and success: Research and policy agendas for the 1990's.* New York: Falmer Press.

Valencia, R. R., Henderson, R. W., & Rankin, R. J. (1985). Family status, family constellation, and home environmental variables as predictors of cognitive performance of Mexican American children. *Journal of Educational Psychology, 77,* 323–331.

Velez-Ibañez, C. G. (1988). Networks of exchange among Mexicans in the U.S. and Mexico: Local level mediating responses to national and international transformations. *Urban Anthropology, 17*(1), 27–52.

Villa, K. M. (1982). *Mexico: A study of the educational system of Mexico and a guide to the academic placement of students in educational institutions in the United States.* Washington, DC: American Association of College Registrars and Admissions Officers.

Walberg, H. J. (1984). Improving the productivity of America's schools. *Educational Leadership, 41,* 19–27.

Weiss, B. J. (1982). Introduction. In B. J. Weiss (Ed.), *American education and the European immigrant: 1840–1940.* Chicago: University of Illinois Press.

White, S. H. (1977). Social implications of IQ. In P. L. Houts (Ed.), *The myth of measurability* (pp. 23–44). New York: Hart.

White, S. H., Day, M. C., Freedman, P. K., Hartman, S. A., & Messenger, K. P. (1973). *Federal programs for young children: Review and recommendations.* Washington, DC: Department of Health, Education, and Welfare.

Whiting, B. B., & Edwards, C. P. (1988). *Children of different worlds: The formation of social behavior.* Cambridge, MA: Harvard University Press.

Whiting, B. B., & Whiting, J. W. M. (1975). *Children of six cultures: A psycho-cultural analysis.* Cambridge, MA: Harvard University Press.

Williams, P. H. (1938/1969). *South Italian folkways in Europe and America.* New York: Russell & Russell.

Willis, P. (1977). *Learning to labour.* Lexington: Heath.

Wong Fillmore, L. (1992). Against our best interest: The attempt to sabotage bilingual education. In J. Crawford (Ed.), *Language loyalties: A source book on the official English controversy* (pp. 367–376). Chicago: University of Chicago Press.

Wrigley, J. (1989). Do young children need intellectual stimulation? Experts' advice to parents, 1900–1985. *History of Education Quarterly, 29* (1), 41–75.

Zacharias, J. R. (1977). The trouble with IQ tests. In P. L. Houts (Ed.), *The myth of measurability* (pp. 66–81). New York: Hart.

Zavella, P. (1987). *Women's work and Chicano families: Cannery workers of the Santa Clara Valley.* Ithaca, NY: Cornell University Press.

INDEX

ABOUT THE AUTHOR

Guadalupe Valdés is Professor of Education and Professor of Spanish and Portuguese at Stanford University. A native of the U.S.–Mexican border area, she commuted across the border from Juárez, Mexico, to attend Loretto Academy in El Paso, Texas, during her elementary and high school years. She then left the border area to reside in Florida for an eight-year period. In Florida, Dr. Valdés completed her education and received both her master's degree and her doctorate in Spanish from Florida State University, in 1968 and 1972 respectively.

After completing her doctorate, Valdés returned to the border area where she joined the faculty of New Mexico State University. She remained in New Mexico for 14 years, during which time she carried out research in the areas of sociolinguistics and applied linguistics, focusing on the English–Spanish bilingualism of Latinos in the United States. In 1986, she left the border area for northern California, where she became a member of the faculty of the School of Education at the University of California, Berkeley, where she remained until 1992.

Most of Valdés's work is concerned with discovering and describing how two languages are developed, used, and maintained by individuals who become bilingual in immigrant communities. Her research has described language use in bilingual settings (e.g., code-switching, language accommodation, language maintenance, and the use of language in school and courtroom settings) and applying the information obtained from such descriptions to the educational context. Valdés's current work includes *Bilingualism and Testing: A Special Case of Bias* (1994); "When Does a Witness Need an Interpreter? Preliminary Guidelines for Establishing Language Competence and Incompetence" (*La Raza Law Journal,* 1990); "*Consideraciones teórico-metodológicas para el estudio del bilingüismo Inglés–Español en el lado Mexicano de la frontera*" (*Mexican Studies,* 1990); and "Bilingual Minorities and Language Issues in Writing: Toward Professionwide Responses to a New Challenge" (*Written Communication,* 1992).